THE AUTHOR Professor Robert Cole teaches Modern European History at Utah State University in America and has lectured at British colleges. He has travelled extensively throughout France. His published work includes several articles on British wartime propaganda and a book on British propaganda in European neutral countries during the Second World War.

SERIES EDITOR Professor Denis Judd is a Fellow of the Royal Historical Society and Professor of History at the Polytechnic of North London. He has published over 20 books including biographies of Joseph Chamberlain, Prince Philip, George VI and Alison Uttley, historical and military studies, stories for children and two novels. He has reviewed extensively in the national press and in journals, and has written several radio programmes.

Other Titles in the Series

A Traveller's History of Spain
A Traveller's History of Greece
A Traveller's History of Italy
A Traveller's History of Russia and the USSR
A Traveller's History of England
A Traveller's History of Scotland

In Preparation

A Traveller's History of Ireland
A Traveller's History of Turkey
A Traveller's History of Egypt
A Traveller's History of India
A Traveller's History of London

A Traveller's History of France

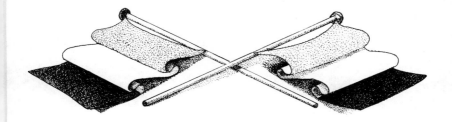

A Traveller's History of France

ROBERT COLE

Series Editor   DENIS JUDD
Line drawings   *ALISON HEPBURN*

INTERLINK BOOKS
An Imprint of Interlink Publishing Group, Inc.
NEW YORK

Updated edition 1992

First American edition published 1989 by
INTERLINK BOOKS
An imprint of Interlink Publishing Group, Inc.
99 Seventh Avenue
Brooklyn, New York 11215

Library of Congress Cataloging-in-Publication Data

Cole, Robert
    A traveller's history of France/Robert Cole; line drawings,
    Alison Hepburn. — 1st American ed.
        p. cm.
    Bibliography: p.
    Includes index.
    ISBN 0-940793-47-4
    1. France—History.   2. France—Description and travel—1975–
—Guide-books.   I. Title.
DC39.C56   1989
944—dc20   89–15346
                                                                    CIP

ISBN 0-940793-47-4

Printed and bound in Great Britain

À Catherine Taylor,
n'oubliez jamais ces merveilleux moments
aujourd'hui disparus

Table of Contents

Preface

Few nations have affected the modern world as profoundly as France. For many centuries she was the colossus of Europe, dominating her neighbours and pursuing a policy of territorial aggrandizement at their expense. Heavily populated, richly endowed, fertile, prosperous and centralised, France was the fulcrum of the continental balance of power. With the Age of Discovery, French commercial and maritime enterprise made a global impact from Canada to India, from the Far East to Louisiana and the Caribbean. By the end of the nineteenth century, the French Empire stood second only to that of Britain, and had incorporated much of North and tropical Africa, Indo-China and many Pacific islands.

But France was not merely a great military and imperial power. French philosophers, French writers and painters, French architects, scientists and engineers inspired and challenged their contemporaries. Two hundred years ago the French Revolution shook the established European order to its core and liberated forces that have yet to be subdued. Even today, with her Empire gone and her frontiers fixed, France is a dominant founder-member of the EEC and enjoys a worldwide cultural influence. Above all, French style is pervasive, and seductive, from the great fashion houses to the dining table, from the boudoir to the international film and motor shows.

In this comprehensive, scholarly and lucid book, Professor Cole explains how the French nation emerged from pre-history to take its place as a world-shaping force. In the process he unravels many myths and puts the inevitable prejudices of France's neighbours in their proper perspective.

Hundreds of thousands of travellers visit France each year. The glories of the French countryside, the essential harmony of much of French architecture, the wealth of historical remains and associations, the enormous variety of experience that France offers, act as a perennial and irresistible attraction. For these visitors, this lively and useful guide provides the essential clues to any understanding of France's past, and present, in entertaining and sometimes surprising detail.

Denis Judd
London, 1988

CHAPTER ONE

The Land, People, and Culture of Early France

FRANCE, like other European nations, is a phenomenon born out of conscious striving rather than from the natural affinity of its parts. Conflict has characterized France throughout its history. The historical landscape sets province against province, province against crown, authority against individuality, Christianity against paganism, church against state, papacy against crown, town against country, the country against the centre, and France against its neighbours. It has been wryly observed that all Frenchmen love France, but decry all other Frenchmen for demeaning her. There is the central theme of French history: the French created France almost in spite of themselves.

Geography

If French history is complex and diverse, so too is the geographical landscape over which it unfolded. Even the great plain stretching from beyond the Rhine river to Brittany and south to the Pyrénées is cut by deep river valleys, high plateaus, and the low hills of the Armorican Massif. It covers roughly three-quarters of the country in a triangle. The Atlantic and English Channel coasts form two sides, and a line of westward-facing hilly escarpments from Toulouse in the south to Verdun in the north-east form the third. The other quarter consists of hills and mountains.

The Alps and Pyrénées, with the Mediterranean coastline between them, define France's southern and south-eastern frontiers; and the Vosges, Massif Central, and Ardennes are rugged hills which break the landscape also in the east and south. Geographical detail varies greatly from one region to the next: the sheer walls of the Pyrénées, the soaring peaks of the Alps with Mont Blanc over 4000 metres, bizarre volcanic cones in the Puy-de-Dôme of the Massif Central, park-like expanses in the Loire Valley, wooded hills in the Paris Basin, flat plains to the east of La Rochelle, granite cliffs on the Breton coast, marshlands in Burgundy, and treeless plateaus in Champagne, to mention only some of what catches the eye.

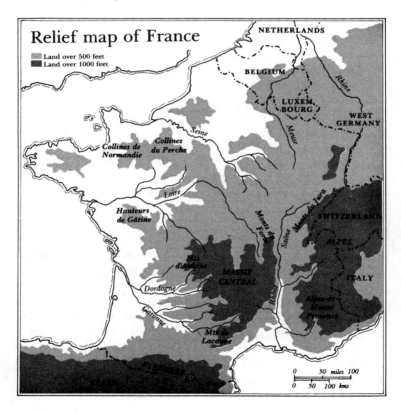

CLIMATE

All of the country escapes extremes of heat and cold, save the highest

Alpine peaks; but a damper, cooler climate prevails across the north and north-east, while dry, hot, Mediterranean conditions characterize the south and south-west. Wine is produced nearly everywhere, but the principal areas are in the warm Mediterranean or semi-Mediterranean areas: the Loire Valley south and south-east to the Languedoc region, and along the Rhône River between Lyon and Arles. Mediterranean France also is subject to the legendary *Mistral* and *Sirocco* winds. The *Mistral* is a cold, winter wind originating in the central plateau, which blows down the Rhône Valley. The *Sirocco*, either moist and warm or dry and hot, blows out of North Africa. Both are said to produce unusual, even bizarre, behaviour among people living in the areas affected.

Climate and geography influenced the course of French history, but did not dictate it. A mild climate and vast, rich agricultural plains, plateaus and river basins made France attractive to settlement and then to acquisitorial competition from neolithic times to the present.

RIVERS

Long river systems (the Loire is over 1000 kilometres long) provided direction and invitation for migration, trade, invasion, and conquest – and still more acquisitorial competition. France, on the extreme western edge of the European continent, lies at the end of a great plain extending unbroken north and east to western Siberia. It has been a highway for the movement of peoples and cultures for thousands of years. Only the Rhine separates France from this plain to the east, and the Rhine has proved no barrier at all. Meanwhile, four great river systems quarter France, three of them in the great plain area. They served as conduits for the settlements and movement of peoples. To some extent the history of France can be written in terms of how the Saône-Rhône, the Garonne, the Loire, and the Paris Basin (Seine) evolved from areas of primitive habitation into centres of warring duchies, counties and kingdoms. Only the Rhône drains into the Mediterranean. The others follow the gentle slope of the western and northern plains to the Atlantic. Over the centuries, this Atlantic orientation has prevailed, for these are the richest watersheds. The economic and political centre, when there was a centre, lay northward, and eventually the Paris Basin emerged as the hub around which the wheel of the French nation revolved.

Paleolithic

The presence of Paleolithic or old stone age remains in the Dordogne Valley indicates clearly that 25,000 years ago and more there were thriving communities, however rudimentary, in what became France. These people moreover were capable of making sophisticated art as well as assorted simple flint tools. Cave paintings abound in the Dordogne east of Bordeaux, most famously in La Grotte de Lascaux at Montignac. Fleeing reindeer and charging bison are rendered in rich and vivid colour and in such motional fluidity as to be nearly photographic in their realism. The human form by comparison is rendered only symbolically. It is absent from the paintings, and appears only in crude statuettes of females with huge breasts, stomachs and buttocks, suggesting their function as fertility goddesses.

A cave painting at Lascaux

Neolithic

In the Neolithic or new stone age 12,000 years ago, human habitation reveals far more. Pottery and architecture join other remains to provide a fuller picture of the peoples then in residence. Agricultural villages were established in the Paris Basin by 4600 BC. Similar settlements from the same era appeared in the Rhône Valley and along the Aude in Languedoc.

Neolithic life flourished in all four river systems, and appears to have been both solidly established and increasingly sophisticated culturally, politically and economically. Indeed, the Neolithic period faded gradually into the earliest metal period, the Bronze Age, and it is clear that Neolithic and metal cultures sometimes existed side by side. But before they disappeared, the Neolithic peoples established settlements, developed rudimentary social organization, fought one another, and laid the foundations of organized, or at least ritualized, religion or mythology. Decoration and burial practice indicate the latter, while pottery, kitchen-middens (refuse heaps) and architectural leavings illuminate the former. The remains are plentiful in all categories, at Cys-la-Commune and Berry-au-Bac in the Paris Basin, Il Corrège in Languedoc, La Grotte des Fées in the Haute-Rhône, Villeneuve-Tolosane and Saint-Michel-du-Touch in the Garonne Valley, Saint-Rémy-la-Varenne in the Loire region, and Carnac in Brittany, among other sites. Menhirs (standing stones), cromlechs (circles of menhirs), and dolmens (flat stones atop menhirs), formed into burial and ceremonial megalithic structures, indicate communities capable technically and socially of considerable achievement. Moreover, between 4600 and 1000 BC Neolithic and early metal cultures in the four major river systems evolved social hierarchies, simple political structures probably organized around the figure of a petty chieftain, colonization practices and far-reaching trade networks which may have connected the Atlantic and Mediterranean well before the appearance of Celtic peoples during the 1st millennium. Thus appeared the first features of a social and political landscape in France more than 60 centuries ago.

Only a handful of remnants survive from this epoch to identify actual peoples: the Ligurians gave their name to the Genoese Riviera, Liguria, and are recalled also in a few Provençal place names. The Iberians left only the name of the south-western tip of the European peninsula. The theory that the Basques, with their peculiar and untraceable language and distinctive physical appearance, are present-day remainders of the Iberians, remains only a theory.

Celtic Gaul

The Romans so named the region of modern France which was populated after 1000 BC by a metal-age people from northern and central Europe, known generically as Celts. Their identity is not precise, since 'Celtic' connotes variously race, language and tribe, and the Greeks and Romans used Celts interchangeably with Gauls to denote the people of the region. Julius Caesar, who described Gaul as being in three parts, recognized only one of the three as truly Celtic. Even so, in Roman eyes the Gauls were Celts; and whether they were called Belgae, Cimbri, Alemanni, Boii, Marcommani, Arverni, or some other name, they were much the same. Only the Aquitanians (Iberians) were descriptively different, and the Belgae were *said* to be different, but probably were not. Perhaps the Romans' practical turn of mind led to lumping the peoples of Gaul together into this Celtic category for convenience.

More is known about the Celts, or Gauls, than any other western European people from this epoch. If Neolithic dwellers left megaliths and pots, Celts left weapons, armour, tools, ornaments, traces of language and other evidence of a lively wide-ranging cultural, political and economic life. Gold and other precious metals were widely used, though for decoration as much as for money. Caesar, Germanicus, and other Roman travellers identified them as tall, blond or red-haired nordic types, organized into a complex social-political system. More recently, archaeologist Daphne Nash described this system as warrior-agrarian, in which peasant labour was the most important source of social wealth and was appropriated by the nobility through contractual and military relationships; in short, a structure similar to later feudalism.

The Greek geographer, Strabo, from his vantage point at Massilia, the Greek colony which would become Marseille, depicted a trading network encompassing the four river systems, the English Channel, and western and southern England. It began with the Celts and was co-opted by early Greek and Roman traders. The first-century cross-channel wine trade was a thriving concern, indicating that 'our claret, chianti or vino tinto, is very much old wine in new bottles'.

CELTIC DOMINATION

The Celts moved into Gaul as part of a general European migration spread over a thousand and more years, the result of population pressures, warfare and territorial acquisitiveness. They also crossed the English Channel to Britain as early as the tenth century. Over the next half-millennium Celts imposed their domination throughout Gaul, and became a great nuisance to Republican Rome, which they sacked and burnt in 390 BC despite, as historian Albert Guérard put it, 'the watchful and patriotic geese of the Capital', whose excited honking at the Celts' stealthy approach went unnoticed. For four centuries the Celts mastered Gaul, challenged Roman hegemony in northern Italy, and built up a culture, though hardly a civilization, which spread from Cornwall to the Alps.

CELTIC RELIGION

They practised a form of organized religion which held forests, streams and mountains to be the sacred places of naturalistic spirits. A priestly order, the Druids, famous equally in Gaul and Britain, was the fount of Celtic religious expression. The Druids practised human sacrifice and worshipped mistletoe as the sacred symbol of life and a panacea. The Druids also fulfilled a judicial function in the sense of providing arbitration in disputes between nobles.

None of the features of Celtic Gaul prepared its ruling peoples to compete with the Romans, however. The Celts never were a united force, only a marauding one. They fought among themselves as frequently as against others. Celtic Gaul was never more than a geographical expression and bequeathed little of substance to the French – neither language, faith, institutions, nor customs – save for a long-standing trade in wine moving westward and eastward out of Bordeaux.

Roman Gaul

The Romans first entered Gaul in the second century BC for defensive reasons, and stayed for trade and conquest. The first Roman soldiers in Gaul were mercenaries defending Nice and Antibes in 153 BC for Marseille, Rome's Greek ally. These soldiers and their descendants remained for six hundred years. Marseille lay just east of the Rhône

The Roman amphitheatre at Nîmes

estuary and the Romans simply followed others in using the river systems as conduits. By 121 BC Roman control extended up the Rhône Valley to Vienne, and up the Garonne Valley to Toulouse. Military and trading posts soon turned into cities in the Roman style such as Aix, Arles and Nîmes, and Roman engineering was applied to communications (a road system which spread from Aix to Boulogne eventually) and the water supply (Pont-du-Gard, a three-tiered aqueduct near Nîmes).

Actually, while the Roman presence began in response to Celtic or Ligurian marauders around Nice and Antibes, it was motivated in a larger context by the general movement of peoples out of Germany into southern Gaul and northern Italy. In the early first century, the Roman general, Marius, annihilated the Teutons in Provence and the Po Valley. This saved Rome, but it remained for Julius Caesar, beginning in 59 BC, to check this barbarian pressure and roll these Germanic peoples back to the Rhine.

JULIUS CAESAR

Caesar came to Gaul by invitation of the Celts as an ally against the Germans. But in his words, he came, saw and conquered Gaul. Caesar acted as ally, liberator and arbitrator between warring tribes and factions, and then as exploiter when he used his arbitrator's role to expand Roman power. In the process he did not flinch from the massacre, mutilation, and enslaving of the Celts. Such behaviour created a backlash, and in 52 BC Vercingetorix, an Arvernian chief, led a 'popular' uprising against Caesar. A bitter struggle followed with great battles at Bourges, Clermont, and Mont Auxois on the Côte d'Or. His back to the wall, Vercingetorix finally surrendered. The young chief was imprisoned, dragged behind Caesar's chariot in a triumphal procession in Rome, and then executed. Thereafter the Romanization of Gaul proceeded swiftly and surely.

THE ROMANIZATION OF GAUL

The people of Gaul actually welcomed Roman civilization, and in the end embraced it. With Rome came sound government, high technology, profitable trade, and in time, Roman citizenship. More cities developed on the Roman model, beyond the early examples at Arles and Aix: Narbonne, Lyon, Paris, Trèves, Toulouse, Bordeaux and many others. Latin replaced Celtic everywhere: classical Latin among educated and aristocratic Celts, and the slang Latin of soldiers, traders and slaves, blended with Celtic, among the rest. It was not French, but it was moving in that direction. Education flourished in the great schools of Autun, Reims, Toulouse and Bordeaux. Professors were well paid and men such as Eumenius of Autun and Ausonius of Bordeaux were among the great personages of the epoch. Rome gave the Celts internal peace and security, a frontier corresponding roughly to modern France, and a model administrative centre in the capital, Lyon. It is no surprise that the Celts took to Romanization, and held on to it for five centuries.

THE DECLINE OF ROME

But it couldn't last forever. Rome itself was falling apart in the fourth century AD and barbaric pressure increased. The Roman military machine was still up to confronting it (Stilicho's victories at Pollenzo and

Verona in 402–3, and Aetius' at Châlons in 451, for example), but the political will was fading. Jaded and jealous emperors had a proclivity for murdering their best generals – such was the fate of Stilicho and Aetius. Chaos then was not far off. First Gaul, then Italy itself, was threatened, invaded and overrun by barbarians. In 410 Alaric the Goth sacked Rome; it was Genseric the Vandal's turn in 455; and Attila the Hun came close. Driving all before him, the 'Scourge of God' invaded Gaul in 451, but was checked in a great battle on the Champs Catalauniques, near Châlons, the last great Roman victory in Gaul. The next year Attila entered Italy, but died before reaching Rome.

Barbarian Gaul

Once more Gaul was a region of warring factions, division and barbarian settlements: Visigoths in Aquitaine, Burgundians in the valley of the Saône-Rhône, Alemans in Alsace, a self-styled Roman king tenuously ruling north of the Loire, and Franks between the Rhine and the Somme. One of their chiefs, Merovech of the Salian (Salt Sea) Franks, had fought with Aetius against the Huns at Châlons. Of the great Roman past, Christianity, a vulgarized Latin – yearly more vulgarized by the infusion of barbarian dialects – a network of cities and roads, and many southern aristocrats styling themselves *patricii*, remained. No doubt the stability of the Roman influence was missed, but as the pope advised, 'go with the power'. And they did, while in Arles, Avignon and other Roman cities, Roman literary and philosophical tradition lived on.

Christian Gaul

It would be wrong to depict the fifth-century barbarians as quite the rough and ready marauders of earlier times – except for the Huns, of course. For one thing, many of them were Christian. Christianity came early in the Roman era, brought by Greek and Jewish converts. It was the third step in Gaul's known religious history after Druidism and a Greco-Roman pantheon into which many Celtic deities were assimilated. Christianity would be the last step, for it was monotheistic, radical, and uncompromisingly bigoted against paganism. Early Christians were hardy and welcomed martyrdom. In Gaul, the early martyrs added impetus to a faith grounded in humility, salvation and an apocalyptic world view. Persecution of the Lyon church in 177 by Marcus Aurelius provided some famous martyrs, while the beheading of the aged Bishop Denis of Paris on Montmartre (Martyr's Hill) in 262 provided both a martyr and a miraculous legend. Denis supposedly picked up his severed head, washed it, and walked 6000 paces to the north before expiring. Later, the Abbey Church of Saint-Denis was built on the site, and its patron, Dagobert I, was the first of many kings to be buried there.

THE RISE OF THE CHURCH

In 312 Constantine the Great embraced Christianity and made it the Roman state religion. Thereafter the Christian Church was virtually unassailable within the empire. Indeed, Christians insisted upon an end to paganism. Martin, bishop of Tours, waged a holy war against paganism in the late fourth century. He founded monasteries and destroyed pagan monuments. Most of urban Gaul and certainly the aristocracy were Christianized by the end of his life. It took much longer for Christianity to settle in fully with the peasants, who kept alive pagan traditions for centuries. Mistletoe, for example, has had a very long religious history, and shows no sign of fading in our own time. Meanwhile, the Church, in alliance with the state and the landed aristocracy, took over, flourished, and by the end of the fifth century played a great role in governmental as well as spiritual life for all of the people of Gaul. Church property was largely untaxed, each Gallo-Roman city was a bishopric (64 in all), and there were 17 seats for archbishops or metropolitans. Many offences were adjudicated by church leaders, rather than by civil authorities. Often, too, they organized local defence against barbarian invaders, like Bishop Lupus at Trèves and Bishop Aignan at Orléans.

The critical moment for Christian Gaul occurred when the Church adopted Clovis the Frank as the 'sword of the true faith', at the end of the fifth century. This action gave the Church a formidable secular support in place of a Roman empire now gone from Gaul, save for Aquitainian or Burgundian kings who fancied themselves Roman in outlook. It also gave the Franks sanction above rival barbarians. 'Clovis fought, the bishops conquered,' was the way it worked, and out of this union of Frankish power and Roman Church eventually evolved the foundation of France itself.

Paris

At the centre of the Seine Valley, long before Caesar, a tribe of river people lived on and around several islands in the Seine, the largest of which was just 1000 by 300 metres. It eventually became the Ile de la Cité, the heart of Paris. Of this city Michel de Montaigne wrote in the sixteenth century: 'I am French only through this great city, great above all things and incomparable in its variety, the glory of France and one of the most noble ornaments of the world.'

Paris wasn't quite Montaigne's vision in 53 BC when Julius Caesar established the Assembly of Gaul at Lutetia Parisiorum, the village closest to territories then in rebellion. A few days later he left, and the Parisii (boat people), the local Celtic tribe, joined in the uprising led by Vercingetorix. The Romans returned and the Parisii were subdued, fittingly, in a battle waged on the present site of the Champs-de-Mars and the École Militaire. The Romans established a permanent garrison on the Ile de la Cité and the life of Paris – called Lutetia until the fourth century – began.

THE ROMAN TOWN

River trade passed through Paris in increasing volume under Roman jurisdiction. The village prospered and a votive column to Jupiter was raised in thanksgiving exactly where Notre-Dame Cathedral now stands. Roman soldiers garrisoned on the Ile took the boat of the river people as their central symbol, and Paris was on the way to becoming integral to the life of Gaul under Rome. Soon the island in the river was too small for the community developing on it, and Paris expanded onto the Left Bank. Meanwhile Gaul was pacified and Romanized, and the village became a town and a crossroads to France. Now roads pushed outward in all directions – to Melun, Meaux, Soissons, Pontoise, Rouen, Dreux and Chartres, and Paris became a hub at the centre of a communication system. The main road remained Caesar's road to Orléans, which was so heavily travelled that a relief road was built to parallel it. This road, the *via inferior*, or *via infer*, survives in the name Avenue Renfert-Rocher.

Within the expanding town a bath appeared where the Musée de Cluny now stands, an amphitheatre on the site of Arènes de Lutèce, and a theatre near Place de l'Odéon. That this was a Gallo-Roman town is remembered in the name of the Latin Quarter on the Left Bank.

Roman Paris was only two centuries old when Christianity arrived in the person of Denis, bishop of Paris, who challenged the interdict against Christianity imposed by the official Roman religion. His tomb became a holy place, and contributed enormously to the later importance of Paris. When Dagobert chose the Abbey of Saint-Denis as his burial place, the abbey became 'the royal necropolis'.

If the Emperor Constantine made Christianity prosper by making it the state religion, he could not improve the Parisian economy. By the early fourth century the barbarians were again on the move, and Paris suffered a decline along with every other northern Gallo-Roman city. Paris might have gone into eclipse had not Julian the Apostate arrived in 351 to drive out the encroaching barbarians. This restorer of pagan religion came as a military commander and administrator to secure the frontier, but left, in 360, at the insistence of the legionaries, to take the imperial throne by force if necessary. During this time, Paris was the seat of government. Never again would it be an inconsequential village on the River Seine.

Neither Julian nor his successors in Rome or Constantinople could keep the barbarians from the door, and one after another various Teutonic tribes passed through the Paris Basin. They fought each other as well as the empire, confusion reigned, and Paris faced continual threat. Aetius made it the seat of his administration as a strategic centre from which to campaign against the Alemans, Burgundians, and Huns. The Huns, indeed, were the greatest threat.

GENEVIÈVE

The Huns inspired the second great Paris miracle after Saint Denis. Attila was on the march into Gaul in 451. The Roman government withdrew first to Orléans, then Tours, and finally to Bordeaux, where they made cause with the Visigoths of Aquitania against this common enemy. The Parisians prepared to flee – until a girl of 15, a zealous *religieuse* burning with Christian fervour, promised them that if they would pray to God and remain in the city, Attila would not come. The girl was Geneviève. As it happened Attila did not appear. The people rejoiced, and in its good time the Church canonized her. Geneviève became the patron saint of Paris. She was still alive 40 years later when Clovis, grandson of Merovech, king of the Salian Franks who fought with Aetius against Attila, 'cast an acquisitive eye on Paris from his temporary capital at Reims'. This time she did not keep the invader at bay, and a new era opened for Paris and for Gaul.

CHAPTER TWO

From Clovis to Hugh Capet
500–1000 AD

It is only after Frankish domination began in Gaul that the foundations of France were truly laid. These foundations had as much to do with diversity as with unity. Frankish Gaul was a collection of ethnic, political and philosophical communities, linked in many ways but self-consciously distinct from one another. This period, when the Franks' Gallic lands, called Francia, were held together only by a loose central authority which reigned rather than ruled, has been termed the Dark Ages. It is not altogether an accurate description. There was a life of the mind in France even before Rabelais.

Gallic community

Community evolved on many levels in the five centuries of Frankish rule: Goths, Basques, and Gascons in Aquitania from the Loire to the Pyrénées; Burgundians, Alemans, Alans and Romans in Burgundy and Provence; and Bretons and then Normans (Scandinavians) in the north and west. All retained a measure of tribal identity, and sometimes political power, distinct from the Franks and often in opposition to them and to each other. The cultural outlook of south and east retained a Roman character up to the sixth century, and in Provence well into the tenth. Roman landowners continued to dominate Aquitania and Provence as aristocracy and church leaders, and referred to themselves as *patricii* (patricians). Law codes reflected Roman and local custom, as in Aquitania north of the Garonne where the Franks recognized the Code of Euric, a fifth-century Romanized Goth and king of Aquitania. Only the Salic Law in the north, a compilation of Frankish codes, or rather

Cologne ■
AIX-LA-CHAPELLE
(Aachen) ■

✝ Rouen   • Soissons
■ PARIS   • Châlons

• Auxerre
Tours ✝   • Dijon
Autun •
• Poitiers

• Saintes
LYON ■
• Vienne   ✝ Milan
Bordeaux

Nîmes •   ✝ Aix-en-Provence
Arles ✝   • Marseille
Narbonne ✝

✝ ROME ■

● Important towns & cities
✝ Archbishoprics
–·– Boundary of Roman Gaul (approx.)
///// Greatest extent of the Frankish
      Empire under Charlemagne

Roman Gaul and Early
Medieval France

0   50   100   miles 200.
├───┼───┼────────┤
0 50 100   200 kms

several compilations, was distinctly and solely Germanic as opposed to Gallo-Roman.

THE STRENGTH OF ROMAN INFLUENCE

Towns retained their Roman character in varying degrees and the countryside, never as Romanized as the towns, reverted quickly to tribal conventions. In the towns, where the basic elements of civilization were carried forward, Rome remained the standard, especially in the south and east. Toulouse, Narbonne, Arles, Aix, Marseille, Lyon and Clermont retained their Roman character for at least another two hundred years. Provençal cities actually *were* Roman for the same period. In Provence the Roman Empire held out the longest against barbarian incursions. Even today Arles, for example, holds bull fights, an entertainment introduced by the Romans, in a second-century Roman amphitheatre.

Throughout Gaul towns were often governed by a bishop or archbishop, frequently elected by the populace rather than appointed by the papacy or the local lord as would become the case in later centuries. These churchmen functioned in a similar manner to that established by the Romans for their provincial administrators. Indeed, bishops and archbishops often were Rome's administrators in the latter days of the empire. Towns built walls when barbarians came, behind which urban dwellers and nearby residents sheltered in wartime. The walls remained to offer similar protection from quarrelling local dignitaries in the Frankish period and after. Walled towns also made for a very effective separation of town officials from territorial aristocracy later on. In time, as effective Roman power broke down and local dialects overtook Latin, towns dropped their Latin names and took over old tribal designations: Lutetia became Paris, after the Parisii, and Augusta Trèves, after the Trevarii.

RELIGIOUS SCHISMS

The apparent religious unity of Gaul, where Aquitanians, Burgundians and even Franks were or were becoming Christianized, was frail. The papal writ ran much deeper in theory than in practice, and the Church itself was split for a significant period at the beginning of Frankish rule, between the Arian heresy which argued that in the Trinity the Son is not equal with the Father, and the Trinitarian orthodoxy which said that they were equal. Burgundian and Aquitanian Christians often were Arians. Clovis, king of the invading Franks, embraced Trinitarianism and thus gained Church backing for his enterprises in conquering Gaul. Also, Jews were quartered in every important town and Islam thrust into Aquitania after the seventh century. Among the common country people pre-Christian and pagan traditions continued to exist side by side with Christian orthodoxy, or in place of it. Bishops despaired. Peasants were 'lustful, drunken, and irreligious', and only in the eighth century was anything done systematically to ensure baptism and some knowledge of Christianity among them. The Latin *paganus* (countryman) may well be the origin of the French *paysan* (peasant).

LANGUAGE DIFFERENCES

Language likewise resisted unity for centuries. By the eighth century, out of a combination of vulgarized Latin, German, and, even earlier, local dialects, there had evolved two distinct variations of what would become French. Romance, or *Langue d'Oïl (yes = oïl* or *oui)* was the language of the north. In the south, from Provence to the Atlantic coast and north to the Loire, *Langue d'Oc* (yes = *oc*) prevailed, save in Gascony and the Basque regions of the Pyrénées, where a variant of *Langue d'Oc* existed along with the Basque *Euskara*. The latter is not an Indo-European tongue at all. Meanwhile, settlers from southern England established Celtic as the language of Brittany, and a Scandinavian vernacular for a short time competed with *Langue d'Oïl* in Normandy, though the Vikings adapted to the local tongue within a generation. Latin remained the language of the educated, of church and school and of law and administration. In the end, for political and economic reasons, *Langue d'Oïl* prevailed. But many centuries passed first and *Langue d'Oc* remained the language of civility for this Frankish epoch and beyond. As Gallus, a Belgae, put it: 'When I remember that I am a Gaul and am going to hold forth in front of Aquitanians, I am afraid that my rather rustic speech may offend your over-civilized ears.' Of course, he may have spoken tongue-in-cheek.

Clovis

Despite diversity, power in Gaul centred in the north and east for the second time after the Franks came in the late fifth century. However much power might be dispersed at various times thereafter, it settled in the Seine Valley from which the Franks first imposed their rule in Gaul, and from which France eventually evolved.

The warlike Frankish king, Clovis (482–511), started in 486 by defeating the Gallo-Roman King Syagrius at Soissons. In 493 he made a far more important conquest by marrying the Burgundian Clotilda, the only Catholic princess in Gaul. On that occasion he 'bowed his proud head' and accepted baptism in the Roman church. Thereafter he and his Frankish successors became the strong right arm of the Church. Frankish king and Roman Church made a powerful combination. After his baptism, Clovis could do no wrong. According to Bishop Gregory of Tours, miracles followed him everywhere. A dove from heaven brought the vial of holy chrism with which he was anointed; a white doe showed him a ford for his army across the River Vienne; and a mysterious white light illuminated Poitiers Cathedral and guided his army towards their victory over Alaric II of Aquitania. This was all Church propaganda, of course, meant to strengthen the link with Frankish power, and to make that power appear sacred so that linkage with the mundane would not blot the ecclesiastical escutcheon.

Clovis was appointed a Roman consul by Anastasius, the emperor in Constantinople, presided over a council in Orléans which confirmed the clergy in their privilege, and for all of this was made 'invincible by God'. At least Gregory thought so. 'Thus day by day God brought low his enemies before him, so that they submitted to him and increased his kingdom, because he walked before Him with an upright heart, and did that which was pleasing in His sight.' This too was propaganda. Clovis warred against his neighbours and murdered his relatives, lest they become rivals for the throne. He then complained that he had no one to turn to in case of need. If any kinsmen did remain, none stepped forward to claim this dangerous honour. Piously, Clovis built a church for each murdered relation. Historians recognize his significance, but find Clovis 'a detestable character' all the same.

THE MEROVINGIAN DYNASTY

Clovis was the first Merovingian. Over the next century the dynasty brought most of Gaul under its sway. This was not a unitary kingdom however, but rather a family enterprise containing four 'natural and more permanent divisions': Austrasia in the east (Metz), Neustria in the north-west (Paris), Burgundy to the south-east (Lyon), and the semi-independent duchy of Aquitania north of the Garonne (Poitiers). The monarchs of these regions, like the later Roman emperors, neither ruled nor governed so much as they reigned – they led armies, presided over ceremonial, rewarded their followers, and left government to servants such as the mayors of the palace. Of these more will be said presently. Clovis and his successors left behind a dreary trail of murders and atrocities to rival the worst excesses of the legendary court at Byzantium.

THE NOBILITY

An aristocracy at once powerful and undisciplined contributed greatly to Merovingian blood-letting. Gregory of Tours' description of Guntram Boso of Austrasia during the reign of Chilperic depicts a typical member of this aristocracy: 'an unprincipled man, eager in his avarice, covetous beyond measure of the property of others, giving his word to all, keeping his promise to none.'

Brunhild

The treatment of Brunhild, widow of King Sigebert of Austrasia, by the Austrasian royal dukes is a better instance. Brunhild was accomplished by any standard. Brought up in the Roman manner, she spoke classical Latin and had an uncommon grasp of general ideas and political concepts. Her qualities of decision, command and perseverance were equally superior. Brunhild was friendly to the Church and attempted to curb aristocratic lawlessness and restore the declining dignity of the kingly office. That was her undoing. None of Brunhild's accomplishments or aspirations impressed these aristocrats, and she had to fight them at every turn, usually with their own weapons. Her husband, King Sigebert, and sister were murdered by the Neustrian branch of the

Merovingians, so she instigated the murder of the Neustrian ruler, Chilperic. She then purged many of the Austrasian aristocrats from involvement in royal affairs, and tried to play king-maker. At that the magnates rebelled, led by Clothar II, son of King Sigebert's murderer, and took Brunhild prisoner. She was tortured, led through the ranks of the soldiers on a camel, and tied by her hair, one arm and one leg to the tail of an unbroken horse, which cut her to pieces with its hooves as it ran.

At the time of her death Brunhild was a white-haired grandmother and beloved by her less exalted subjects, who took a dim view of these proceedings. It was in Brunhild's era, wrote Gregory, that the common people grew apart from the aristocracy and chafed at their arrogance and venality, on occasion even attacking unpopular nobles.

Dagobert I

This Merovingian was perhaps the last effective ruler of the line. Through the instrument of the Edict of Paris in 613 – 'a mixture of pious wishes for law and order' – and the taxation policies of his predecessors which were single-mindedly implemented by Eligius, bishop of Noyon, Dagobert (628 – 637) attempted to restore the Frankish kingdom after the civil strife which had dominated Brunhild's career.

Eligius was only one of many bishops employed by Dagobert in civil administration, from Rouen to Metz and Paris to Bordeaux. As the Edict gave him the right to appoint bishops, it may be that the use of such 'loyalists' as royal agents was Dagobert's way of holding the kingdom together in the face of self-aggrandizing aristocrats. Eligius was the most important bishop under this king. He attracted a general attitude of loathing among the populace for his taxation policies, and upon the death of Dagobert retired hastily to Noyon with a Paris mob speeding him on his way.

Dagobert's restoration project succeeded only briefly. When he died in 637 the kingdom again split between royal sons, and the Merovingian dynasty began its descent into the succession of *rois fainéants*, or 'do-nothing' kings, in the eighth century. These Merovingians were remote from their subjects, and given over to debauchery, gluttony and internecine plotting. Merovingian princes in these years often ended up in monasteries, and not always by choice. By the end of the eighth century effective government throughout Frankish Gaul was in the hands of the mayors of the palace.

MAYORS OF THE PALACE

For several generations the Merovingians employed managers of the royal estates called mayors of the palace: *major domus*. These were royal officials and presumably aristocrats as well. Their power waxed in lieu of effective kings, and with a victory in battle over Berchar the Neustrian mayor at Tertry in 687, one Pepin of Heristal established both the supremacy of Austrasia in the Frankish lands and of his own house in Austrasia. Anarchy reigned for a generation afterward, until his bastard son, Charles Martel (the Hammer), routed all serious opposition to this wealthy Moselle Valley family, and a new power was established. With Charles Martel began the Carolingian line which was to include his grandson Charlemagne, the greatest of all Frankish Kings.

Charles Martel

Austrasia and Neustria were torn by internal clashes. Meanwhile, Aquitania, Burgundy, Gascony, Provence and Moslem Septimania (the coast between the Rhône and the Pyrénées) fiercely resisted submitting to Frankish rule. This gave Charles his opportunity. The Hammer smashed the Arabs at Tours in 732 and the Burgundians in a campaign in 734, after which he rewarded his followers with confiscated lands. A significant gesture: such awards were technically reserved for kings to make. He campaigned in Aquitania in 735, in Burgundy again in 736, in Provence and Septimania in 737, and against the Saxons in 738. Charles soon won a great reputation and became the centre of power in the Frankish lands. He never proclaimed himself king, but he was virtually king and in documents of the time was often designated *rex*. Further, when King Thierry IV died in 737, 'Charles did not even bother to look around the monasteries for another one'. The Hammer's son, Pepin known as the Short, had no qualms about being king and in 751 had himself crowned Pepin I.

Martel and his grandson Charlemagne were heroes in their own time, but were castigated by later descriptions. Einhard's biography of Charlemagne is virtually hagiography, but church writers in the ninth century treated both him and Charles Martel as sinners doomed beyond redemption. In the 850s Hincmar of Reims wrote down the 'vision of Eucherius', wherein this eighth-century bishop of Orléans, once exiled by Charles Martel, had been led into Hell by an angel. There he saw Martel burning. Eucherius told his story to Boniface of Mainz and Fulrad of Saint-Denis, who ordered Martel's tomb opened. A snake slithered out and the walls were blackened as if by fire. (The fact that Eucherius had actually died *before* Charles Martel was not mentioned.) Similarly, a story circulated at the same time that Charlemagne was a denizen of Hell, where for all eternity he had to suffer his genitals being torn at by a wild animal in punishment for his debauchery on earth. What inspired these revisions? Simply that they *were* sinners, guilty of the greatest sin that the Church could conceive: they confiscated church lands and distributed it among their secular followers.

Pepin I

The debunking of the great Carolingians occurred in the ninth century, at a time when tension between Church and crown was rising over the issue of pre-eminence. The seeds of the issue were planted in Gaul in the reign of Pepin I (751–768), Martel's son and premier Carolingian king.

The Church always resented royal interference in clerical affairs, but needed secular power for its security in tempestuous times. Both Pepin I and Charlemagne made good relations with the papacy central to their policy. In 751 Childeric III, the last Merovingian, was deposed by Pepin and sent, naturally, to a monastery. At Soissons, 'by election of all the Franks, the consecration of the bishops and the submission of the great,' Pepin became king. (Not too much should be made of the similarity of language between this declaration and preambulary sections of the Magna Carta in England four-and-a-half centuries later, attractive though the parallel might appear.) Pope Zacarius sanctioned this usurpation by observing that 'it is better to call king the man who has the power rather than the man who is deprived of it'.

This papal declaration, which got Pepin over some sticky moments with subjects who regarded him as overly self-aggrandizing, warmed Pepin's heart. In 754 he offered the new pope, Stephen II, on the run from Byzantines and Lombards, sanctuary in the Abbey of Saint-Denis. There on 28 July in the same year, either in gratitude or as a ploy to bind the Frankish king to the papal cause, Stephen anointed and crowned Pepin in the basilica. The act had monumental significance. Never before had a Frankish ruler been anointed or crowned in this sacerdotal manner. Thereafter kingship in Gaul was sacred; it was bestowed as a divine right. To oppose the king was to commit sacrilege, a principle of great value to any monarch. In the end it even helped overcome the greatest burden faced by kings of France, the resistance of great magnates to the centralization of authority.

Pepin was happy to become the 'sword of God', the strong right arm of the Church. So was Charlemagne. Henceforth the clergy were treated in Gaul as a privileged class – which did not, however, prevent Charlemagne from expropriating ecclesiastical property, an action which was taken in part to forward ecclesiastical reforms and break the power of truculent aristocrats. The clergy saw it otherwise. Actually, had the anointed king been both temporal and spiritual head of the Church in one, there would have been no problem. However there were both king and pope. This meant that power had to be tested, and more than one king was excommunicated and pope imprisoned in the centuries ahead. But for the time being the arrangement between pope and king was a happy one, and the events of 28 July gave Pepin I the blessings of the Church for his wars against the Aquitanians and Burgundians, who still resisted Frankish rule. In 768 Pepin died with these territorial questions unresolved. But the linkage with Rome was firmly established, and with it the principle of sacerdotal monarchy.

Charlemagne

As was Frankish custom, Pepin's kingdom was divided upon his death between his two sons, Carloman and Charles. Carloman died three years later and Charles, soon to be known as Charlemagne, a man of strength, resolve and boundless ambition, seized the whole of the kingdom for

The Palatine chapel at Aachen, consecrated in 805

himself. Charlemagne (768–814) was proof that the power of medieval kings lay in their character and personality. Institutional rule was for the future. This, the greatest of Carolingian rulers, was physically powerful and energetic, a great warrior, dominating, colourful, accessible and jovial. He maintained his capital at Aachen (Aix-la-Chapelle), an old Roman spa where the whole court and often the palace guards as well would frolic together in the baths.

Charlemagne was also cruel and unyielding. He christianized Saxony at the point of a sword, beheaded four-and-a-half thousand men at Verdun, and dispersed a third of the Saxon population to Franconia and Alemannia. And he was judicious. Charlemagne rewarded loyal supporters. He treated the Aquitanians and Burgundians with respect – he dressed his young son in Aquitanian garb before naming him king of Aquitania – and there were few rebellions against him from these quarters. He brought the sons of the aristocracy to court for their education, ruled according to law (more or less), patronised scholars and made Aachen the cultural centre of Europe. Scholars such as Alcuin of York and Einhard went to Aachen. A great cathedral and a school were built there. In a time that is often termed the Carolingian Renaissance, Aachen surpassed every city in Europe including Rome.

As a ruler, Charlemagne appeared to think that a mix of personal magnetism, generosity and tyranny, overlaid by an appeal to vanity, was the way to get results. Within limits he was right. By his death in 814, after a rule of 47 years, the Carolingian Empire incorporated central and western Europe, save for Spain, Britain and part of Italy. That it was an 'Empire' referred again to the Carolingian alliance with the papacy. On Christmas Day, 800, Pope Leo III crowned and anointed Charlemagne in Rome as 'most pious, Augustus, crowned of God, great and pacific Emperor of the Romans'. The act became significant only later, and more for Germany than for France.

One achievement escaped Charlemagne, and it makes an interesting commentary on the Franks as a people. They entered Gaul four hundred years earlier, took over and ruled a country both Romanized and relatively sophisticated, wherein lay many centres of literacy if not of learning, embraced many customs and some of the language of the Roman Empire – but remained, in the eyes of Aquitanians and many others, barbarians. Perhaps Charlemagne gives a clue to this. Great emperor, *patricius* and Protector of the Roman Republic, patron of scholars and instigator of great buildings, ecclesiastical and otherwise, Charlemagne never learned to read or write. According to Einhard he tried, 'taking the opportunity of moments of leisure to practise tracing letters; but he had begun too late and the result was poor'.

SYSTEM OF GOVERNMENT

Being illiterate did not prevent Charlemagne from creating a kingdom with a structure more advanced than that of his predecessors, although similar to it. The kingdom lasted only his lifetime, for there was little of the modern state about it. Charlemagne's rule was strictly personal. The fundamental unit was the county, governed in the king's name by a count and appointed by him. Most counts were drawn from the local aristocracy, whether Frank or other. Charlemagne oversaw their work personally, and frequently called them away to consult, serve in war, or simply to interrupt any rebellious thoughts they might be entertaining. He instituted the office of viscount to deputize when the count was away, and made certain that these officers had ample reason not to take the count's side against kingly authority. Counties on the extreme edges of the kingdom were grouped into 'marches' and overseen by a military prefect, later called a 'marquess', in German 'margraf', and in French 'marquis'. Austria and Brandenburg Prussia began as Carolingian marches. Charlemagne also employed special emissaries, the *missi dominici*, invested with considerable powers to root out corruption, injustice or disobedience among his subjects throughout the empire.

One part of kingly rule was to keep subjects from rebelling. Under Charlemagne the *missi* as well as his own watchful eye were deployed for this purpose. So too was the process of securing loyalty by establishing personal bonds between king and subject through the oath of fealty and the institution of vassalage. This process began well before Charlemagne, but certainly he expanded on it. From the process derived the horribly complicated and unwieldy, but ultimately inescapable, concept of feudalism.

FEUDALISM

'Better not even to use the term', wrote historian Edward James, who preferred simply to describe what happened between ruler and subject on the matter of the personal king-subject relationship. A vassal – a count, let us say – placed his hands between his lord's, swore an oath of loyalty (fealty, to be faithful), and 'commended' himself to the lord. Often the oath was sworn over holy relics, giving it the quality of sanctification so that violation put the swearer at risk of eternal damnation. It cut both ways, of course. Charlemagne laid down that if a lord mistreated his vassal – tried to kill him, reduce him to slavery or seduce his wife, for instance – the fealty owed to the lord was forfeit. The language of the feudal relationship evolved over time until meaning changed. Vassal originally meant slave; by Charlemagne's day it meant only one subordinated by fealty to his lord. By the ninth century everyone from the top of society to the bottom was part of the system. Ordinary people were easier to control within the system than were aristocrats. To ensure aristocratic loyalty beyond the oath, it became customary to award fiefs, which term was a specific of the more general term benefice. The vagueness of this term is a major reason why feudalism is such a variable concept. One historian has found 41 different shades of meaning for benefice. In time, granting fiefs naturally worked to undermine the system by creating 'over-mighty subjects'.

HEREDITY

Meanwhile, as feudalism evolved, the element of heredity appeared and became part of it. Charlemagne allowed his counts to pass their counties to their heirs, since revenue from these lands supported the counts. Soon all titles were regarded as hereditary. Whatever specific meaning they once or still had – duke, a great leader, marquis, guardian of a march, count, administrator of a district, or viscount, deputy for a count – they began to take on a quality of territoriality that went well beyond simply administrative or military responsibilities. This advance was a privilege not taken lightly or surrendered easily. In one famous instance in 877 when Louis the Stammerer thought to revoke many benefices, as he had the legal right to do, and redistribute them among personal followers, the whole aristocracy rose in rebellion against him and the plan was abandoned.

This point should not be misunderstood. The *power* of these rising 'territorial' aristocrats still derived from their role as agents of the crown. The identification of power with landedness would come later. The same was true of obligation and landedness: it was only in the north of France and in Belgium at this time that the bulk of the peasantry were tied to the land through legal obligation, the condition which evolved into serfdom. In much of the rest of the countryside there were many free peasants, particularly in Languedoc, living on their own allodial land; even when they merely were tenants of a lord, they discharged their obligations through payment of rent rather than through service.

Charlemagne's Heirs

Briefly upon Charlemagne's death, the centre held. Charlemagne, just before dying, crowned his son Louis. Louis, who tortured his nephew to death and then felt remorse and did public penance, was called 'the Pious'; he declared that the empire would continue undivided. His sons objected, fearing the loss of their inheritance, and the aristocracy protested, fearing the loss of privilege. Over the next half-century compromises were made and, in the best Frankish tradition, the empire was divided after all. In 817, 843 and 855 the Frankish lands were parcelled out. The kingdom of West Francia emerged as part of the subdivision. These divisions constituted the regional framework within which the aristocrats would build their own small empires. The Carolingians survived until the end of the tenth century, each generation becoming less able to hold on to the once proud family tradition. West Francia was France; however its Carolingian kings held it in name only. Francia resembled by AD 1000 a patchwork quilt in which the royal domains (the territorial lands personally possessed by the king) were smaller than those of the dukes of Normandy, Burgundy, Aquitaine and Gascony, smaller even than those of the counts of Brittany, Flanders, Provence and Toulouse. There were no mayors of the palace in these late days, but there were powerful aristocrats, landed now and able to oppose their king. One such was Robert, count of Anjou and lay-abbot of Marmoutier near Tours, known as the Strong.

Robert the Strong

In 856 Robert the Strong was deprived of some of his power when Charles II the Bald made his son Louis the Stammerer king of western Neustria (Brittany and Normandy). Robert rebelled. He was made marquis of the Breton marches in exchange for abandoning the rebellion, an indication perhaps that local power was fully in the ascendant against the centre. In 865 he was given power also in Burgundy, and Charles, frustrated by the Stammerer's incompetence as military leader against marauding Vikings, made him give up this role to Robert. Robert was killed in 866 in battle against the Vikings, but left behind two young sons under the protection of Hugh the Abbot. They grew up to be, each in turn, counts of Paris and kings of West Francia. The Robertian line, as it was called, was established. It led straight to Hugh Capet.

Odo of Paris

Paris, already important for economic reasons and as a crossroads, was now to become the power base of the kings of France. Robert's eldest son, Odo, was appointed count of Paris by the emperor, Charles III the Fat. There Odo made his name with his defence of Paris against a Viking attack in 886. The Vikings were unable to force a surrender, thus greatly enhancing Odo's reputation both as warrior and organizer. Then Charles, who was both emperor and king of West Francia, lost all respect among the Parisians for his weak-kneed intervention when he appeared with a vast army before Paris after long delays and, rather than fall upon the Vikings, allowed them to negotiate a safe passage for themselves up the Seine and into Burgundy. There they subjected the region 'to the worst winter it had ever known'. After that Charles was a broken reed. When he died in 888, the bishops, counts and other magnates refused to have another German prince in West Francia, and elected Odo king. It was a large kingdom, but royal power was strictly limited by powerful local magnates perfectly capable, oaths of fealty notwithstanding, of throwing in their lot with other 'kings': Rudolph in Upper Burgundy, Louis and Guy in Provence and Burgundy respectively, and Rannulf in Aquitania. Even so, the Robertians were strong and from this moment dominated from their centre in Paris.

It was a confused domination however, and a limited one. The country was afflicted by usurpations, rival claimants to the throne, rebellious aristocrats, invading Vikings, weak kings and powerful kingmakers. Odo was followed in 898 by a restored Carolingian, Charles III the Simple (king of West Francia, but never emperor), who was not so much confused, as this sobriquet might suggest, as straightforward and honest. Better had he been duplicitous, as were those around him. He was deposed in 922 by Robert I, the second son of Robert the Strong, who was killed the following year by supporters of the deposed Charles. However, Ralph of Burgundy took Charles prisoner and seized the throne for himself, leaving Charles to rot in prison where he died six years later. Ralph died in 936 and was followed by Louis IV, called the Foreigner because he returned from exile in England to be king. Louis too was a Carolingian, urged upon the magnates by Hugh the Great, a Robertian playing kingmaker. Then came Lothaire, and another

Carolingian, Louis V, who had no sobriquet but might well have been named 'the Last'. He was killed in a hunting accident after a reign of only one year. Hugh Capet, son of Hugh the Great and grandson of Robert the Strong, followed him to the throne of West Francia. The Robertians were triumphant and with them Paris, future hub of France. It was, however, a hub of which Gaul yet was only casually aware, and concerned about not at all.

Hugh Capet

So-called because he favoured a short cape called a *cappa*, Hugh Capet (987 – 996) ascended a throne nominally over all of western and southern Gaul, but practically only over the north. He was nominated for the throne most eloquently by Archbishop Adalbero of Reims. His brother, Henry of Burgundy, and his brother-in-law, Richard of Normandy, were his chief supporters. The great southern princes such as William Ironarm, count of Poitou and duke of the Aquitanians, had no objection to him so long as he did not interfere in their affairs. Hugh was, so far as can be determined, the first king of 'France'. He actually controlled (as distinct from reigned over) a territory 200 kilometres long by less than 100 kilometres wide.

Hugh was a famous warrior, as were all of the Robertians, and a powerful Francian duke as well as count of Paris. His capital was Paris in so far as it was anywhere. There was a palace, where now stands the Palais de Justice on the Ile de la Cité. In reality the capital was wherever the king was, and Hugh moved regularly among Étampes, Poissy, Senlis and Orléans. He was crowned, probably, at Noyon, once the seat of Eligius, Dagobert's hated tax collector, by Archbishop Adalbero of Reims. Succeeding Capetians were crowned at Reims. Hugh's hold on France was tenuous owing to the fragmentation of actual power at the end of the tenth century. But he had several moral advantages. He was a sacerdotal figure, the legacy of Pope Stephen anointing Pepin; and, as king, he had most of the great magnates bound to him by oaths of fealty. While this was no guarantee against disloyalty, it at least provided the king with recourse of a legal and moral nature when subjects did rebel. Hugh Capet was shrewd. He understood his limitations, and reigned rather than ruled outside his personal domain, the Ile de France. He interfered in local affairs only when asked. France now was governed by castle-holding magnates who might be intimidated by a strong king, but could in turn intimidate a weak one. It still was much a matter of personality.

Normandy

In 793 Viking longships landed on Holy Island off the coast of Northumbria and sacked the famous Lindisfarne monastery. 'May God preserve us from the fury of the Northmen,' intoned many a monkish prayer thereafter. By contrast, the monastery of Mont-St-Michel, also on an island, on the coast of lower Normandy, was too well-fortified to be successfully attacked. Over the next century and more, the Vikings continued to assault Britain, and travelling up the Seine, Loire and Rhône, conduits for invaders and conquerors since Neolithic times, plagued Gaul almost beyond endurance.

They first appeared among the Franks in the 840s, striking swiftly, brutally and successfully. The Vikings were a pagan culture in search of movable wealth, usually precious metals (although in the cartoon strip Viking Hagar the Horrible often brings wife Helga dresses from chic Paris designers), which meant they preyed on churches and towns. Both were very vulnerable.

The Vikings' great advantage in Gaul was the political confusion of the ninth century when magnates, emperors and kings quarrelled constantly among themselves and could not mount any sustained, unified campaign against these northern marauders. Robert the Strong, for example, was killed in 866 fighting the Vikings but that was chance. He spent a great deal more time at war with Charles the Bald and Louis the Stammerer, his overlord and neighbour. It was understandable, then, that Charles the Simple decided to deal with the Vikings by making them respectable. In 911 he bought off the Viking chief Rollo, known as the Ganger, by appointing him count of Rouen with a substantial grant of land to support the honour. Rollo then left Charles alone, although he and his followers, at least through the reign of Rollo's successor, William Longsword, continued to regard Brittany as fair game. Actually, attacks on Brittany were often retaliation for Breton attacks on Normandy and elsewhere, and therefore part of Rollo's obligation as a count. Meanwhile, the bishop of Coutances fled in panic from his Norman See, despite Rollo's promise in the agreement of St-Clair-sur-Epte not to raid the church. The bishop of Rouen remained in place to oversee the Christianizing of these pagans and apparently was not molested by them.

Rollo proved to be a competent administrator. So too were his successors, becoming over the next decades Christianized, pacified and, to some degree, Frankified. For himself, Rollo, who became Christian as part of the bargain, left nothing to chance and on his death bed ordered both benefactions to Christian churches and human sacrifices. But his death signalled the passing of the 'old guard' so to speak, and his successors married Franks – for instance, Richard I married the daughter of Hugh the Great, thus becoming Hugh Capet's brother-in-law – and the Normans learned to speak the local dialect. Some of them in time entered monasteries or joined the clergy, and in due course became as French as anyone else in West Francia. The duchy of Normandy, as it soon became, grew strong and rich, a duchy to be reckoned with. It was to contribute to the fragmentation of Gaul at the end of the tenth century as it became yet another powerful feudal territory quarrelling with its neighbours and maintaining a great degree of autonomy. The feudal relationship was complex enough, given the weakness of those who held the Ile de France. It was to be complicated a hundredfold when one of the great Norman dukes, William II, bastard son of Duke Robert I, went off to become king of England in 1066.

CHAPTER THREE

Capetian France
987–1328

Political power was fragmented in the France of the Capets until reconsolidation began in the thirteenth century. Territorial princes and lesser nobles had real power, and it was greater the further they were from the Ile de France. There was no clearly defined feudal hierarchy to subdue this regionality. Even in the north, ties of vassalage and fief were little more than treaties to be broken at will, whether between king and noble, or noble and noble. It varied in degree, but generally a kind of aristocratic anarchy reigned involving princes, nobles, castellans (keepers of castles) and knights.

Territorial princes

Each major feudatory of France (Brittany, Normandy, Aquitaine, Champagne, Toulouse, Gascony and Anjou, among others) was ruled by a duke or count acting with sufficient independence and power to be regarded as virtually a kingly equal. Fulk Nerra of Anjou, Odo II of Blois, William II of Normandy and William X of Aquitaine, for example: dominating personalities, able rulers, renowned warriors. They were vassals of the king, and lesser lords and knights were their vassals. But this was often a formality, enforceable in the last resort only by the deployment of armed strength. Meanwhile these princes ruled virtually without hindrance, imitated the ceremonial, language and practice of royalty, and often made war against the king as well as against each other. The only difference was that the royal title, conferred by crowning and anointing, gave the kingly office a sacred and special feudal dimension beyond mere territorial titles.

In some regions hierarchical feudal relationships were firmly fixed: in Normandy, Flanders and Aquitaine, for example. Regarding these regions the Ile de France often sustained itself only by making alliance with one set of princes against another.

However, while the princes were often virtually independent of the king, none among them ever disputed the existence of the royal office. Odo II of Blois often said – with tongue in cheek, no doubt – that he did not wish to be king, but the king's master. By the middle of the eleventh century the Francian (French) monarchy had arrived to stay, and the main currents of French history thereafter swirled around it.

Royal Power

Crowning and anointing made kings 'clean different' from their subjects, as England's Charles I was later to put it. Even so, they had first to be chosen by an assembly of nobles, knights and clerics from the royal principality, and then consecrated and blessed by the bishops (who had transferred the sacerdotal tradition and their political loyalty from the Carolingians to the Capetians), anointed with holy chrism, invested with sword, ring, sceptre and rod (also by the bishops), and crowned and enthroned. The king was then recognized as lawgiver, the keeper of God's peace, and overlord of the whole of France, to whom all territorial magnates and lesser lords owed service and counsel as vassals.

The theory was greater than the fact. Capetian power was limited to the Ile de France, that collection of secular and ecclesiastical lands and rights which the kings ruled directly, and any other areas which they could dominate. Within the Ile de France they controlled a primitive government machinery which any vassal could call upon for assistance. This government was usually limited to issuing royal charters. They also held a number of castles and towns, including *villeneuves*, or 'new towns', chartered for commercial or strategic purposes. But even in the royal principality many ancient and powerful hereditary castellan families defied these kings: of these Montlhéry, Montmorency and Montfort were among the most troublesome. On his deathbed, Philip I told his son never to let the tower of Montlhéry out of his keeping, 'Frankly, that tower has made me old before my time.'

Political power, royal or princely, depended upon the personal strength or weakness of rulers, on the extent of feudal pluralism (wherein a vassal commended himself to two or more lords), and on the knightly class which emerged in the tenth century. Knights – mounted war machines supported first as household retainers and then as holders of fiefs and benefices in return for service – were, by 1000, the core of royal and noble armies. Sometimes they were little better than roving mercenaries, and their presence was the 'yeast of anarchy and a threat of disorder for society' – the essence of feudalism, in the historian J.F. Larignier's view.

By 1100 many knights were castellans, but still exhibited the anarchic and savage behaviour of the mercenary. Thomas de Marle of Laon was credited with warring against his father, cutting the throat of his relative, the archdeacon Gautier of Laon, giving sanctuary to the murderers of the bishop of Laon, and confiscating ecclesiastical property. He was excommunicated in 1114, and Louis VI outlawed him. The kings sat at the top and the knights at the bottom of a very loosely constructed feudal pyramid.

The First Capets

Hugh behaved as a territorial prince and did little more than survive. His successors into the twelfth century were not more promising: they fell foul of the church for engaging in sexual *mésalliances*, they warred endlessly with their vassals, and they expanded the interests of the monarchy only slightly, if at all. Robert II, the Pious (996–1031), was the first French king credited with curing scrofula by touching. Henry I (1031–1060) married Anne of Kiev, whose father's court rivalled Constantinople in brilliance. Henry by comparison was a bumpkin, never sure 'he would not have his pocket picked if he ventured more than three leagues from his palace'. Philip I (1060–1108) was 'indolent, fat, and unfit for war,' as was his son, Louis VI (1108–1137). Louis also fathered at least seven illegitimate children, and was noteworthy mainly because Suger, abbot of Saint-Denis, was his principal administrative servant. Not a brilliant beginning for the Capets. At least Henry was credited with having 'put royal power back on the map', if not of actually expanding it. By his day the prestige of the monarchy was such that when Henry summoned vassals to his aid, they usually came.

Normandy and England

In 1066 William II, duke of Normandy, invaded England, overthrew King Harold in a battle near Hastings, and became king himself. The pictorial record of this event, a large, sewn cloth wrongly called a tapestry, hangs in Bayeux in Normandy. Could William, now a king in his own right, continue to swear fealty as duke of Normandy to King Philip, his feudal overlord? That very real problem was soon joined to a much greater one: could Philip maintain his throne in the face of William's enlarged prestige and power?

Philip did much better than some accounts might suggest. He fought successful holding actions against William and his allies, and after William's death encouraged divisive jealousy between William's sons,

The tomb of Richard Coeur de Lion at the Abbey of Fontevrault

William Rufus, king of England, and Robert Curthose, duke of Normandy. Philip continued to fish in these troubled waters when Henry I succeeded William Rufus, but died with nothing resolved. Louis VI simply took up where his father left off: he fought with Henry over Gisors in Normandy, encouraged rebellion among Norman nobles, and even appealed to Pope Calixtus II for aid. It was only the beginning. Anglo-French wars dragged on for the next three centuries.

Crown and clergy

The Church was not the problem for the Capets that Normandy was, but it was a problem all the same. French bishops in the north – at Reims, Sens, Laon, Orléans and elsewhere – made alliances with the throne and expected royal support for their privileges in return. When they did not get it, they were disloyal; as they also were rich and powerful, their disloyalty was both annoying and dangerous. French kings did not care for these uncertain arrangements.

CLUNY

The Cluniac reforms showed a way out. The Benedictine abbey of Cluny in Burgundy, founded in 909 by Bruno of Baume and chartered by Duke William of Aquitaine, led a wide-ranging monastic reform in the eleventh century. It called for the free election of abbots, a direct link with papal authority, guarantees for monastic property (Cluniac monks embraced personal poverty but the Order lived in richly decorated and ornate houses), elaborate liturgical ceremony and prayer, and strict discipline. Cluny soon had two thousand dependent houses, the right to reform others where discipline was slack (such as the abbey of Saint-Denis), and independence from the bishops. The bishops did not care for that, but both popes and kings did, for they were plagued equally by 'over-mighty' episcopal subjects.

There were drawbacks. The Cluniac movement could be used against powerful bishops and archbishops, and often was, by both popes and kings. But the Cluniacs meant what they said and such saintly, and powerful, abbots as Hugh of Cluny brooked no pragmatic nonsense from crown or tiara (as the papal crown was named) on the matter of the 'new morality'. Robert the Pious was a great enthusiast for the Cluniacs; Henry I chafed under them and Louis VI, with his brood of royal bastards, found them annoying. Philip I preferred them to independent and uncooperative bishops, but only just. His sins were as numerous – and of the same sort – as those of his son.

PAPAL REFORM

Worse was to come. In the eleventh century the papacy too was bitten by the reforming bug, and set out to recover prestige and moral authority eroded by weak popes and a corrupt clergy. Leo IX and Gregory VII led the way. They condemned simony (the buying and selling of church offices) and lay investment (clergy receiving symbols of office from lay lords), and asserted papal supremacy over temporal rulers.

French kings, among the worst offenders against ecclesiastical privilege, tried to take it all in their stride. When accused of simony, Henry I ignored the charge and took over more religious houses. Philip I, condemned and excommunicated for his 'marital excesses and self-indulgent way of life', turned without a qualm to bishops Walter of Meaux and John of Orléans, whom he had created, for support against the papacy. They gave it. It was Philip's view that the church existed to be exploited, and that bishops ought to serve the crown in this as in other areas. The role of the bishops has always been ambiguous in the history of Christian monarchy.

THE CRUSADES

Clearly a crisis was brewing when popes, bishops, princes and kings all claimed powerful rights and were unprepared to compromise. (Henry of Germany kneeling penitently in the snow at Canossa was a political chess move against Pope Gregory, not an admission of defeat.) The laity had physical power, but the church held the ultimate trump: moral authority. It also controlled the main channels of propaganda, the pulpits. In 1095 at Clermont, Pope Urban II called for a crusade to liberate Palestine from the Saracens (Moslems). This crusade was eloquently preached across Europe by the papal legate, Bishop Adhémar of Le Puy. The idea caught on, and over the next few decades men and women from every class and condition in Europe participated in holy expeditions *outremer* (overseas), urged on by the likes of Adhémar and Bernard, the firebrand abbot of Clairvaux.

It was a masterful stroke. Could King Philip disapprove as Peter the Hermit emptied his realm of starving peasants, various fanatics, beggars and adventurers for the 'Peoples' Crusade'? Could any prince object to enhanced moral stature gained by 'taking the Cross'? Could the papacy fail to gain from diverting secular energies away from the brewing church-state crisis? Did not nobles who remained at home profit from the departure of their rivals for Palestine? And were not aristocrats with few acres and many sons pleased that the pope now sanctioned abroad the practice of looting, which had been discouraged in Europe by the 'peace and truce of God' movement after the Council of Limoges in 994? The crusades, wrote the historian Elizabeth Hallam, 'canalised the piety, pugnacity and greed of the western nobles and earned much prestige for their lay and ecclesiastical leaders.'

The French above all: by 1099 Bohemond of Hauteville, Godfrey of Bouillon, Hugh of Vermandois, Raymond IV of Toulouse, Robert Curthose of Normandy, and Robert II of Flanders had established four Latin states in Palestine. The crusades degenerated thereafter into wars between Christian princes.

Suger of Saint-Denis

Suger, abbot of Saint-Denis, was the invaluable right-hand man of Louis VII (1137–1180), the first French monarch to take the cross. Perhaps Louis, who left for his crusade in 1146, went as penance for having burnt a church at Vitry with 1500 people inside in about 1143. Neither he nor France profited from his venture abroad, nor from much else that he did. The best part of his reign was the service given him by Suger, whom he 'inherited' from Louis VI.

Leaving Suger in charge, Louis went off to Palestine with his wife and an army. The crusade was a débâcle, and Louis spent his time making pilgrimages to shrines – commendable, probably, but of little military value. At home, his brother Robert of Dreux, who had fallen out with Louis in Palestine, plotted with dissident nobles in Paris to seize the throne. In 1149 Suger called them to an assembly at Soissons and in eloquent phrases (including threats of excommunication) talked them out of it. He wrote to Louis urging him in strong language to come home. The king was alarmed and, disgruntled with events in Palestine, came at once. Suger died soon after, exhausted from his efforts on behalf of Louis's throne. He was a great churchman, and a greater administrator; a most loyal ecclesiastical subject. Best of all, he was patron of the new basilica for the abbey church, which introduced that highly decorative, pointed-arched and rose-windowed church-style that is called Gothic, and which replaced the simpler but no less elegant Romanesque style. Saint-Denis was the model for the cathedrals of Chartres, Amiens, Reims, Notre-Dame, and many others.

Twelfth-century Gothic carving at Cunault Church

Eleanor and Louis

Louis VII's failure on his crusade was of small account compared to his failures at home. Duke William X of Aquitaine bequeathed his duchy to his daughter, Eleanor, and both of them to Louis VI. In 1137 Louis married Eleanor to his son, who as Louis VII and ruler of Aquitaine ascended the French throne as a *puissant prince* (as the troubadour literature of Eleanor's duchy termed it), at least on paper. He relished this view of himself.

Louis intervened in the affairs of Anjou, Normandy and Champagne, and worked hard, behind Eleanor's urging, to expand the interests of

Aquitaine. He was not remarkably successful, losing, in the end, more than he gained. Above all, he was no match for the strong-willed, vigorous, vivid and brilliant Eleanor, who always put Aquitaine ahead of France. She produced only daughters for Louis, which disgruntled him. Their relationship deteriorated steadily, and when he insisted that she accompany him on crusade, Eleanor had had enough. In Antioch she 'fell into the arms' of her youthful uncle, Raymond of Aquitaine, with whom she was accused of 'lewd and improper' behaviour. When she returned to Paris she was pregnant, probably by Raymond.

In 1151 Louis also had had enough, and procured a papal annulment of the marriage. Eleanor went happily, taking Aquitaine with her. A year later she made a brilliant match with Henry Plantagenet, son of Geoffrey 'the Bel' of Anjou, who was soon to be King Henry II of England. They married in 1152. For him Eleanor bore four sons, each of whom proved to be, in some degree, a disaster. By contrast her daughter by Louis VII, Marie of France, did well. She married Henry of Champagne and wrote Arthurian romances on a par with Chrétien de Troyes.

The Angevin Empire

Eleanor's marriage was a blow to Louis VII. In 1154 Henry mounted the English throne as master of England, Normandy and Aquitaine; a quarter of a century of vigorous warfare later, and he had created the vast Angevin Empire: Scotland, Ireland, Wales and England; Normandy, Anjou, Aquitaine, Brittany, Gascony, and Béarn (the Pyrénées). The French crown barely hung onto the royal principality.

Actually, Henry acknowledged the feudatory status of his French holdings. When he set off to attack Toulouse in 1159, Louis backed Count Raymond V and occupied the city. Henry was not prepared to lay siege to his suzerain and withdrew. Thus the feudal system perhaps worked better than is supposed; or, more likely, Henry thought that to attack the king from whom he held Normandy and other French lands might give ideas to his own vassals in England, a surly and contentious lot at the best of times.

Louis had other ways of resisting which also met with some success.

When Thomas à Becket, archbishop of Canterbury, fell out with Henry and fled to Louis for protection, the French monarch gave it, thereby strengthening his ties with the Church. When Becket was murdered and blame fell on Henry, Louis's reputation expanded greatly as the godly king who had protected the martyr. Finally, Eleanor set her four sons against their father when they grew up, still in the interest of Aquitaine, discord which Louis did everything in his power to encourage. By 1175 he was still confronted with overwhelming Angevin power in France, but had managed to contain it. In 1179 he crowned his successor, Philip *dieudonné* (gift of God), his son by his second marriage to Adela of Champagne. Things were about to change dramatically in royal France.

Philip Augustus

Philip II, Augustus (1180–1223), was intelligent, prudent, cunning and successful. He reversed the Angevin trend and expanded royal power into Picardy, Normandy, Anjou, Maine, and Languedoc. He married Isabella, daughter of Baldwin V of Hainault, which gave him Artois, access to other properties and young Louis, his heir. When Isabella died he married Ingeborg of Denmark, whom he disliked immediately they were wed. He set her aside in favour of Agnes of Méran. Like many Capetians, Philip Augustus found it difficult to work out the dynamics of successful marital relations.

In 1182 an alliance with the ageing Henry II, arranged at Gisors on the Seine, Henry's favourite Norman château, gave Philip support in his wars with Flanders and Champagne. In the later 1180s he and Henry fell out over Brittany, and Philip, like Louis before him, played off the Plantagenet sons against their father. Eleanor was also involved. Philip made alliances with her and with Richard Coeur-de-Lion, the future King Richard I of England. When Henry died in 1189, all of his sons, his wife and Philip were plotting against him.

Philip made war against the Plantagenets over the Angevin Empire until little of it was left. King John of England was known appropriately as Lackland for all the French territory he lost, notably after his disastrous defeat at Philip's hands at Bouvines in 1214. Philip used every channel open to him to advance the interests of the crown against the

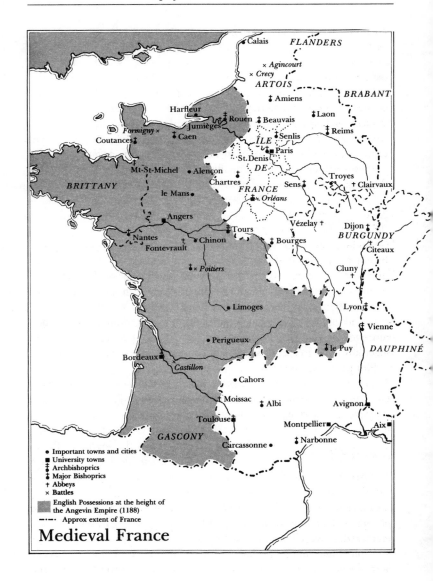

Medieval France

• Important towns and cities
■ University towns
‡ Archbishoprics
⚕ Major Bishoprics
† Abbeys
× Battles

English Possessions at the height of
the Angevin Empire (1188)
—·—· Approx extent of France

Angevins, and against his own recalcitrant vassals, including paying lip service to, and participating briefly in, the crusades in order to gain favour with the papacy and divert the attention of his rivals. His efforts did not go unopposed.

Many territorial princes continued to behave as independently as their personal power allowed, and in the 'liberated' Angevin lands they often showed their gratitude to the monarch of France by backing the English. This was true especially in the south-west where the Bordeaux wine trade with England was very old and very lucrative.

Philip backed the church against the Albigensian heresy (centred in the episcopal city of Albi, it was anti-Rome and anti-clerical) in Toulouse and Languedoc, acted as law-giver and patron of church-building, and advanced Paris as the commercial centre of France. In Paris, he built hospitals, rebuilt many churches, including Saint-Geneviève, caused the work on Notre-Dame cathedral, begun by Bishop Maurice de Sully in Louis VII's reign, to go forward, oversaw the first cobbling of Paris streets (it was said that he tired of having to wade in mud every time he left the palace), and created a form of a metropolitan police force. In 1200 he codified the study of medicine, and civil and canon law. When Philip died in 1223 royal lands were three times as extensive as in his father's day, and Plantagenet holdings had shrunk merely to Gascony and Béarn.

Philip's son, Louis VIII, reigned only until 1226. Thus between Philip Augustus, arguably France's greatest monarch, and his grandson Louis IX, arguably its most pious, almost nothing intervened save a spectacularly bloody campaign against the Albigensians.

Social Change

The growth of the Capetian centre was in the context of economic, social and urban change, which may indeed have encouraged it. During the eleventh and twelfth centuries much forest land was cleared for the plough and colonized at the landlords' urging. Long-distance trade increased, inspired by the rising demand for luxury goods. Local markets multiplied and money became a more common medium of exchange. Serfs declined in numbers as a group, and rents and dues often replaced labour service for peasants. Urban communities grew in importance and independence, with many now able to negotiate successfully for charters granting them privileges separate from the surrounding countryside: Orléans, La Chapelle, Aude, Étampes, and Souvigny offer examples of the general nature of this development. Extravagant lifestyles for the nobility created an ever-increasing burden of debt, an affliction also of many religious communities. In consequence many territorial lords became patrons of trade and commerce. The counts of Flanders and Champagne, and Philip Augustus himself adopted deliberate economic policies. It may have been the result of changing climatic conditions which favoured agriculture in the rich lands of Picardy and the Ile de France, and of the invention of the horse-drawn iron plough.

ABÉLARD AND THE UNIVERSITY OF PARIS

At the dawn of the twelfth century, Peter Abélard, a Breton, arrived in Paris and challenged and surpassed the teaching supremacy of Guillaume of Champeaux at the cathedral school. The young philosopher was brilliant, poetical and musical, and attractive. He set up his rival school in the cloister of Sainte-Geneviève. Students came to him in droves, leaving Guillaume high and dry. One of these was Héloïse, niece of Canon Filbert of Notre-Dame and Guillaume's patron.

The attraction for her was not wholly intellectual. Soon Héloïse was pregnant. Abélard took her away to Brittany where they were secretly married, and she bore a son. Canon Filbert was not pleased. He hired some ruffians and a barber to abduct Abélard and perform such rough justice on him that he was forced into a life of chastity. Abélard became a monk and persuaded Héloïse to enter the convent at Argenteuil. There she wrote her famous letters which prove that the flame burning within her was anything but spiritual. Abélard took up teaching again, and began writing the books which prove him to have been among the greatest minds of that or any other age.

As a thinker, Abélard was always at the centre of controversy. His early work was condemned and burnt at Soissons because of its personalized theology. This did not deter him, and thereafter he produced some of the great writing of the Middle Ages, including the famous rationalist treatise *Sic et Non*. Abélard claimed that he was now 'the only philosopher on earth and saw no rival whom I need fear'. False humility was never a problem for him. The last great confrontation for the ageing philosopher was against Bernard of Clairvaux at a council at Sens in 1140. Bernard, fearing he was intellectually no match for Abélard, refused to debate and merely read off 17 prepared propositions condemning Abélard's work. The monk stormed from the session and retired to a Cluniac priory at Châlons where he ended his days.

Intellectual life in France 'took off' after Abélard. When the University of Paris was founded, chartered, and officially recognized by Pope Innocent III and Philip Augustus a generation later, Abélard's school at Sainte-Geneviève was the embryo. True to his character, the university began life amid controversy: brawls and rifts between students and the *prévôts* (police officials) and citizens of Paris were customary. These have continued to be part of university life, on and off, ever since.

THE CHURCH

In the early thirteenth century the Capetians took control in the endless task of sorting out church-state relations. Louis VI granted and chartered religious houses, and aided popes against emperors. But he reformed monastic houses on his own, used ecclesiastical office to enrich his family, and insisted upon his regalian (royal) right to supervise episcopal and abbotical elections. Louis VII acted similarly, although perhaps less dramatically, and despite his great reputation for piety never relaxed his control over royal churches. Often he used his pious reputation for gain, as in his aid to Thomas à Becket: it was 'piety with valuable political consequences'.

Philip Augustus paid well-publicized deference to church and clerical rights; but in practice he did not allow any extension of papal power in France. He allowed free clerical elections, but let it be known he expected his candidates to be elected. The Church and churchmen complained, fulminated, cajoled, excommunicated, pleaded, threatened, plotted and manipulated on behalf of their privileges. But by the end of Louis VIII's short reign the crown controlled most of the French church, and more importantly, the French church gave its loyalty to the king before the pope.

Saint-Louis

Louis IX (1226–1270), the only French king to be canonized, continued strongly in the established warring traditions of the house of Capet: he fought England (under Henry III), his own territorial vassals, the Saracens and the Albigensian heretics. He also built churches (most famously the Sainte-Chapelle on the Ile de la Cité in Paris), was pious, (just), supported the papacy (so long as it did not encroach upon his domain), dressed simply and, so far as a king could be, was humble. Louis died while on a crusade. For these things and for providing what his chronicler Joinville called good government, he was canonized.

His canonization simply shows up the importance of propaganda even at that early date. Louis' exploits were substantively no greater, if as great, as those of his grandfather, Philip Augustus; but they were of the sort to impress the Church. The Church was grateful for them; hence Saint-Louis. However, the only truly distinctive thing about his reign was the remarkable women it brought to light.

Blanche of Castile

Louis came to the throne as a minor with his mother, Blanche of Castile, as regent. Henry III of England, various French territorial magnates and members of Louis's own family tried to forward their interests at his expense: even, as in the case of the counts of Boulogne and Brittany, to dethrone him. Blanche held France for Louis, 'a remarkable achievement for a foreigner and a woman in a land where politics were dominated by men,' with the aid of loyal castellan families. Among those, ironically, were the Montmorency and Montfort, who had made life so difficult for Philip I and Louis VI. Blanche played a key role in consolidating royal power.

Margaret of Provence

Louis married Margaret in 1234. Blanche hated her from the start, for fear that she would dominate the royal household. For a time Blanche held her at bay, but after 1244 Margaret's influence with the king grew while Blanche's influence waned. Louis took his wife on a crusade in

1248. The campaign was a disaster, and Louis himself was taken prisoner and had to pay a huge ransom. Meanwhile, Margaret held the Egyptian seaport of Damietta for him, and gave birth to their son, John Tristan, at the same time. She was the sister of Henry III's wife, Eleanor, and probably influenced Louis to side with Henry against the Provisions of Oxford, imposed upon the English king by his barons in 1263 to reaffirm the Magna Carta. Margaret survived Louis by 25 years. In that time she was no less spirited on her own behalf, wresting concessions from Charles of Anjou, her brother-in-law, regarding her Provençal inheritance, and furthering the interests of her son, Philip III. In the end Margaret received Beaufort, Baugé and Anjou itself, which she administered effectively until her death.

The thirteenth century produced a striking collection of women in France, beginning with Eleanor of Aquitaine, who lived well into it, and including Blanche, Eleanor's granddaughter, and Margaret. There also were Alice of Cyprus, who fought an unsuccessful war for the possession of Champagne, and Isabella of La Marche, widow of King John, who organized resistance to the French king in Poitou in league with her husband, Hugh. She was consigned to the abbey of Fontevrault for her trouble. In centuries to come there would be others. It remains a mystery why the assumption grew up that women could not manage affairs with as much cunning and strength of will and intellect as could men; or why French women received the vote only in 1945.

The Last Capetians

Fifty-eight years remained to the Capets after Saint-Louis. Between 1270 and 1328 five kings reigned: Philip III (1270–1285), Philip IV, the Fair (1285–1314), Louis X (1314–1316), Philip V (1316–1322) and Charles IV (1322–1328). Only Philip III and Philip IV lasted longer than a half-dozen years, but all saw advances in the prestige and power of royal France. By 1328 more of the country than ever before was under the royal house, directly or through lands attached to members of the family. The royal administration, judicial court (*Parlement* of Paris), and style of the monarchy was increasingly urbane and sophisticated; the Church was humbled; and the economy waxed strong. Even so, there were clouds on the horizon as well as bright sun at the zenith of the royal day.

THE ALBIGENSIAN CRUSADE

During the thirteenth century, the Capets appeared to profit from nearly every venture, so long as it was in France proper. Between 1209 and 1330 the crown made war in Toulouse and Languedoc against the Albigensian heretics, who were backed by the counts of Toulouse and other southern nobles. This heresy was inconsistent in its beliefs except that it opposed the corruption of Rome and antedated the Protestant reformers. Successive French kings campaigned against the Albigensians with the blessings of the Church, seizing, burning and slaughtering: in one day in 1245 royal officers and members of the Inquisition burnt 200 heretics at Montségur. When the smoke cleared the traditional independence of these principalities was broken along with the heresy, and they were brought under royal control.

THE TEMPLARS

Another crusade of a different but equally profitable nature was Philip IV's suppressing of the Templars, one of the holy orders of knights created during the crusades. Rich and powerful, they were a particularly tempting target for a king both pressed for cash and anxious to rid himself of any form of opposition from ecclesiastical sources. First the Templars had to be discredited. This was managed by Guillaume of Nogaret, Philip's principal hatchet-man and a skilful propagandist.

In 1307 Templars were arrested throughout France and made to confess under torture to the most diabolical practices, including witchcraft and Satanism. Pope Clement V condemned all of this and did not believe what he was being told about the Templars. Nogaret then produced public confessions by the Grand Master, Jacques de Molay, and other leaders. Finally after more than 70 Templars confessed before the pope on his visit to Poitiers, Clement compromised and the suppression was carried through to its bitter conclusion.

Templar property was transferred to the Hospitallers, another knightly order, who were compelled to pay Philip huge sums for it. The rank and file were pensioned off to religious houses, but de Molay and other leaders were condemned and burnt. The chronicler Villani concluded: '[The king] ... made secret arrangements with the pope and caused him to promise to destroy the Templars, laying to their charge many articles of heresy; but it is said that this was more in the hope of extracting money from them ...' There was nothing new in all of this: even the pious Saint-Louis extracted money from the Church in the name of crusading causes. Philip merely surpassed others in the brutality of his extractions.

AVIGNON

Clement V was elected pope through Nogaret's intervention, and even though he eventually gave in over the Templars, Philip had him seized and removed to Avignon in Provence, virtually a prisoner of the French monarch. (Provence then belonged to the counts of Anjou, feudal vassals of the king.) There the papacy remained until 1377, freer under Clement's successors but still surrounded by French cardinals.

THE PRINCES

With the church humbled and Toulouse and Languedoc gained for the crown, the appearance of royal supremacy achieved by 1328 is compelling. Princely power, however, was only constrained; it was not broken. Indeed it was gathering itself even as royal supremacy was acknowledged. Europe marvelled at Philip IV's authority; but it was a power maintained at great strain and cost, and could easily be disrupted by any significant wrench in society or in the body politic. Professor J. Le Patourel suggested that in the thirteenth century the great territorialities were compromised; in the fourteenth they began reconsolidating their power; and in the fifteenth they again dominated the crown. In Brittany, by 1297, the count was a duke and peer of France, with his own *parlement* and financial institutions. In the 1340s the Breton dukes, with English backing, claimed that Brittany was a kingdom. In the 1390s they claimed it was not part of France at all. This was an extreme case, but it suggests that the Hundred Years War in the fourteenth century was a civil war as well as a struggle with England.

SOCIAL CRISES

Over the centuries, strong economic differences emerged from region to region, usually reflecting geography and climate. For example, the Ile de France and Picardy were agriculturally advanced and prosperous, while less lucrative subsistence farming and stock-raising characterized Languedoc and the Massif Central. The former comprised rich, well-watered soil; the latter were dry and rocky. Montaillou, a village in Foix in the Pyrénées, and a Cathar (Albigensian) stronghold, is well documented in the records of the Inquisition. It is a good example of the poorer sort of place: landless peasants working as shepherds; landed peasants raising poor crops on poor soil; and the difference between them of personal wealth much less than would have been the case in Blois or the Vexin. The *châtelain* had very little more land than the Clergues, a comparatively rich peasant family. The Clergues dominated village life. One of them was a womanizing priest, which, added to Montaillou's heresies, probably explains why the villagers resented the Roman church more than they did the local nobility.

Montaillou represented marginal living at all social levels, and its inhabitants might be thought easy prey in hard times: to extremist causes, to *jacqueries* (peasant uprisings) and to exploiting landlords. They were, but no more so than their more affluent counterparts in the north. Landlords always tried to expand their seigneurial rights in hard times in order to make ends meet, no matter where they were, and famines and crop failures devastated social tranquillity and stability equally wherever they occurred.

Consider the example of the north in the opening decades of the fourteenth century. Economic and social crises loomed in the Ile de France. Long years of warfare had brought royal expansion and apparent prosperity; they had also drained economic resources and weakened the social fabric. Then weather patterns abruptly changed and bad harvests followed: food shortages in Paris in 1305; grain scarce everywhere in 1309; bad harvests in the Ile de France in 1314; and freezing rain and flood-ravaged coastal areas throughout the summer of 1315, destroying crops on a wide scale. The psychological impact was horrendous. The price of wheat reached unprecedented levels, and starvation, disease, crime and even cannibalism followed. A chronicler in 1317 described a prayer procession to Saint-Denis in which poor people were barefoot and wholly or nearly naked. In 1320 a great band of poor men and fanatics roamed the land massacring Jews. In 1321 a similar massacre of lepers took place. The more economic conditions deteriorated, the more Philip's administrators manipulated the currency: they raised living costs, diminished the value of fixed incomes, created hardships for everyone, and sought to solve financial problems through such expedients as suppressing the Templars. No wonder the reign of Saint-Louis began to look like a Golden Age. The situation only worsened when the Hundred Years War began in 1339.

ORIGINS OF THE WAR

In 1328 Charles IV died leaving only a daughter. The throne passed to Philip VI of Valois (1328–1350), a grandson of Philip III. However the succession was clouded. The last Capets produced many daughters but few sons, and it was an erroneous presumption that the ancient *Lex Salica* of the founding Franks denied that royal inheritance could pass through the female line. This actually was an excuse to deny the claims to royal lands put forward by these daughters or their sons – or to the throne, a claim made by Isabella of England, daughter of Philip IV and mother-regent to the boy-king Edward III. When Edward grew up he did homage as lord of Gascony to Philip VI. Then in 1337 Philip seized Gascony, and Edward asserted his claim to the whole of France as Philip IV's grandson. He backed his claim with force, and in 1339 the Hundred Years War began. It reduced the crown to destitution, but raised the territorial princes to new heights. France again fell prey to the tensions and antagonisms of its disparate parts. It was to take a woman to sort it out.

CHAPTER FOUR

The Lily and The Lion
1328–1515

The Hundred Years War

The Hundred Years War effectively ended the French Middle Ages. The reign of Louis XI which followed it represented a bridge to the Renaissance.

'Hundred Years War' is a term less descriptive than symbolic; that is, it was a war and it lasted a very long time. But since the major feature was the struggle between France and England – the Lily and the Lion – for control of French lands, it could be argued that the war began in 1066 and only ended when England gave up Calais in 1558. Even the conventional dates, 1337–1453, are well beyond one hundred years. Nevertheless, the term provides a convenient handle for the war which started because Edward III, king of England, duke of Gascony and Philip IV's grandson, argued that his claim to the French throne was superior to that of Philip VI of Valois.

Philip, enthroned in 1328, naturally did not share Edward's views. In 1336 Edward, as duke, renounced his homage to Philip, who proceeded to seize Gascony and the war was on. It was in part a civil war: Edward was more French than English, and his Gascon barons gladly followed him against their French compatriots. Admittedly, they also expected that a king in distant England would be less interfering than one closer to home.

The war brought clearly into focus several long-standing issues: the perpetual struggle between the centralizing Paris monarchy and the independent-minded territorial princes; the question of who should control the crown, quite apart from the person wearing it; the conflict between the great lords for control of the economic resources upon which the royal government could call; and the security of the wine trade between Bordeaux, the principal Gascon city and port, and England. Ultimately, the war devastated wide areas of France and precipitated drastic alterations in internal social and economic relationships.

Edward tried to raise an anti-French coalition in the Low Countries, supported by the counts of Hainault and Brabant and wealthy merchant Jacob van Artevelde, who led an urban workers' revolt which drove out pro-French Louis of Nevers. But the revolt petered out, and with it the coalition. After 1339 the war settled into its 'heroic' phase: thirty years of the great, if often brutal, generalship of Edward III and his son, the Black Prince, and periodic *chevauchées*, 'scorched earth' campaigns in which English armies ravaged the countryside destroying and killing at random. There were also great battles which pitted French chivalry against English bowmen, to the former's discomfiture.

The English were singularly successful in the heroic period. In 1340 they destroyed most of the French fleet off Sluys, near the Scheldt River mouth in Flanders. It was the beginning of a very uncomfortable time for the French monarch, whose court, claimed King John of Bohemia, offered 'the most *chivalric* sojourn in the world'. Prophetic words: it was the chivalric mentality of French arms, the undisciplined, arrogant, glory-seeking individualism of the mounted knights, which brought defeat after defeat over the next 70-odd years.

After Sluys Philip was forced to levy additional taxes: the *gabelle*, a salt tax, which was extended to the whole nation in 1341, followed by a hearth tax in 1342. The *paysans* and townspeople regarded these taxes as extortionate and soon rebelled against them.

CRÉCY

The opening *chevauchée* occurred in 1345 in Poitou, the first of many over the coming years. It was followed in 1346 by the campaign which culminated in the Battle of Crécy, in Artois. After capturing Caen, King Edward's idea was to withdraw from Flanders before the ponderous French feudal army could be mobilized. He feinted towards Paris, then looked for an undestroyed bridge across the Somme. There were few left, and he was delayed several days. The French caught him at Crécy.

Badly outnumbered, the English fought a defensive, almost a guerilla, action. The infantry shot arrows from their longbows from behind hedges and fences at the French knights, who charged in reckless disorder. Edward's style of warfare was not chivalric, but it was effective. The French cavalry, wrote the chronicler Froissart, tried to push ahead of each other 'from mere pride and jealousy'. It was impossible to call a retreat even when it was clear the knights were being slaughtered to no purpose. Philip was lucky to escape from the débâcle. Edward too was lucky to leave Crécy unscathed, for he had been caught in a position where the skilful use of French cavalry could have turned English victory into a devastating defeat. But he came away whole, and pushed on to Calais were six townsmen (their sacrifice immortalized in sculpture by Auguste Rodin) surrendered their lives so that Edward might spare the city. Why they had to die is not clear.

Back in Paris Philip summoned the Estates, the representatives of church and nobility who advised him. There were recriminations. The Estates complained that Philip had humiliated French chivalry by losing the battle; Philip argued that the Estates were niggardly in providing him with adequate supplies.

The Black Death

'[In] men and women alike there appeared ... certain swellings, either on the groin or under the arm-pits, whereof some waxed of the bigness of a common apple, others like unto an egg ... and these the vulgar named plague-boils.' Then came black and red blotches on arms and thighs, until the body was covered, 'a very certain token of coming death ...' Thus Giovanni Boccaccio described the bubonic plague introduced into Europe probably from China, which reached France and England in 1348. An estimated third of the French population was wiped out with dramatic consequences: manpower shortages drove up labour costs; rural productivity and town manufacturing declined; the import market dried up, creating economic dislocations elsewhere in Europe; and the nobility, often facing bankruptcy, forced royal government to impose edicts freezing labour and rent obligations owed by peasants and labourers, so that aristocratic privilege would not be curtailed. The immediate consequence of these edicts was the *jacqueries*, the peasant uprisings of 1358 and 1381. But the clock could not be turned back, as these edicts with their strong hint of revitalized serfdom and even slavery attempted to do. Labour acquired a new value and the relationship between the landed classes and the peasantry was altered forever. Feudalism was doomed by the Black Death. The devastation of subsequent *chevauchées* and the outmoded military styles of French chivalry would finish it off.

The Dauphin

In 1349 France acquired control of Dauphiné, remote, rugged and backward, east of the Rhône and above Provence. Nominally Dauphiné was part of the Holy Roman Empire, that loose confederation of Germanic and some Italian regions (the legacy of Charlemagne's 'special relationship' with Rome), which came permanently under the rule of the House of Hapsburg in the fourteenth century and was the basis of their power through the eighteenth. Henceforth Dauphiné was an *apanage* for the royal heir, who would be known thereafter as the dauphin. Coincidental circumstance made successive dauphins supremely important in coming years.

The Black Death only briefly curtailed the war. The first dauphin replaced Philip in 1350, with the war in full swing. This was John II, the Good (1350–1364). He was not especially good, either as military leader or as king. Blunt, honest, even kindhearted on occasion, this king was also stubborn, narrow-minded and inflexible. John was unlucky as well: he had to concern himself from the start with Charles of Navarre, a cruel, thoroughly evil man who murdered Charles of Castille, the Constable of France, and made deals with the English. At Poitiers in 1356 John not only lost an important battle, but was taken captive into the bargain. The responsibility for France and for containing Charles of Navarre then fell on the none-too-sturdy shoulders of John's son, the dauphin Charles.

While John enjoyed a comfortable captivity (his captors treated him like royalty), Charles faced uprisings in Paris. Étienne Marcel, a rich merchant, and Robert Le Coq, bishop of Laon, channelled popular discontent over the evils and deprivations attending the war, and made the dauphin their virtual prisoner. He was forced to watch as two of his friends and counsellors were murdered. The Paris riots spread beyond the city and turned into the *jacquerie* of 1358. But the dauphin escaped from Paris and made his peace with Charles of Navarre. The dauphin and Navarre were enemies, but anarchy and riot among the common people threatened them both. They could always continue their quarrel later.

In 1360 the dauphin agreed to the Treaty of Bretigny with England, by which France had to pay three million gold *eçus* ransom for John, and the English were confirmed in possession of the Calais area and Aquitaine. John reigned for four more years, creating confusion and difficulty before he died.

Charles V

The dauphin became Charles V, the Wise (1364–1380). He actually was wise, or at the very least prudent. Charles found men of ability to serve him – the abbot Fécamp, Hugh Abricot, *prévôt* of Paris, and Bertrand du Guesclin, a Breton mercenary who understood the changing rules of warfare. Despite the annoyance it caused both his chivalric nobles and the English, Charles refused to fight more than minor engagements. In exasperation Edward III called him 'that lawyer', and it was not meant as a compliment. Perhaps Charles, not a strong, robust military figure on the lines of his father, simply followed his natural inclinations.

It was the correct policy. By 1374 France regained most of what had been lost, and even penetrated Gascony, where the usually pro-English nobility were rebelling against the Black Prince's efforts at streamlining the administration. Efficiency, they found, interfered with their privileges. The Gascons did not now resist the French king with their former enthusiasm.

Unfortunately for France, Charles's successor was a minor. In turbulent times almost nothing could be more destabilizing, and the accession of Charles VI, the Fool (1380–1422), brought out the royal uncles to take charge of him and to use this excuse of a royal minority to enhance their power as territorial lords. In 1388 Charles's brother, the duke of Orléans, goaded him into taking a stand, something the timid and none-too-bright king had remained reluctant to do even as an adult. But now he acted, dismissing the uncles and gathering around him able counsellors – called the Marmosets – some of whom had served his father.

Civil War

Sadly, Charles VI became deranged following an attempt on his life in 1392. The uncles returned, expelled the Marmosets and busied themselves exploiting crown resources for their own interests. Soon the duke of Burgundy was involved, and a civil war broke out. Burgundy encompassed part of the lands once comprising Lotharingia, a subdivision of the Frankish empire after Charlemagne, and had always been autonomous even though its dukes were vassals of the French king. Their autonomy made the dukes a natural rallying point whenever control of France was being contested. One side followed Burgundy's lead; the other, the so-called Armagnacs, adhered to the duke of Orléans and crown interests. It was a desperate time: the king was mad and his son, the future Charles VII, was unequipped to act decisively. Moreover the uncles had married Charles VI to Isabella of Bavaria, a woman of strong sexual appetites, who put it about that the dauphin was not the king's son.

Again a common enemy came to the rescue. In 1381 there had been another *jacquerie*, just after Charles was enthroned; in 1413 Simon Caboche, a butcher, led an uprising. These events were separated by three decades, but nonetheless reminded both sides that more was at stake than merely who controlled the poor, sick king or his irresolute son. The Caboche rising united the warring noble factions – just in time to confront a resurgent English army.

AGINCOURT

After 1377, with both King Edward and the Black Prince dead, the English were hampered by domestic quarrels and weak leadership. The war petered out until the accession of Henry V in the early fifteenth century. Strong, ambitious, anxious to reassert Plantagenet claims in France, he resumed the war. In 1415 Henry campaigned in Artois, took

Harfleur, and then at Agincourt faced a far superior force of French cavalry. Once again English archery prevailed. By 1415 armour was a complete metal cocoon; on horseback a knight, encased in seventy pounds of metal plating, was impregnable. If, on the other hand, the horse was shot from under him and he fell to the ground, the knight was helpless and easily dispatched by mallet-wielding infantry. At Agincourt the English longbow drove the last nail into the coffin of French feudalism. However, Agincourt was to be England's last major victory in the Hundred Years War.

THE TREATY OF TROYES

In 1420 Charles VI was forced to accept the Treaty of Troyes: the dauphin was disinherited in favour of Henry V; France was divided for purposes of administration between England (Aquitaine and a much enlarged Normandy including Anjou and parts of Brittany) and an Anglo-Burgundian alliance; and Henry would marry Catherine, Charles's only daughter, and upon Charles's death would become king of France. The dauphin was stuck in Bourges, maintained only by remnants of the Armagnac faction and seemingly a lost cause.

Joan of Arc

Henry and Catherine married and produced a son. Eight months later both Charles VI and Henry V were dead. The dauphin claimed the throne; so did the English on behalf of the Plantagenet heir. They held Paris and the baby Henry VI of England was duly enthroned. But with a child of such tender age as their king, the English lords immediately fell out over who should actually govern. Preoccupied with this internal struggle they left the dauphin unmolested in Bourges, where he seemed content to wait until doomsday. But, in fact, he delayed only six years, until Joan of Arc entered the picture and forced him into action.

Joan, the Maid of Orléans, was the stuff of which legends are made. Only she was no legend. This daughter of Jacques d'Arc, a well-off peasant from Domrémy on the Meuse, was 'a young woman of robust flesh and healthy blood, full of courage and tenderness, of common sense and racy humour'. Instructed by what she believed were the voices of the saints Michael, Margaret and Catherine, she set out in 1428 to save France. The moment was opportune. In October the English besieged Orléans. The dauphin Charles by then had sold his last jewels, had to have sleeves patched into his old doublet, could not get credit from a cordwainer for new shoes, and had only four crowns in his purse. He needed a miracle. What he got was Joan: much the same thing.

At first no one listened to Joan. But in this age, people believed in miracles. Finally Durand Laxart, her cousin by marriage, took Joan to the Sire de Baudricourt. Joan was compelling and convinced the Sire to take her to Chinon, to the dauphin. Joan persuaded the dauphin that she was directed by her 'voices' to throw the English out of France. He put her in charge – spiritually at any rate – of any army to raise the siege of Orléans. It was a curious but effective force including among its captains: Gilles de Rais (the legendary Bluebeard); La Hire, a good soldier and author of this unique soldier's prayer: 'God, I pray You that You will today do for La Hire what You would wish La Hire to do for You, if La Hire were God and You were a man-at-arms'; and Dunois, bastard son of the duke of Orléans, an exceptional soldier and Joan's devoted companion-in-arms. The army believed in her, took Orléans, and marched on Reims with Charles in tow where he was crowned in the cathedral. Joan's mission was complete; the rest was up to the king. She continued with the army, however, and in an attack on Compiègne in 1430 she was wounded and then captured by the Burgundians.

They sold her to the English who hated her (she was called a whore by her English guards who threatened to rape her on several occasions), and who gave her to the church for trial as a heretic. It was a show trial, of course, carried on at Rouen in Normandy, deep in English territory. The earl of Warwick masterminded it and Pierre Couchon, bishop of Beauvais, prosecuted. Joan was convicted, condemned, and on 30 May, 1431, burnt at Rouen. Charles did nothing to save her. Historian Martin Scott observed: 'Alive she would have been an embarrassment; as a martyr she formed a telling witness to the brutality of the English.' Her final achievement, it seems, was to become a propaganda weapon.

By 1432 Charles VII (1422–1461) sat firmly on a throne made available to him by Joan of Arc. But he was not out of the woods. Burgundy still sided with England, and he had yet to live down his reputation as the do-

Agnes Sorel, the favourite of Charles VII

nothing 'King of Bourges'. To aid him, Charles had merchant-banker Jacques Coeur of Bourges, the richest man in France, forward-looking military planners who understood the uses of gunpowder, and an Estates which understood the need for a regular army supported by regular taxes. Not for nothing was Charles VII called 'the Well-Served'.

It was to take another generation, but by 1453 English power in France was broken once and for all. Joan of Arc created the momentum which made it possible. Her presence generated the popular enthusiasm which goaded Charles to action in 1429, to a reconciliation with the duke of Burgundy in 1435, and to the victories at Formigny in 1450 and Castillon in 1453, after which English civil and military administration was withdrawn entirely from Normandy. The war was then over.

The Impact of the Hundred Years War

The Black Death, *chevauchées, jacqueries:* together they left an indelible mark, a scar of vivid hue, on the face of fifteenth-century France. A late fourteenth-century priest of Cahors recorded that he had seen nothing in his lifetime but war, and that in his diocese '... neither cock nor hen is crowing,' instead 'wolves and beasts of the forest' furrowed the fields. The Italian Petrarch wrote in 1360 that the English 'have reduced the entire kingdom of France by fire and sword to such a state that I, who had traversed it lately on business, had to force myself to believe that it was the same country I had seen before. Outside the walls of towns, there was not, as it were, one building left standing.' A century later French chronicler Thomas Basin wrote:

> From the Loire to the Seine, and from there to the Somme, nearly all the fields were left for a long time ... not merely untended but without people capable of cultivating them, except for rare patches of soil, for the peasants had been killed or put to flight .... We ourselves have seen the vast plains of Champagne, Beauce, Brie, Gatinais, Chartres, Dreux, Mainz and Perche, Vexin, both French and Norman, Beauvais, Caux, from the Seine as far as Amiens and Abbeville, Senlis, Soissonnais, Valois, as far as Laon and, beyond, as far as Hainault, absolutely deserted, uncultivated, abandoned, devoid of all inhabitants, overgrown with brushwood ...

Exaggerations? Probably not, particularly when considered in the context of the Black Death and the slaughter of peasants in putting down the *jacqueries*. When Louis XI ascended the throne in 1461 the waste of the war was such that the desperate need for labour enabled many serfs to win freedom, and many peasants to gain advantageous terms for their tenantry. Many nobles were impoverished, and towns and townsmen had grown stronger (for this was what the insurrections led by Étienne Marcel and the butcher Caboche really signified) relative to the nobility. The age of the bourgoisie was beginning even as the bonds of feudalism were weakening.

EDUCATION

Meanwhile, the horizons of the intellect deepened and widened during this era of war and devastation, expanding upon foundations laid in the eleventh and twelfth centuries. Primary education was hit and miss:

children learnt to read and write at home, in 'dame school' or in chantry, or not at all. Grammar schools were better and more formally organized, and were not uncommon by the fourteenth century. After the manner of Bernard of Chartres, they used Latin in the upper and vernacular in the lower forms, although vernacular was not taught expressly as a subject, whereas Latin was. Universities expanded in number and between 1300 and 1500 13 universities were founded in France beyond the University of Paris, including Caen and Bordeaux in 'English' France, where the idea was to draw students away from Paris.

There was no doubt that Paris was the intellectual centre of Europe, and its university was the reason. The courses were in rhetoric, logic, metaphysics, moral and natural philosophy. The faculties enjoyed great intellectual freedom and were remarkably independent. True, successive kings forbade the discussion of church-state questions and Sorbonne theologians were obliged to argue the king's position in the Great Schism regarding the Avignon papacy; but this was minor secular interference compared to the count of Provence who fined Provençals for attending any university but Aix. Medicine and Law, long established at the Montpellier University in Roussillon were added to the Paris curriculum in the fifteenth century, and the time required to complete the Master of Arts degree was reduced.

In the fourteenth century, Scholasticism promoted fierce debates in Paris between adherents of 'realism' (the real existence of abstractions) and 'nominalism' (abstractions useful only as intellectual devices for speculation). Those who debated were among the finest minds Europe has produced: Thomas Aquinas, Jean Gerson and Roger Bacon, among others. Their intellectual conflicts led directly to the methodological division which has informed western science and philosophy ever since. The French followed 'realism' straight to René Descartes in the seventeenth century, who linked it with modern mathematics to make 'rationalism'; the English endorsed and promoted 'nominalism', which led to Francis Bacon, Descartes's contemporary, who advanced the methodology common to modern science, and known as 'empiricism'.

VERNACULAR LITERATURE

In popular literature the vernacular had been the currency for generations. *Chanson de Roland*, the romance in *Langue d'Oïl* about the betrayed Carolingian hero Roland dying in defence of the pass at Roncesvalles against the Basques, appeared around 1100. It was in the heroic *chanson de geste* tradition. Meanwhile, in *Langue d'Oc* and *Langue d'Oïl* Troubadour poetry, the literature of 'courtly love' – a far cry from the men-only *chanson de geste* – captured the fancy of the literate population of Europe. The Troubadours (among them William IX of Aquitaine and Richard I of England) told of ladies worshipped from afar by knightly lovers who sought their favour by displaying the chivalrous virtues of patience, constancy and prowess in war. The genre was probably instructional, meant to curb the savage behaviour of uncultured knights in eleventh-century Aquitaine. Meanwhile, maidens were exhorted to remain chaste for the marriage bed. The moral lessons of Troubadour writing were clear and so was its earthiness. Jean Gerson thought the poetry encouraged lewd behaviour, and wrote a denunciation of *Roman de la Rose* as engendering lustful thoughts. Professor G.G. Coulton reckons that Gerson failed to understand the mentality of his own age: 'Moral at one moment and immoral at another, without any great effort to paper over the cracks.'

One other vernacular tradition both delighted and irked its public. The goliard poets were 'literary outlaws', roaming France and singing of bawdy subjects: drink, seduction, and corrupt clergy. *Passions of our Lord the Pope of the Romans according to the Gold and Silver Marks* was an outstanding and tasteless example. As often as not goliards ended their days at the end of a rope, or worse.

Prose was also popular by the fifteenth century, particularly in the chronicles of men like Froissart and Chastellain. Vernacular commentaries on religious and political subjects also appeared. Philippe de Commynes's *Memoirs*, for instance. The older forms remained and grew even more popular. In Paris, François Villon carried on the goliardic tradition, and like the goliards, remained just one jump ahead of the law until finally he was destroyed by it.

ART AND ARCHITECTURE

As we have seen, Suger of Saint-Denis introduced Gothic, the architectural style which replaced Romanesque in the twelfth century.

It incorporated the pointed arch, cross- or rib-vault, flying buttress and rose window. Churchmen such as Suger and Bishop Maurice de Sully of Notre-Dame inspired the Gothic; less well known are the names of its architects: Pierre de Montreuil for Saint-Denis and Sens, Jean Langlois for Troyes, and Jean de Challes for Notre-Dame. Gothic dominated well into the Renaissance, until Michelangelo and Bramante revolutionized church architecture with Saint Peter's Basilica in Rome.

The Gothic church illuminated the bible for the illiterate faithful: the church buildings became the Bible of the Poor, as Henry Adams made clear in his famous book *Chartres*. Every statue, window, gargoyle, and carving informed and reminded the worshipper of the essentials of Christianity. St Peter held a key; Christ raised his fingers in benediction; rose windows described in their colours the indescribable beauty of the Divine; other stained glass told biblical and inspirational stories; and the gargoyles reminded the wicked that terrible beasts waited to tear the flesh of the damned. Religious manuscripts were illuminated in order to shed the light of glory on the word of God. François Villon had his illiterate mother say: 'I am a poor, old woman who knows nothing, who cannot read. But in church I see Paradise painted, and Hell where the

The tympanum at Chartres

damned boil.' In time, similar techniques, materials, and probably designers, came to be employed in the construction of châteaux and the decorating of secular windows and manuscripts – Books of Hours in particular – and often for the same purposes.

THE CHURCH

By removing Clement V to Avignon in 1307, Philip IV set in motion events which Gallicanized the fifteenth-century church in France. French influence at Avignon remained considerable after Clement V. Every pope between Clement, who died in 1314, and Urban VI, elected in 1378, was French; and of 134 cardinals created in those six decades, 116 came from France. The Italians thought they should own the papacy, and when it returned to Rome in the 1370s they determined to remove French influence. The outcome was the Great Schism, with popes elected at both Rome and Avignon. Charles V had the Sorbonne declare for Avignon, while the Holy Roman Emperor backed Rome. All Europe divided over support of the two papacies and for a time it looked as if the ancient unitary concept of church and Christian civilization would be broken in Europe. In France it was.

With the tiara restored permanently to Rome, the Conciliar movement (the idea that councils of cardinals are superior to popes) took root in France. Jean Gerson was among the strongest Conciliar advocates. The issue came up in Councils at Constance (1415), Pavia (1423), and Basle (1431); papal bulls were issued and episcopal rebuttals circulated. In the end, papal supremacy triumphed in Europe; but Charles VII issued the Pragmatic Sanction of Bourges in 1438, whereby the French clergy were by law made independent of the papacy. This established Conciliarism in France. Later, Louis XI revoked the Sanction; Gallicanism (the church dependent not on the pope but on the king of France) had triumphed all the same. The tendency was too well-seated to disappear; Gallicans believed that the government was devoted to the Catholic faith, and prefered its suzerainty to Rome's. Gallicanism disappeared only when the state was thoroughly secularized; even then it reappeared on such bizarre occasions as the infamous treason trial of Captain Alfred Dreyfus at the end of the nineteenth century.

'SEE THAT THERE ARE NO SLIP-UPS'

This was the favourite admonition given to his servants by Louis XI, the Spider (1461–1483), probably the greatest of the Valois kings, when he sent them off to execute his policies. Francis I, builder of the fabulous Château Chambord, shone brighter than Louis XI, but with less substance. Louis grew up in the latter days of the Hundred Years War. As dauphin to an impoverished, war-racked crown he acquired a taste for streamlining government, improving the economy and centralizing royal authority – which meant bending the great territorial lords to his will. As king he had the energy to implement these authoritarian tastes.

Louis had no great love for his father, Charles VII, not least because he resented the king's mistress, Agnes Sorel, perhaps the greatest beauty of her era. Louis led an abortive rebellion against Charles when he was only sixteen. Afterward Charles was sufficiently suspicious to deny Louis access to his *apanage* of Dauphiné until the prince was into his twenties. Once in charge there, Louis's 'advanced' ideas of government made enemies for him among the great feudal lords. Charles took their side and Louis fled to the protection of his uncle, Duke Philip the Good of Burgundy. There he remained until the crown was his in 1461.

While at Philip's court Louis became friends with Francesco Sforza, duke of Milan, and Philippe de Commynes, Philip's, and later his own, principal advisor on state affairs. He also made the acquaintance of a future enemy, Charles, count of Charolais, heir to the Burgundian throne. At this court Louis learnt the Machiavellian skills which when he was king would earn for him the sobriquet 'the Spider'. He had to: in Burgundy, at Genappe, he was 'the man without a place', and his uncle Philip's benevolence extended only so far.

Louis XI accomplished many things, but nothing more significant than finally subduing the great feudal lords. After Louis, the French nobility never again dominated the crown as they had in his father's reign. In 1465, after four years of his 'shabby, toilsome, efficient, saddle-hardened' government, carried on by 'fearfully hard-working and fearfully intelligent and disgustingly low-born fellows', the French feudal lords had had enough of Louis.

Led by the duke of Bourbon, they issued a propaganda manifesto on behalf of the great lords, the lesser nobility, the churchmen and the poor, on behalf, in short, of the *bien publique* (public welfare), proclaiming their intention 'to remedy injustices and to sweep away taxes which were driving the realm to perdition'. The collaborators were the dukes of Berry (Louis's brother), Brittany, Nemours and Calabria, the counts of Charolais, Anjou, Armagnac, St Pol and Dunois, and various barons. When Louis discussed their grievances with them, it soon was clear that this, like other noble uprisings, had much less of *bien publique* at heart than it did of *bien particulaire* (private welfare).

Louis met the challenge. Through his intrigues, calculations, manipulations and straight military manouevres and battles he put the feudal lords in their place. By his death in 1483 all of France bent the knee to royal authority more completely than ever before: Burgundy, Normandy, even Brittany succumbed in the end; and Louis added Picardy, Anjou and Bar in the north, and Roussillon, Cerdagne and Provençe in the south (the latter bringing with it Marseille, a great prize) to the royal holdings. Paul Murray Kendall, Louis's biographer, wrote: 'In the south of France, once swarming with semi-independent lords, there remained no prince to defy royal law.'

Louis used professional civil servants to enhance government administration, tax collection and law enforcement and adjudication. He encouraged trade and new industry, and at his death had far-reaching plans for developing 'famous Marseille', for abolishing the irrational and uneconomic local customs which confounded economic development, and for creating a national standard for laws, regulations, weights and measures.

The King maintained a network of diplomats, special investigators, secret agents and officers of foreign states in his pay throughout his feudality and Europe, through which he was kept informed and on top of the complicated foreign relations which characterized his reign. Through a combination of intimidation, manipulation and warfare (as a last resort), Louis broke the Anglo-Burgundian connection and brought the last great independent territorial princes (Burgundy and Brittany) to heel. Philippe de Commynes recounted Louis's policies in intimate detail. The Emperor Charles V called the Commynes *Memoirs* 'a textbook for kings'.

Louis XI was a bridge between the Middle Ages and the Renaissance.

He was a medieval king in that he ruled from horseback, convened his lords as advisors, believed that where possible the king should live on his private revenue, and hunted incessantly during which time he often lived rough. But Louis also was a Renaissance prince. He attended to trade and commercial regulation, made foreign policy into an art, opened government to commoners of ability, exercised his mind vigorously (he corresponded with scholars, and as dauphin enrolled as a student at the University of Louvain), commissioned a 'modern' Loire château (Langeais, designed by Jean Bourré), and may even have learnt the new game of tennis which was all the rage at the court in Burgundy. Louis's 'new' ideas were not altogether new. But in the fifteenth century, for the first time in six centuries, at a time when feudalism was dying of its own decrepitude, they could be implemented. Significantly, in 1484, a year after Louis's death, the Estates met and for the first time included a Third Estate representing the commons of France.

After he died, the nobility tried to overturn Louis's accomplishments. They had only limited success, despite the fact that his son, Charles VIII (1483–1498), ruled neither wisely nor well. On the strength of bad advice and against the urging of his much abler sister, Anne of Beaujeu, Charles embroiled France in the Italian wars. In consequence he lost Roussillon, Cerdagne, Artois, Franche Comté (part of Burgundy), and 'gold by the shovelful'. Charles died unlamented at Amboise, replaced by his distant cousin, Louis XII (1498–1515).

Out of weakness, Louis XII practised docility. 'He had a kind heart,' wrote the historian Albert Guérard. Under Louis 'the country knew internal peace: no "foolish war", no "League for the Public Weal". Prosperity was abounding: his reign and the first decade under Francis I are among the happiest moments in France's chequered life.' Not for nothing was Louis XII known as the Father of his People. Tranquillity reigned along with him; but inevitably it could not last.

CHAPTER FIVE

Renaissance, Reformation and Raison D'État
1515–1661

It is difficult to make sense of France between 1515 and 1661. There seems to be no symmetry, no inner historical logic. The Renaissance (when, according to eighteenth-century writers, France was rescued from barren medievalism) gives way to savage religious civil war which is followed by a cynical and pragmatic opportunism. Apparently, there is only confusion. But appearances can be deceptive.

The Renaissance

The Renaissance, characterized by the rebirth of classical learning and humanism (ancient wisdom allied with human reason) and new forms in art, literature, learning and politics, percolated out of fourteenth-century Italy and climaxed in France during the reign of Francis I (1515–1547). This king seemed the perfect model of a Renaissance prince. In the words of Guillaume Budé, whose patron he was, Francis 'is educated in letters ... and also possesses a natural eloquence, wit, tact, pleasant manners; nature, in short, has endowed him with the rarest gifts of body and mind . . . .' Francis possessed *virtu*; he was born to rule; he was, simply, a Renaissance Prince.

Francis I

The king patronized Leonardo da Vinci, Andrea del Sarto, Benvenuto Cellini and Jean Clouet, built or remodelled châteaux at Chambord and Blois in the Loire Valley and Fontainebleau near Paris, and commissioned Pierre Lescot to renovate the ancient Louvre in Paris, a palace

The Francis I staircase at Blois

made by Philip Augustus out of a castle erected by Hugh Capet. Francis made Budé Master of the King's Library, a collection which formed the foundation of the Bibliothèque Nationale, today one of the great research libraries of the world; set up four regius professorships – the *lecteurs royaux* – at the university of Paris; and encouraged humanism in theology and letters. Francis tried, without success, to lure the great Dutch humanist, Erasmus, to France, and created an atmosphere of sufficient intellectual freedom to encourage Rabelais to produce his humanistic satires, *Gargantua* and *Pantagruel*.

Renaissance 'types' included the prince, artist and scholar, but also the merchant, royal servant (noble or otherwise), courtesan and intellectual. Francis was singularly fortunate in the 'types' around him, some of whom were his relatives and all of whom were useful. Jean de Beaune, Baron de Semblançay, a merchant, directed royal financial administration until his fall from favour. The oddly named Anne de Montmorency, Constable of France, espoused a Machiavellian view of princely power which suited Francis's self-image perfectly. The queen mother, Louise of Savoy, intelligent, educated, even gifted, twice acted as regent for

Francis and in 1529 negotiated the Peace of Cambrai on his behalf. She took a 'liberal' view of religious heresy, as did her daughter Marguerite of Angoulême.

Marguerite too was gifted, a writer, foreign-policy formulator, and author of a poem, *Mirror of the Sinful Soul*, which the Sorbonne blacklisted – on a technicality, they hastily assured the king, who resented any apparent affronts to royalty. Anne of Heilly, duchess of Étampes, the most important of several royal mistresses, was described by the imperial ambassador as 'the real president of the king's most private and intimate council'. She played politics with the best of them, and was a patron of the arts despite not being on cordial terms with Cellini. Queen Claude also played her part by providing Francis with abundant heirs. But that was hardly a function of the Renaissance spirit.

PRINCELY STATECRAFT

In 1518 Budé wrote *L'Institution du Prince*, which urged Francis to be an absolute ruler. The king followed this advice, or tried to. The *Parlement* of Paris, a law court and quasi-legislative body and the most important of a number of *parlements* throughout France, was forced to give in to Francis over the Concordat of Bologna. By acquiesing to this agreement with the papacy, the *Parlement* enabled Francis to bend the Gallican church and its theologians of the Sorbonne to his will also. Meanwhile he centralized patronage, which increased royal control over the provincial nobility. They and the higher clergy were thereby made more susceptible to royal pressure. The king relied upon assemblies of notables for counsel and dispensed with the Estates General, a body he considered not only useless but dangerous. The structure of royal government was still too feudal to provide for absolute rule, but Francis at least took a step in that direction.

The king's foreign policy did not quite achieve its aims either, but in form did lay the foundations of the *raison d'état* style of later French statecraft. Francis's policy centred upon rivalry with England (Henry VIII) and Spain and the Holy Roman Empire (Charles V) over Italy and the Low Countries. He fought five wars in 1515, 1526, 1527–29, 1536–38 and 1542, and juggled his rivals diplomatically, seeking alliance with first one and then the other. Francis considered alliance too with German

Protestant princes against Charles after 1530, and in 1533 made a treaty with Sultan Suleiman of the Ottoman Empire, Charles's great enemy in the Balkans. This shocked Christian opinion and did Francis no good at home. Other treaties, more acceptable but of no particular advantage – save for the first – included the Concordat of Bologna (1516), the Field of the Cloth of Gold (1520), Cambrai (1529) and Crépy-en-Laonnois (1544).

Francis's constant objectives were control of the duchies of Milan and Burgundy, and, until Charles was elected, of the Holy Roman Empire. What he got was a victory at Marignano in 1515; better relations with the papacy, but also greater control over the church in France from the Concordat; improved relations with Henry VIII out of his approach to the German princes; brief security for Normandy but the loss of his Italian claims out of Cambrai; and from Crépy-en-Laonnois the promise that through marriage his third son, the duke of Orléans, would inherit the duchy of Milan – which did not happen because Orléans died before the marriage took place.

Otherwise, nothing much came of the treaty with the Sultan, and Francis was captured by Charles at Pavia in 1526 and forced to pay a huge ransom as well as leave his sons in Madrid as hostages. The meeting with Henry VIII at Val Doré near Calais, the Field of the Cloth of Gold, was a great but empty gesture; two Renaissance princes out to cut a figure postured and pranced, erected gorgeous tents, wore dazzling clothes, put on splendid tournaments, and possibly engaged in a royal wrestling match which French records say Francis won handily, but which English records do not mention. Then they went home. Nothing of any lasting significance had taken place.

Meanwhile, the cost to France of having Francis on the throne mounted. There were war debts and general social and economic deterioration, a condition blamed on corruption rather than on the increased taxes, steady inflation and rising population without an attendant increase in productivity which really caused it. Francis borrowed heavily from Parisian and Lyonnais bankers in order to keep going, which mortgaged the throne. By selling revenue-producing offices he created a hereditary bureaucracy and thus mortgaged the future of royal administration. Sale of offices extended patronage and produced revenue in the short run; in the long run it extended 'bastard feudalism' as the fundamental structure of political relationships. This guaranteed the formation of new power blocs across the country.

Francis died in 1547 in debt to the equivalent of nearly a year's royal revenue. By then, too, the peasantry had suffered from general impoverishment, and conflict between royal officials, traditional landed nobles and higher clergy was on the rise.

STATECRAFT AND MARRIAGE

Royal marriage was traditionally an important element of statecraft. Francis continued the tradition. His sister, Marguerite of Angoulême, married Henry of Albret of Navarre, allying that Pyrénéean kingdom to the Valois house. Marguerite's grandson became Henry IV, the first Bourbon king of France. The dauphin (Henry II) married Catherine de Medici, who lived to be queen mother to three kings through whom she virtually ruled France for thirty years. One of the three, Francis II, married Mary Stuart of Scotland, thus linking France with England's most ancient enemy.

After Francis I

Henry II (1547–1559) ruled neither wisely nor well. He kept his father's foreign policy, thus weakening France internally with more war and more debt, and made no more substantive efforts at fiscal reforms than had Francis. In 1559 peace was agreed at Cateau-Cambrésis, ending France's long war with the Empire. But while jousting in the tournament celebrating this peace, the hapless Henry was speared and killed. It was probably an accident rather than the assassination many romanticists later claimed; it was an ill-omen all the same. Henry's limitations were many compared to his father, and that his mistress, Diane of Poitiers, is best remembered as a model for magnificent classic statuary (the duchess of Étampes at least had a brain) may be a more than adequate epitaph for him. Diane occupied the Château Chaumont-sur-Loire, which Catherine de Medici owned. Henry made no contribution to the arts beyond visiting Diane. Francis II (1559–1560) survived little more than a year, and after his death Mary Stuart returned to Scotland to become a thorn in the side of Elizabeth I of England. Charles IX (1560–1574) then entered upon his reign, just in time for the half-century of religious warfare sometimes called the Era of Politics by Assassination.

The Reformation

The era opened with religious reformation, but religion soon sparked conflict which involved ancient issues of class and politics. With access to the new printing technology, all sides made effective use of propaganda in focussing the views of people of every class and condition. Opinions turned into bigotry; bigotry became persecution; and the wars began. Louis Le Roy, a Parisian humanist writing in the mid-sixteenth century, thought spreading religious sectarianism was a malady worse than venereal disease which was also on the increase.

The Protestant Reformation had many causes, but its catalyst was Martin Luther, Augustinian monk in Wittenburg, challenging Roman orthodoxy and being excommunicated for his pains. This was the work of Pope Leo X, backed by the new Holy Roman Emperor, Charles V. The Empire was mainly German and Italian, and Germany was full of petty principalities and semi-autonomous merchant cities which chafed under papal taxes and interference in their affairs by an absentee ruler who, in any case, was a Spaniard. The princes began it, rebelling in the name of their rights and their nationality (discovered when Luther translated the Bible into German). Their peasants followed suit, which led the princes to conclude that Luther's teachings meant freedom for princes but obedience for peasants. He agreed, and the peasants were put down with great bloodshed in 1525–26. Then the princes organized themselves into a league poised against Charles, and made war against him until the Peace of Augsburg in 1555. Augsburg provided that a prince could decide if his realm would be Catholic or Lutheran. For the first time Christian Europe was divided into two religious parts, both having official status. Soon the French were right in the middle of it.

REFORMATION IN FRANCE

The immediate impact of the Reformation was muted in France. But impact there was all the same. In 1519 the Sorbonne condemned Luther's writings out of hand; in 1523 the *Parlement* seized all Lutheran books from Paris booksellers; and in 1526 Louise of Savoy ordered the extermination from France of the 'evil and damnable heresy of Luther'. The queen mother's career as a liberal on reform was over. That same year a weaver from Meaux became the first French protestant martyr. Meanwhile, Bishop Briçonnet of Meaux (Semblançay's nephew) undertook to envangelize his diocese and invited famous preachers like Guillaume Farel to take part in the process. Jacques Lefèvre of Étaples translated the scriptures into French and published humanistic textual criticism. Marguerite of Angoulême wrote evangelical verse, corresponded with Briçonnet, and patronized and protected humanists like Étaples. Francis I contemplated an anti-Habsburg alliance with the protestant princes.

Then, in 1534, the Affair of the Placards produced scurrilous anti-Catholic propaganda in Paris and throughout the country, driving orthodox mobs to frenzy. The king decided that Lutheranism was both heresy and sedition and a wave of repression and persecution began, involving both the burning of heretics and the censoring of heretical writings. Many French reformers headed for cover. Among them was a humanist evangelical and former University of Paris law student from Noyon, Jean Calvin.

Jean Calvin

In 1536 Calvin published his reformist doctrines in *Institution of the Christian Religion*. In 1541 he was in Geneva undertaking to establish a church according to the sacraments, litany, patterns of worship, catechism and discipline of *Institution*. Within a decade and a half it was achieved and integrated with city government so that Geneva became a theocracy. Once in power, these 'Calvinists' dealt summarily with opposition. (Servetus was condemned and burnt for criticism.) In 1557 French exiles flooded into Geneva; in 1560 they flooded back as Calvinist missionaries. Royal edicts condemning their activities had no effect on the traffic either way.

Persecution produced martyrs, whose blood, Calvin preached, was the seed of the true church. Jean Crespin's *Book of the Martyrs*, periodically updated between 1554 and 1609, was effective propaganda for Calvinism in France. By 1570 twelve hundred Protestant churches dotted France: heavily in Normandy, Poitou (in La Rochelle Protestants actually outnumbered Catholics), Dauphiné and Languedoc; lightly in Picardy, Champagne and Burgundy; and not at all in Brittany and the Vendée where, the local clergy feared, Christianity of any sort was as unknown among the inhabitants as among the natives of the New World.

HUGUENOTS

French Protestants, mostly Calvinist, were called Huguenots. No one seems to know why. Opinion on who they were varied widely. Gaspard de Saulx-Tavannes, Marshal of France, believed they mainly were townsmen, vagabonds, women and children; Jean Michieli, Venetian diplomat and spy, said they were the nobility 'under forty years old'; Blaise of Monluc, ultra-Catholic Lieutenant of Gascony, pointed to royal officials and financiers in his region; Florimond de Raemond, judge, believed schoolmasters had much to answer for, having taught pupils to read, think and act for themselves; in Gaillac, rich merchants were blamed for Protestantism, and in Toulouse, one judge held that it was all the fault of rich young men and beautiful young women – which judgement contains some interesting implications. Clearly Huguenot heresy aroused much excitement and hostility, but it seemed to be a tidal wave which nothing could hold back. In 1560 Charles IX issued a general amnesty to Protestants, mute testimony to the failed legal repression of Huguenots.

CIVIL WAR

By 1561 the Huguenots believed victory for Protestantism in France was imminent. That summer they sang psalms in Rouen, Toulouse, and throughout urban France. Many Huguenots ran printing presses (like Jean Crespin in Paris) and Protestant literature spread widely. It was often vicious and satiric: *Muster of the Archers at the Popinjay* (an attack on the papacy); or the woodcut, widely circulated, called *The Great Marmite Overturned*, which showed the pope and his minions trying to prop up

Church wealth (a great stew pot) whilst the light of the Holy Gospel inspired common people to pull it down. This propaganda frightened the orthodox as it revealed the 'menacing public face of the blossoming new faith'. Catholic-Huguenot animosities grew – and provided the perfect arena for old clan feuds and traditions of violence.

Civil war began in 1562 when the prince of Condé raised the Huguenot standard at Orléans, claiming that the fight was for both religious freedom and the political rights of princes of the blood. Calvin approved this. Anne de Montmorency, the Constable, led royal forces against them, aided by his eldest son and his old enemy, the ultra-Catholic duke of Guise. Montmorency's Châtillon nephews (Gaspard of Coligny, Admiral of France, and his brother Odet of Châtillon, count-bishop of Beauvais and a cardinal) and the constable's younger son were in the Huguenot camp. The war soon became a Montmorency-Guise struggle. The aim of the civil war, whatever justifications were stated, was to seize power.

Catherine de Medici

The queen mother tried to contain the crisis. Intelligent, determined, and politically supple and devious, Catherine was also tolerant and extended the olive branch to Protestants at court and in the country. Nothing worked, and the English (backing the Huguenots from their base at Le Havre) and the Spanish (invading Protestant-held areas of the Low Countries) were soon involved in the civil war. Catherine personally rallied the army to defend their new young king against 'English traitors'.

The battle of Dreux in 1562 was a narrow victory won by the duke of Guise. Catherine thereupon organized a peace which granted some Huguenot demands. Between 1564 and 1566 she took King Charles around the country, reinforcing loyalties and damping down disputes. Unfortunately, she met with the Spanish duke of Alba in 1565, which the Huguenots read as a plot against them. The war resumed in 1567.

SECTARIAN VIOLENCE

Dreux, Jarnac and Montcontour were the only major pitched battles of the civil war, and there were a few sieges: Rouen and Orléans, for example. Mainly the war was outbreaks of mob violence and acts of assassination and sabotage, which fed the propaganda of both sides, and which in turn fed hatred and fuelled the violence.

In 1563 the duke of Guise was assassinated; in 1568 a Huguenot nobleman was slaughtered by masked men outside his home in Mâcon; the prince of Condé was killed in 1569 at Jarnac.

In 1562 the *parlement* of Toulouse legalised the slaughter of heretics; Huguenots everywhere committed sacrilege against the sacred host, statues of the Virgin, the Crucifix, Holy Oil and fonts and holy-water basins; and mobs of the orthodox frequently fell upon Huguenots and tore them to pieces. All of this was faithfully recorded in pamphlets and broadsheets. King Charles once rebuked the duke of Guise for reading such a broadsheet during Mass.

ST BARTHOLOMEW'S DAY

On 18 August, 1572, Henry of Navarre, Condé's cousin and a Huguenot, married Charles IX's sister, Marguerite, at a ceremony in Paris. Many Protestant leaders attended. On 22 August with the newlyweds still in Paris, Admiral Coligny was wounded in an assassination attempt. The next day Huguenot nobles threatened retaliation against the royal family, whom they accused of betrayal. In a panic, Charles and his mother consented to a scheme to finish off Coligny and other Huguenot nobles with him. Henry of Navarre saved himself only by promising to return to orthodoxy, a promise he abandoned once he was away from Paris.

The scheme was put into play early on 24 August, which was St Bartholomew's day. A Paris mob got wind of this, took it as a sign, and began slaughtering every Huguenot they could find. Thousands died in Paris and elsewhere as the news spread. The result was disastrous. Never again would Huguenots trust the word of a Valois; and never again would Paris Catholics offer the olive branch to Protestants.

THE CATHOLIC LEAGUE

When Henry III (1574–1589) succeeded his brother Charles IX, he reckoned the time had come for concessions to the Huguenots. The

Catholic backlash was immediate and a league was formed to defy the crown and reopen the war against Protestantism. Henry barely saved the day by naming himself head of the Catholic League and declaring war against the Huguenots. The League was then disbanded.

In the 1580s Henry's questionable court favourites, called sneeringly *les mignons* (literally, 'the sweets', but meant here to imply unnatural sexuality), and economic dislocations and heavy taxes accumulated by the civil war, brought royal prestige to an all-time low. The Catholic League revived and mobilized not only country aristocrats but lower-class fanatics in the towns. The League put forward the Cardinal of Bourbon (a Guise) as a rival heir to the throne to Henry of Navarre, and Pope Sixtus V backed them by denying Navarre's right to succeed. This revived Gallican resentment of Roman interference in French affairs, and weakened the cardinal's candidacy.

In 1587 Queen Elizabeth of England, tired of Mary Stuart's continuous intrigues against her, allowed the Scottish queen, who was her prisoner, to be executed. The next year Philip II of Spain, partly in retaliation, launched a massive naval expedition, the Armada, against England. It was wrecked by Admiral John Hawkins, Francis Drake, an English fleet, and a strong wind propitiously blowing eastward so that the duke of Alba could not sail out from the Spanish Netherlands as reinforcement against the English warships. Catherine de Medici died that year, and Henry was murdered in 1589 by the League in revenge for having arranged the death of the duke of Guise and his brother, the Cardinal of Bourbon. Henry of Navarre at once claimed the throne as Henry IV (1589–1610), the first Bourbon monarch. Sitting securely upon it was another matter.

Henry IV

Henry's task was daunting enough: to restore political order, rebuild a war-ravaged country, reconcile contending forces, sort through the foreign-policy complications created by religious war, actually secure his throne, and make himself popular.

The new king was shrewd and able, and above all a pragmatist. He never actually said 'Paris is worth a mass', as older histories maintain, but he did abjure the abjuration of his 'conversion' in 1572. This, and a number of military successes against the Catholic League, finally got him to Paris in 1594. Thereafter he even tolerated the Jesuits, the religious order founded by Ignatius Loyola with the support of François Xavier, as the cutting edge of the Catholic response to Protestantism. Naturally his former Huguenot comrades were not pleased. They distrusted the newly Romanised monarch, and to ease their minds, he arranged the Edict of Nantes in 1598 which gave political and religious protection to Huguenots. Henry also made a Protestant, the duke of Sully, his principal advisor. For a few years something like peace settled over the bitterly divided country.

The depth of Henry's Catholicism is suspect. His foreign policy was pro-Dutch, which is to say pro-Protestant, and anti-Spanish, which is to say anti-Habsburg and anti-Catholic. Throughout he held his cards close to his chest, and with the adept seigneur of Villeroy as his foreign minister, neither Spain nor Rome knew that Henry subsidized the Dutch and their Protestant allies. Meanwhile, he procured a papal sanction for his divorce and his subsequent remarriage to Marie de Medici in 1600.

Henry appeared more forthright on matters touching royal authority. He overrode the *parlements* and other courts regularly, intervened arbitrarily in provincial affairs, dictated marriage alliances among the great houses (thereby keeping the nobility at each other's throats instead of at the king's), and used more 'new' men and fewer old nobles as royal servants than any king before him: Villeroy, Sully and Brulart of Sillery, the chancellor, among others. This practice advanced the *noblesse de la robe*, the clerical and state bureaucracy, which became a mainstay of royal absolutism during his reign. The traditional nobles, who began to

fear for their power, prestige and wealth, were therefore not drawn to Henry. Moreover, as the expanding *robe* nobility had to provide for their progeny just as did their landed counterparts, a new venue was opened for venality which in the long run could only weaken absolutism.

It is not clear that Henry achieved much of lasting value by making royal authority absolute, nor did he make substantive improvements in fiscal or administrative operations. The sale of offices continued as did tax farming, and inflation was still treated as a problem of corruption without considering that economic factors might lie beyond it. Taxes too were increased and their burden distributed without regard for long-term effects. This was not the king's fault alone: the *parlements* and *cours des aides*, courts of registry with power to block tax and other reforms, often did exactly that when class interests were, or appeared to be, threatened. One minor triumph was Sully's success in ensuring that the Dutch subsidies were subtracted from France's debt to England.

Both Henry and Sully undertook economic rebuilding by increasing agricultural production (Sully) and encouraging manufacturing (Henry). The silk industry of Nîmes and Lyon, glass and pottery works in Paris and Nevers, and various metal, tapestry (such as Gobelins in Paris), carpet and linen manufactories were started up with Henry's support. Sully oversaw the recovery of swamplands in Bas-Médoc (the Gironde) and worked to remove export duties on corn to encourage trade.

Perhaps this first Bourbon king was not sufficiently open in the pursuit of his policies. At any rate, in 1610 he was assassinated while his carriage was stuck in Paris traffic. The assassin, François Ravaillac, thought he was performing an act both patriotic and Catholic. At least it was the last such act of great significance in an epoch distressingly full of terrorist acts.

Marie de Medici

Louis XIII (1610–1643) was eight when his father was killed. His mother, Marie de Medici, acted as regent and it was a surprisingly quiet time. She bought off those nobles most likely to be troublesome, arranged marriages for Louis with the Infanta Anne of Austria, and for his sister with the future Philip IV of Spain (only a temporary deviation from France's anti-Habsburg policy). Marie reaffirmed the Edict of Nantes, which helped keep the ever-suspicious Huguenots quiet, and summoned the Estates General in 1614 to help head off a revolt by the prince of Condé. When the Estates had done that, they took issue with the crown over fiscal and other reforms. The session was hastily wound up, and the Estates did not meet again until 1789, when they helped to start a revolution.

In 1617 the duke of Luynes persuaded Louis to cut the apron strings and let him, Luynes, run things. The duke succeeded only in provoking another Huguenot revolt, and was killed trying to put it down. The way to power was open for Marie de Medici's personal chaplain and advisor, Cardinal Richelieu, bishop of Luçon.

The Thirty Years War

This began as a religious war in 1618, but turned into a primarily political struggle long before it ended in stalemate in 1648 and only involved France after 1632. It also was unprecedentedly destructive, a monument to the price central Europe had to pay for the purely dynastic desires of the Holy Roman Emperor, the Habsburg Ferdinand II, who pressed the war as emperor solely in order to re-establish Habsburg rule in Germany. The war began when Protestant Bohemian nobles threw two Jesuits representing Ferdinand (who also was king of Bohemia) from a high window in Hradčany Castle in Prague. A propaganda war ensued. The Catholics claimed that the Jesuits survived because angels caught them up and bore them gently to earth; the Protestants countered that they had survived by falling into a dung heap. Whatever the truth, the war was on, and in 1620 imperial forces crushed the Bohemians at the battle of White Mountain. This should have ended the war. But the mercenaries Ferdinand hired for his huge army had caught the scent of plunder, and they continued the war on their own. The emperor now used them as an excuse to launch a campaign of reconquest.

White Mountain made the Huguenots feel insecure, and they rose in the rebellion which killed the duke of Luynes. From 1624 onward the war spread, and after the Edict of Restitution in 1629, by which

Ferdinand declared his intention to make all Germany bend the knee to the Catholic emperor, France became involved in the war – but only indirectly.

Cardinal Richelieu and Raison d'État

Richelieu, who had dissembled so well that until 1632 it appeared he was willing to give the Habsburgs a free hand in Europe, now unfolded the policy which justly won for him the reputation of the first great exponent in France of *raison d'état*. Everything Richelieu did was meant to further the interests of France abroad, and of the French state, the royal administrative power structure through which government operated. This was *raison d'état*. To implement it Richelieu needed to be a supreme pragmatist and dissembler, and an expert manager of the royal person. He was all of this, and Louis, aware of the cardinal's great gifts, stood loyally behind him even when he chafed at being 'managed'. For his part the cardinal was always straightforward with the king, if with no one else.

FOREIGN POLICY

Richelieu was subtle, even ambiguous. He arranged a marriage between Henrietta Maria, Louis's sister, and Charles Stuart of England, which recognized an Anglo-French anti-Spanish venture in the Netherlands. In 1626 he made a treaty with Spain while Dutch Protestants made peace with Spain through English mediation. Then came the Edict of Restitution, and as Habsburg domination of Europe was not in the French interest, Richeleiu offered subsidies to the Lutheran King Gustavus Adolphus II of Sweden, to enter the war and fight against the Emperor. He paid subsidies to other Protestant princes as well after Gustavus was dead, to keep the war going. All the while a Habsburg was queen of France.

In the 1630s, French foreign policy for the future emerged: Balance of Power, that is, the idea that no one state should dominate Europe, and that this might be prevented by juggling combinations of states. Ironically, only the French themselves overturned the balance, or sought to, between 1648 and 1815. Each time the other powers employed

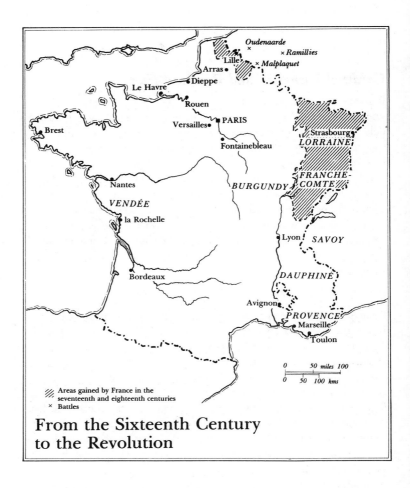

Oudenaarde
× Ramillies
Lille × Malplaquet
Arras
Dieppe
Le Havre
Brest
Rouen
Versailles PARIS
Fontainebleau
Strasbourg
LORRAINE
FRANCHE-COMTÉ
Nantes
BURGUNDY
VENDÉE
la Rochelle
Lyon *SAVOY*
DAUPHINÉ
Bordeaux
Avignon
PROVENCE
Marseille
Toulon

0   50 miles 100
0   50 100 kms

/// Areas gained by France in the
    seventeenth and eighteenth centuries
× Battles

From the Sixteenth Century
to the Revolution

Richelieu's conception to put things right. The essence of Richelieu's policy was articulated two hundred years later by the British foreign secretary Lord Palmerston when he said: 'In foreign policy there are no permanent alliances, only permanent interests.'

GOVERNMENT

Richelieu was little better here than were his predecessors. He used patronage as a means of control, and once it was distributed used it to squeeze money out of those dependent upon it. This alienated a significant portion of the body politic. Meanwhile, he did little to curb the recalcitrance, or limit the traditions of independence, of the *parlements* and *cours des aides*. Their periodic rebellions against centralized fiscal reforms did not cease. On the other hand, the cardinal raised the *intendants*, servants working directly for the crown and with power to interfere directly in the operations of the regular bureaucracy in any part of the country (not unlike Charlemagne's *missi dominici* in this regard), to new and greater powers. They now became a permanent fixture of government, and by 1642 were responsible for fiscal administration, tax collection and supervising the bureaucracy.

The *intendants'* task, or tasks, required the best and brightest that France could produce. Doors opened wider for talent, strengthening Richelieu by further weakening the traditional nobility, but in turn weakening the cardinal by strengthening the resentments of this nobility and the older elements of bureaucracy. It was no different from Henry IV's time. Nevertheless, through his professionals Richelieu undertook developments in trade and industry, built up the navy and attempted administrative reforms. However, the system of *intendants* fell under Richelieu's concept of patronage, and many of them were his 'creatures', as they came to be called, creating jealousy throughout the government. Eventually the *intendants* became like other *noblesse de la robe*: rigid, self-serving and hereditary. But until then they had much to do with strengthening the qualities of absolutism in the French state.

FRANCE OVERSEAS

In the sixteenth and seventeenth centuries, France joined other European nations in overseas expansion. Jacques Cartier explored eastern Canada; a cartography school was opened in Dieppe; France started trade with Portuguese-claimed areas in southern America; Henry IV established a great naval base at Toulon on the Mediterranean; overseas commercial treaties were made with the Hanseatic League, Denmark and Sweden; and finally, colonies were laid down in Canada, plantations in the West

Indies, and trading factories in India. French colonialism would ebb and flow over the next three and a half centuries. In Richelieu's time its tendency was to flow.

North America was an important beneficiary of the 'flow'. French fur trappers followed Cartier, and soon Québec was established, along with French settlements in the Ohio river valley. Québec became an integral part of Canada, and maintained strong cultural ties with France, even after it was amalgamated into British Canada. Canada is officially bilingual today, as a result. Other French communities did not fare so well at British hands. The British took over Acadia (Nova Scotia) in 1713, and expelled the Acadians, who fled to Louisiana. In time, 'Acadian' was perverted into 'Cajun,' by which the descendents of these emigrés are now known. Louisiana was the southern tip of a territory that spread as far as the Pacific Northwest, and which Napoleon Bonaparte sold to the United States in 1806 (the 'Louisiana Purchase'). French traditions remain in the name Louisiana, in *la vieux Carré*, or French Quarter, in New Orleans, and in Cajun culture itself.

REBELLION

Richelieu's years of supremacy also saw sporadic rebellions, of a religious or social nature, against the government. Rebellion was endemic by the early seventeenth century. The Huguenot wars ended finally in the 1640s, but their great cost had forced tax increases which townsmen, peasants and nobles alike frequently rebelled against paying. One element was added, and if it was not new it was at least more prominent than in the past: the urban poor and the peasants were linking up in opposition to nobility and the upper bourgeoisie.

Revolts were endemic, but one deserves special mention simply because of its bizarre ending. In 1641 the count of Soissons led a rebellious army, including some Spaniards, into eastern France, and won an impressive victory at La Marfée. As the smoke cleared, the count paused to survey his triumph. He raised the visor on his helmet with his pistol and accidentally blew his brains out.

AFTER RICHELIEU

Richelieu died in 1642 and Louis XIII in 1643. Louis XIV was only five.

Cardinal Mazarin emerged as first minister of the regent, Anne of Austria. They got on well and may even have been secretly married. Louis's uncle, Gaston, duke of Orléans, always a thorn in Richelieu's side, emerged now as a helpful addition to royal administration. Even so, under Mazarin France was afflicted by war and rebellion, and his tenure was only a sort of line-holding. He did successfully negotiate the French position in the Treaty of Westphalia ending the Thirty Years War in 1648, a treaty which firmly established the balance of power principle; but no sooner was it signed than the French nobles were in rebellion behind the prince of Condé (Condé rebellions against central authority had become a family tradition by this time) in an attempt to reverse the absolutist trends of the monarchy.

The Fronde was the most significant rebellion of the seventeenth century. It was also nearly the last; only the Bordeaux and Breton revolts in 1675 approached it in scale. Between 1648 and 1661 the royal army (in the later days with young Louis XIV at its head) ended the Fronde and established a royal control non-existent before in France. Mazarin died in 1661. Louis, who had not forgotten the humiliations he suffered as a boy at the hands of Fronde leaders, threw off all restraint and took France entirely into his own hands. Now the age of French absolutism began in earnest.

Did this epoch lack symmetry? Was there no inner historical logic from the accession of Francis I to the death of Mazarin? Francis I glittered without substance and planted the seeds of political and religious upheaval even as he built the great châteaux and centres of learning. Civil and religious war raged after him. Reforms succeeded only in papering over cracks in the administrative and fiscal systems. Rebels often protested against the administrative corruption and the grinding taxation. Cynical ministers vied with arrogant aristocrats to manipulate government in their own interests. There was symmetry to this era after all: the tension between the whole and its parts which had characterized French history for more than half a millennium was alive and well. There should have been a revolution, all things considered. Instead there was Louis XIV, and that which sometimes is referred to romantically, or at least nostalgically, as 'the glory that was France'.

CHAPTER SIX

'The Glory that was France'
1661–1789

In the seventeenth and eighteenth centuries, the French sought first to explain and then to order the world around them; a legacy of both the Renaissance and the Religious wars. Explanation and ordering characterized philosophy and criticism, and influenced art, literature, politics and the social order, at least secondarily. But the French got more than they bargained for. What began as philosophical enquiry ended as revolution – with the aid of economic malaise, corrupt officials, a starving and deprived urban populace, and a grasping and increasingly useless aristocracy. The philosophy, thinking about the relationship – if any – between the moral and physical ordering of things, divided between the Rationalists, who thought that universal systematic knowledge was possible, and the Empiricists, who did not. Rationalism and Empiricism permeated Europe. In France Rationalism held the field, even after the thinking of Isaac Newton, the English empiricist, was distilled into a book, *Newtonisme pour les Dames*, which was read in all of the best Paris *salons*.

RATIONALISM

Michel de Montaigne and other sixteenth-century Sceptics doubted that truth was knowable, arguing that the mind is too dependent on the senses. René Descartes thought otherwise, and in *Discourse on Method* (1637) and *Metaphysical Meditations* (1641) propounded a mathematical equation into a philosophical proposition which distinguished true from false and laid the foundation for a system of universal knowledge. Descartes worked logically through his doubts until he was left with an indisputable single fact which was greater than mere fact: '*Je pense, donc je suis*' (I think, therefore I am).

90

Descartes left an important legacy. He invented a method by which a multitude of instances of the behaviour of a physical object can be expressed by a single mathematical formulation. Broadly speaking, Einstein owed the Theory of Relativity to Descartes. In his own thinking, however, Descartes preferred to deduce reality from primary intuition, as in 'I think, therefore I am'.

EMPIRICISM

Like the earlier Sceptics, the Empiricists doubted that everything could be known, and argued that what could, would derive from learning, not from speculation. Blaise Pascal, a mathematician like Descartes, was also his most severe empirical critic. The existence of God was the theme: Descartes's system, Pascal argued, led straight to Deism, the unsatisfactory view that God existed only in order to give the universe the initial push to set it in motion. But for Pascal human experience could be explained only through Christian revelation. Pascal was also an experimental scientist far in advance of his time, and by keeping his theology and his science so clearly separated he was adhering to the empirical tradition that not everything can be known. There were Empirical Deists, however, but they came into their own in the eighteenth century as *philosophes* of the Age of Enlightenment, such as the *libertin* (free-thinker) François La Mothe le Vayer.

BAROQUE AND CLASSICISM

These terms denote both ornamentation and refinement, and are commonly applied to the sweep of cultural forms in the seventeenth and early eighteenth centuries. The paramountcy of order and stability is recognized in Fréart de Chambray's observation: 'Proportion, symmetry and agreement of the whole with its parts, taught above all by geometry, the source and guide of all the arts.' The centre was Paris, but Toulouse and Aix-en-Provence were not far behind. The exponents of baroque and classicism are legion: Simon Vouet, Sébastien Bourdon, Louis Le Nain, Georges de La Tour and Claude Lorraine in painting; François Girardon, Antoine Coysevox and Pierre Puget in sculpture; Jacques Lemercier, François Mansart (his sloped, flat-topped roof form with dormer windows remains one of the most characteristic architectural features of Paris), Louis Le Vau, André Le Nôtre and Jules Hardouin-Mansart in architecture; Pierre Corneille, François de La Rochefoucauld, Cyrano de Bergerac and Jean-Baptiste Poquelin (Molière) in literature; and Jean-Baptiste Lully, court composer to Louis XIV, Jean-Philippe Rameau and François Couperin in music. There were many others.

They worked mainly because kings, the rich bourgeoisie and nobles patronized them, or hired them to adorn palace, hôtel and château. The *salon* was part of the patronage system for culture, where people such as Madame de Rambouillet, who held the most famous *salon* in Paris, gathered the best of the best, and brought together the upper bourgeoisie and aristocracy to mix in nearly perfect harmony. Later the *philosophes* would dominate the *salons*, and then the tone was less reflective. The *philosophes* wanted their ideas actually to change things.

The Sun King

Political and economic ordering was arranged by the royal government. Under Louis XIV (1643–1715), whose dazzle and grandeur – plus a fanciful costume worn in a ballet – won for him the sobriquet *Roi du Soleil* (Sun King), that government was absolute, or as near as ever it could be. In 1661 he arrested Nicolas Fouquet, Superintendent of Finance and among the wealthiest and most powerful men in France, on charges of corruption. He wrote to the queen mother: 'I told them that I would not have another superintendent ... that I would work on the finances myself with the aid of faithful people who would act under my direction.' Reflecting on his kingly role years later, Louis wrote:

> Nothing is so dangerous as weakness, of whatever kind it may be. To command others, one must rise above them; and after having heard all sides, one must decide on what must be done with an open mind, always keeping in view to order or execute nothing unworthy of oneself, of the character one bears, or of the grandeur of the State ....

He was to keep up these high standards throughout his life.

Louis was hard-working and would accept nothing less from his servants. In 1695 he warned the archbishop of Reims that his nephew, the marquis of Louvois, the war secretary, practised deception, flirted, was never at home and rarely was in his office: '. . . I do not wish to lose the services of your nephew; . . . but that for me, the welfare of the State comes before everything else.' Never had France had such a monarch. Never would it again. He was an absolute prince who believed in the trinity of order, regularity and unity.

Louis was a man for all seasons. Religious and a staunch Catholic, he backed the church – so long as the church remembered who ruled in France. His mistresses were numerous (in this he was a true Bourbon). The most important were Louise de La Vallière and Athénaïs de Montespan. Two wives but only one queen shared the royal bed. Marie Thérèse of Austria, who died in 1683, was the queen, and Madame de Maintenon, whom Louis married in secret because she was a commoner, was simply his wife. She was probably also his only true friend. The king was a patron of the arts, a daring, progressive and skilful warlord, an innovator in government, an able and enthusiastic diplomat, popular, courteous (he even touched his hat to chambermaids), a hunter, a gourmand, and a man with a sense of humour. The king loved Molière's comedies (a passion he shared with Madame de Maintenon), which often were performed at court.

Louis was no intellectual, but he possessed a shrewd and astute mind. He believed it was his Godly duty to work for the good of France and the French state – something which thoroughly distinguished him from medieval kings. Louis identified himself with the State and its paraphernalia, not with a personal domain called France. His unofficial motto was: '*l'État, c'est moi*' (I am the State). This was true only at first. By his death the State was able to get on reasonably well no matter what sort of monarch sat on the throne.

Colbert

Jean-Baptiste Colbert was a draper's son, honest, loyal, dedicated, brilliant and capable, and wholly dependent upon the king for his power, wealth and position. Louis described him to his mother in 1661 as the ultimate 'faithful' person. The king 'inherited' Colbert from Cardinal Mazarin, whose secretary he had been, and used him (and Captain d'Artagnan, a musketeer upon whose character Alexandre Dumas, *père*, based his hero in *The Three Musketeers*) to arrange the downfall of the corrupt Superintendent Nicolas Fouquet.

Colbert then became finance minister. His task (under Louis' supervision) was to make France economically and administratively strong as befitted Europe's most populous nation (20 million in 1661). The minister never doubted who was in charge, once he had received this letter from Louis, sent after Colbert had argued with the king over naval expenditure: '... do not risk vexing me again, because after I have heard your arguments and those of your colleagues and have given my opinion on all your claims, I do not ever wish to hear further talk about it.' One warning was enough.

COLBERTISM

Self-sufficiency was widely held to be the key to power and stability. The finance minister set out to achieve it by bending and manipulating economic development. This, in principle, was Mercantilism, or as it was in France, Colbertism. Tax reforms increased revenues over expenditure. Importing textile, metal, glass, leather and other skilled workers, and promoting scientific and technical research (the Academy of Science opened in 1666), improved industry. Lowered tariff barriers improved overseas trade, and new merchant companies exploiting non-European resources (colonial development, particularly in Canada, took off in this era) for a time made France the overseas rival of Holland, Spain, Portugal and England. Such was Colbertism, and by 1671 king and finance minister had set the feet of France on the path to what Colbert, after summing up industrial activity across the country in 1669, rather breathlessly termed: 'Grandeur and Magnificence!'

Meanwhile, king and minister, but principally king, established sound, strong central government well beyond what Henry IV had attempted: a council of state with four ministers; a cooperative Paris *parlement*; provincial *parlements* brought in line with Paris and limited to judicial deliberations. Municipal government was reformed and mayoral power restricted; the nobility were replaced as *intendants* almost entirely by members of the bourgeoisie; and there was uniform administration of the law (on two occasions Louis decided lawsuits against himself).

The army was also important to Louis's concept of glory and the absolute state, and he introduced extensive modernization carried forward by hard-working, competent professionals. Colonel Martinet reformed military discipline; Monsieur de Bayonet invented a long knife which attached to the end of the musket for hand-to-hand combat; standard uniforms were supplied beginning in 1686; and an astute innovator introduced the portable field kitchen, which greatly improved morale. No longer would soldiers have to subsist on the traditional doughnut-shaped hard biscuit while in the field. Meanwhile, Marshal Sébastien Vauban, an engineer, applied scientific principles to tactics, strategy, defence and supply, and the French army, modern and formidable, was ready for war. A strong government and armed forces was part of Colbertism, in that the idea always was to strengthen the state and thereby France.

VERSAILLES

This too was the idea behind Versailles, the magnificent château twelve miles south-west of Paris. With its 10,000 rooms and as many windows, ordered gardens and extensive park lands, Versailles was more than a house for King Louis. It was a symbol of French glory and unity, and of royal mastery over the forces of disorder. It was safe now to have large windows and extensive gardens instead of fortified walls and barbicans; openness overcame the grim seclusion of the Louvre. Versailles became the centre of the nation and Paris was a kind of suburb.

Louis conceived the grand plan in about 1670, and soon as many as 36,000 men and 6,000 horses were at work building, improving, landscaping and terracing. The king moved in, in 1682. Work continued on the château even then and for much of the rest of the reign. Versailles could never be quite grand enough. One example of its splendours, the *Galerie des Glaces* (hall of mirrors), was 80 metres long with 17 huge windows looking out across broad lawns to fountains, statuary, trees and parks; opposite each window was a mirror of equal size. The *Galerie des Glaces* achieved a fame enduring well beyond Louis and the Bourbon monarchy. In 1871 Bismarck proclaimed the new German empire there; and in 1919 the treaty ending the First World War was signed there – a treaty in part made necessary by Bismarck's act in 1871.

The *Galeries des Glaces* at Versailles

Louis in residence was the working king at home, surrounded by officials and courtiers who were kept on their toes by rigid rules of etiquette (though less rigid than in many European capitals of the time), and by their conviction that to be at Versailles was the ultimate privilege of their class. The marquis of Varde, for example, exiled for twenty years for interfering in Louis's love affairs, was finally allowed to return and appeared wearing the now outmoded clothes he had worn on the day he had left Versailles. He knelt before Louis who raised and embraced him. The marquis wept openly and explained: 'To have displeased your Majesty is to be wretched; to be apart from you is to appear ridiculous.' Of course Versailles bred sycophancy, too, which was the point of the reference in François de Fénelon's famous letter criticising Louis's rule: '... truth is free and strong. You have hardly been used to hearing it.'

Within limits, Versailles was open to the public. The populace could come and watch the king dine, and when the dauphin was ill, Paris fishwives came by to kiss him on the cheek. The château was also the centre of French cultural life. Molière plays were performed, as was the music of Lully, Couperin and, in the eighteenth century, Rameau. Le Vau, Le Nôtre and Jules Hardouin-Mansart were its architects, and the best artists were employed in decorating and redecorating. Versailles cost a fortune to maintain, and Colbert disapproved of developing the château instead of the Louvre.

But Versailles cost little compared to warfare. Unfortunately, Louis spent lavishly on both. He was at war with his neighbours for 35 years. The economic and fiscal advantages gained by his reforms were nullified, and the foundations of absolutism he was at such pains to establish were undermined in consequence.

Holland

For most of his reign, Louis was at war with Holland, England and/or the Empire. He disliked Holland because it was republican, Protestant and most of all, because it was in his way. In 1672 he attacked the Dutch with a well-organized, well-armed and disciplined army of 119,000 officers and men.

THE DUTCH WAR

Louis obtained nearly everything he wanted against the Dutch and their allies. English troops fought alongside the French until 1674, and Louis personally commended young John Churchill for bravery at Maastricht. After England left the alliance, Louis effectively neutralized it through secret deals with Charles II. France gained Franche Comté and half of Flanders, and the king won fame as a military leader and in diplomacy. By 1683 he was master of Europe.

But French glory came at a high price. In the first place, the Dutch war cost £30 million a year, and was soon unpopular because taxes rose to meet expenses. In 1675 a rebellion broke out in Brittany, and at the same time Bordeaux, starved of its wine trade with Holland, conspired with the Dutch against Louis. In the second place, although Louis's neighbours were awed by him, they were also made uneasy. After the Peace of Westphalia ended the Thirty Years War in 1648, England and the Habsburg Empire were committed to the balance of power in Europe. Now Louis XIV was upsetting it and neither England nor the Empire were prepared to let this go unchallenged. In the third place, success made Louis arrogant. He committed precipitous acts certain to rouse anti-French feeling in England.

Prince William of Orange, Stadholder of Holland and commander of the Dutch armies, had married Mary Stuart, daughter of the future James II of England and niece of Charles II, in 1677. In 1685 Louis revoked the Edict of Nantes and began systematic persecution of the Huguenots. Between 1677 and 1683 England had passed through the 'Popish Plot' and Succession Crises, and anti-Catholic feeling ran high. Revocation of the Edict simply focused that feeling against Louis. By 1685 England was in a mood for war with France, and had allies in Holland, the Empire and Brandenberg Prussia, ruled by a Calvinist. In 1688 the Glorious Revolution deposed James II, a Catholic, and brought in his son-in-law, William of Orange, a Protestant, to rule England jointly with his wife as William III and Mary II. James fled to France where Louis welcomed him as the rightful king of England and a true son of the Church. In 1689 the first of two long wars began between France and England in alliance with the Empire.

THE GERMAN WAR

Louis planned to expand French territory to the north-east, and made an alliance with the Turks who were to keep Emperor Leopold I distracted while Louis invaded the Habsburg Rhineland. But in 1683 Leopold won a great victory over the Turks outside Vienna, breaking their European strength. (Viennese bakers celebrated by creating a crescent-shaped bun in imitation of the crescent moon of Islam. This bun later became popular in France as the *croissant*.) When war began in 1689, the Empire was ready to counter-attack in alliance with England, Holland, Spain, Savoy, Brandenberg and Bavaria. The 1689 war did not go well for France as a result. In the Treaty of Ryswick in 1697, King Louis gave up most of the occupied territories, plus Lorraine. What he retained was kept mainly because his enemies were as exhausted as himself.

THE SPANISH WAR

After Ryswick, Louis felt surrounded by enemies and had it in mind to make Spain a permanent ally by promoting a Bourbon as heir to the Spanish throne. This he achieved through diplomacy, and when the Habsburg King of Spain, Charles II, died in 1701, Louis's grandson was crowned Philip VI. The Imperial Habsburgs and the English objected, and war broke out again. In 1702 William III died, and was succeeded by Queen Anne. Louis did himself little good by proclaiming for the exiled James II. Meanwhile, the duke of Marlborough, John Churchill, stepped forward as the power behind Queen Anne's throne. If Louis was prepared to go to war on behalf of his grandson and the Stuart claimant, Marlborough and Prince Eugène of Savoy, the Emperor's principal commander and a general the equal of Marlborough, were glad to accommodate him.

The war ended only in 1713. It was filled with famous battles, most of which France lost. Louis's best advisors were gone (Colbert died in 1683), debts sky-rocketed and public disquiet increased. His great reputation bled away at Blenheim, Ramillies, Turin, Oudenaarde, Lille, Malplaquet and Denain. At Utrecht in 1713, Louis ceded territory, much of it in North America, and kept only the Spanish throne for his grandson, with the proviso that no Spanish Bourbon could ever inherit the French throne. With that the war ended. In 1715, aged, disappointed, weary, much of his life's work diminished by this war, Louis died.

The Enlightenment

Louis died and the Age of Reason was born. Seventeenth-century thinkers wanted system; eighteenth-century intellectuals wanted action, enlightened solutions to specific problems born out of reasoned analysis of what was wrong. The life of the mind in France was never livelier. These intellectuals were critics, satirists, materialists, metaphysicians, anti-clericals, republicans, constitutionalists, radicals, rich and poor. Men like Voltaire corresponded with princes and were also exiled by them. Meanwhile, in the arts this was the Age of Rococo, almost frivolous compared to Enlightened thought, but no less innovative and interesting. Elegant, light and airy, its decorative swirls and curves

Voltaire

teased the symmetrical lines of the Baroque and Classical. Rococo was symbolized by a delicate Antoine Watteau painting, a low-relief horse carved by Robert le Lorrain over the stables of the Hôtel de Rohan in Paris, or a harpsichord concerto by Jean-Philippe Rameau, foreshadowing the neo-impressionism of Claude Debussy a century and a half later.

THE PHILOSOPHES

The intellectuals were called *philosophes*, and they wrote and argued about every subject under the sun. In *The Spirit of the Law*, Montesquieu explained how the separation of powers between legislature, executive and judiciary was the secret to political stability. In *The History of the Reign of Louis XIV, Candide*, and other writings, Voltaire criticized society and urged change. He also championed Deism as the only reasonable alternative to the priest-ridden and corrupt church. Diderot argued for a broader-based science of experimentation and observation, and founded the *Encyclopédie*, wherein the sum of human knowledge would be assembled in rational categories for the enlightenment of humanity. In *Émile* and *The Social Contract*, Rousseau elaborated new concepts in education and an egalitarian society based upon the General Will of the community. Regrettably, he did not leave space for dissent, and Rousseauism led directly to totalitarian concepts of democracy during the Revolution, and again in the twentieth century. The list of contributors to the world of the intellect in eighteenth-century France includes, among others, La Mettrie, Alembert, Maupertuis, Holbach, Condillac, and even de Sade, in his perverse way. They created new expressions for established ideas, and some new ideas of their own. Above all, they created an atmosphere of intellectual ferment in which dissatisfaction with the failings of the *Ancien Régime* was readily expressed and acted upon.

ENLIGHTENED ABSOLUTISM

The Enlightenment appealed to at least some absolutist rulers. Most of the *philosophes* corresponded with princes, and visited them, outside of France. They were less welcome at Versailles, which fact adds credence to the ancient adage that a prophet rarely finds honour in his own land. Voltaire was virtually idolized by Frederick II of Prussia, an intellectual and composer in his own right, despite several disagreements. Catherine II of Russia patronized Diderot so that he would have funds to continue with the *Encylcopédie*. Joseph II of the Habsburg Empire looked for inspiration to the *philosophes* for the reforms he was attempting within his domains. George III of England, though no absolutist, was caught up in the fascination with technics. He dabbled in agriculture and wrote articles about it under the name Ralph Robinson. Frederick, Catherine and Joseph held no brief for democratic principles contained in *philosophe* writings; but they were much interested in the techniques of analysis and reform found there, which were applicable to economics, government or the arts. They reasoned that if properly applied, these techniques would make the state, economy or war machine more efficient and thus would enhance absolutism. They also did not encourage home-grown *philosophes*, despite founding academies right and left; better to import French intellectuals – as Frederick brought in Maupertuis to head the

Prussian academy – and send them packing if they became troublesome.

The Ancien Régime

In the period 1715–1789, the social, economic and fiscal failures of the previous two centuries caught up with the Bourbon monarchy. This was the era of the *Ancien Régime*, the 'old order'. Two kings sat on the throne in this period, and neither could come to grips with these failures. Many specific factors led to revolution in 1789, but decades of failing to provide lasting reforms underscored them.

In the eighteenth century the gap between rich and poor, privileged and deprived, town and country, locality and the centre, widened. The provinces defended their rights against royal authority with heightened vigour, and the *intendants* found their jobs ever harder to do. No real improvements were made in the tax system. Tax farmers made hefty profits as always and resentment among ordinary and landed locals towards them increased. *Parlementaire* powers revived, and those of municipalities and guilds expanded. The old nobility lost virtually none of its privileges, regained some of its power, abnegated all sense of responsibility, and concerned itself solely with defending its social exclusivity. Louis XV (1715–1774) ascended the throne as a five-year-old child with a regent, the duke of Orléans, ruling for him. He was Louis XIV's great-grandson; this did not deter the old nobles, who seized this opportunity to stage a 'palace revolution'. Prophetic words.

Louis XV

The Peers of France (the highest of the ancient nobility) took control of the government in 1715, and with the aid of the reviving *parlements* took back the powers the late king had taken from them. But they made a hash of governing and by 1718 the secretaries of state were again running the bureacracy. Moreover, the arrogance of the peers alienated other ancient nobles, who now placed the protection of their interests in the hands of the *noblesse de la robe* and the *parlement* of Paris (which was also sick of the peers) which the *robe* backed. There aristocratic leadership remained until the Revolution. Absolutism was being dismantled. The process would take a half-century, but when complete, the full poverty of the system begun by Francis I, enhanced by Henry IV and brought to fruition by the Sun King, would be revealed. It should have been Louis XIV, rather than Louis XVI, who said: 'Aprés moi, c'est le Deluge' (After me comes the flood).

Cardinal Fleury

By 1726 French government settled down under the direction of Cardinal Fleury. Royal finances improved and deficits were reduced. However, there was no corresponding improvement in industry, and the conditions of the peasantry remained the same as in the past, or deteriorated.

The *parlements* and tax farmers opposed any reforms of industrial or agricultural policy, and Louis XV had neither the strength of will nor the confidence to impose himself upon the court and government. He quickly learnt to give his minister the lead, and himself up to hunting and his mistresses, the marquise de Pompadour and Madame du Barry, who apparently were more entertaining than his Polish queen, Marie Leszczyńska. The marquise adorned the court lavishly with the latest of everything, which invoked popular criticism about extravagance and waste. But – echoes of Louis XIV and Versailles – her spending was as nothing compared to the costs of the wars which began in 1741 and were paid for with tax increases.

THE SEVEN YEARS WAR

In the decade after 1741 the *parlements*, led by Paris, emerged as the principal obstacles to any attempt by the government at fiscal or provincial reform. The *parlements*, usually behind the façade of defending liberty, became reactionary institutions prepared to drag France into oblivion before surrendering privilege. They had their opportunity with the Seven Years War, which began in 1756, the result of machinations between Frederick II of Prussia, and Prince Kaunitz, chancellor of the Habsburg Empire.

A sudden shift in diplomacy, sometimes called the Diplomatic Revolution of 1756, ranged Britain with Prussia, and France with the Empire and Russia. The war did not go well for France: India, Canada and Louisiana and some islands in the West Indies were lost. The Seven Years War was known by many names, including, in North America, the French and Indian War.

France emerged from the Treaty of Paris in 1763 shorn of empire and heavily in debt. Taxes had to be assessed, and the *parlements* stood four-square against it, just as they had in 1749 when minister of finance Machault d'Arnouville introduced a tax to pay for the War of the Austrian Succession. In 1763 the provincial *parlements* drew closer to their *confrères* in Paris, and between them they first curtailed government plans to prolong war-time taxes as a way to reduce deficits, and second, in the name of Gallicanism, launched an attack on the Jesuits which finally forced Louis to suppress the order in 1764.

More disputes erupted between king and *parlements* over the next half-dozen years, particularly in Paris and Brittany, and by 1771 the kingdom was on the verge of anarchy. Meanwhile, Madame Du Barry became royal mistress, and persuaded Louis to dismiss his foreign minister, the duke of Choiseul. Choiseul was popular with the nobility, but made no effort to conceal his dislike for Du Barry. At that moment, Chancellor René-Nicolas de Maupeou abolished the *parlement* of Paris; he got away with this dramatic act because noble opposition to the crown was not then certain how much power the crown might display. New courts were set up to handle judicial affairs and plans for fiscal reform were scrutinized, including a plan to put a tax on all classes. But at this point Louis died.

Louis XVI

Louis XV's grandson, Louis XVI (1774–1793), inherited an enormously unpopular throne, a noisy capital of perhaps a half-million inhabitants still crammed into a city of medieval proportions (save for the parks and the suburbs – or *faubourgs* – where the nobility had developed elegant hôtels and squares), an economy inadequate to meet the needs of 26 million French people, of whom 21 million lived on the land, and a deficit of 37 million livres which within 15 years rose to 112 million. The tax reform plans did not survive Louis XV. His grandson had no means for dealing with financial problems, and began to rely on financiers.

Anne-Robert Jacques Turgot, the finance minister, wanted to tax landed wealth; this proved to be impossible. After Louis XV died the *parlements* had recovered their strength. Now they engineered Turgot's dismissal for even thinking such revolutionary thoughts. The peasants approved of Turgot however, especially his abolishing the *corvée* (forced) peasant labour on public roads.

AMERICA

In 1778 the count of Vergennes involved France in the American War of Independence, part of a manoeuvre against Great Britain. He helped the American rebels considerably, and a liberal reputation was acquired by the marquis de Lafayette, who served as *aide-de-camp* to General George Washington for a winter. Also, a French fleet helped the Americans win the battle of Yorktown. However, Vergennes did nothing at all for French solvency. The money which paid for America was borrowed from bankers, one of whom, Jacques Necker, a Swiss, looked after the loans as director of state finance.

Calonne

Charles-Alexandre de Calonne emerged in the late 1780s as financial controller with a scheme to restore confidence in the government by lavish spending on public works. He also planned tax reforms, including a universal tax to be administered by new, local assemblies. Calonne advised Louis to summon a carefully hand-picked Assembly of Notables to put these 'revolutionary' proposals over in the countryside. Louis did, but the Notables were no more sympathetic than the *parlements*. Privilege had won again. Notables, *parlements*, pamphlets and orators haranguing crowds in the Palais-Royal in Paris, all demanded the summoning of the Estates General to deal with the problems of the reign and the country.

Meanwhile there were other difficulties, among them Louis' queen, Marie Antoinette, daughter of Maria Theresa and sister of Joseph II of Austria. While France seethed, she built rustic cottages in the Versailles park lands and played at being a milk-maid. When told the poor of Paris had no bread, she probably did not actually say: 'Let them eat cake'; but she might have, for all the difference it made to her reputation.

Moreover, as *l'Autrichienne* (the Austrian) she was suspect in the popular mind. Pamphleteers accused her of heinous things, some of them straining credulity, like the accusation that in a single night she gave her sexual favours to an entire Guards regiment. Anti-royal propaganda was becoming more scurrilous in the 1780s. Furthermore, the court nobles looked down their noses at rustic provincial aristocrats, which isolated the court from the country; nobles keen to make their estates efficient were frequently at odds with those who simply wished to profit by exploiting feudal dues; the upper bourgeoisie had no sympathy with the petty bourgeoisie and the urban worker, who in turn hated rich merchants and bankers; and the humble *curé* and the prince of the church were miles apart. In short, every social category now pursued its own interests, mostly indifferent to any sense of community.

Louis XVI's reign opened with a severe food crisis and grain riots in Paris. Between 1775 and 1788, riots over food shortages and taxes were regular occurrences. In 1788 the Paris *parlement* revolted over Necker's tax plan, and forced the king to summon the Estates General. The *parlement* then demanded that when the Estates met, voting would be equal between the three parts, even though the Third Estate (commoners) would represent 96 per cent of the population. The *parlement* represented privilege, not liberty; they were sowing the whirlwind.

Revolution

Provincial assemblies elected delegates to the Estates General, and in May 1789 these delegates gathered at Versailles. There were alarming developments from the start. The Third Estate rejected aristocratic leadership and insisted on single-member voting in the form of a National Assembly. On 17 June they so renamed themselves, and three days later met at a nearby tennis court where they swore an oath not to participate in any deliberations until their demands were met.

Meanwhile in Paris, radical orators stirred up the *sans-culottes* (the aristocrats' term for the Parisian working people), pamphlets appealed to popular discontents, royal ministers were burnt in effigy, radical newspapers appeared, ideas of the Enlightenment circulated as the revealed wisdom of a new world order, and certain nobles and clergy –

count Mirabeau and the abbé Sieyès, for example – joined with the Third Estate in demanding the formation of the National Assembly. Louis and his ministers gave in, and on 27 June ordered the abolition of the Estates and official formation of the National Assembly.

On 14 July, a heavy, overcast and muggy day, a crowd gathered in front of the Bastille. They claimed (wrongly) that this old fortress prison was filled with political prisoners. Tension increased and the crowd grew violent. They demanded that the Bastille surrender its prisoners, to which the commandant finally agreed, on the promise of a safe conduct for himself and his men. He cpened the gate, and almost at once he and several of the soldiers were killed. The revolution had now begun in earnest. The fallen Bastille, however, was a disappointment. There were only four prisoners, and none of them were political. Revolutionary propaganda gave the impression later that half the population of Paris was inside. In any event, the fortress, a hated symbol of the old order, was soon razed to the ground, and survives today only in the name of a square, a stop on the Métro, and a new opera house.

History can turn on accidents, or so Voltaire claimed when he speculated that the Roman Republic might have survived had Cleopatra's nose been less seductive to Julius Caesar and Mark Antony. Thus we must also remember the count of Soissons and his hair-triggered pistol after the battle of La Marfée, and the incident of the Locked Door.

On the morning of 20 June 1789, the Third Estate arrived at their hall prepared to press demands for the National Assembly. The door was locked. Suspecting the worst, they went off to the tennis court and swore the famous oath, effectively beginning the Revolution. It is supposed that they were locked out as part of a royal manoeuvre to nip their demands in the bud, and thus reassert government control of the situation. But another version has it that the door was locked because the porters had not finished cleaning, and they refused to open up until they had. Did the porters start the Revolution by default? Probably the Revolution would have occurred whatever the state of the door. No doubt the count of Soissons would have been amused by the question all the same.

CHAPTER SEVEN

The Era of Revolution
1789–1852

In 1789 the dam broke. France entered upon sixty years of social, political, economic and intellectual upheaval. In this era the French nation was born, and Paris emerged as its beating heart.

Paris

In 1789 a half-million Parisians lived in an eight-by-six-kilometre area characterized by poor hovels, rich hôtels and palaces, churches, narrow and crowded streets and only a few avenues. Six bridges crossed the Seine, of which the Pont Neuf was the largest. It offered strollers entertainments, a view of the river (the Pont Neuf had no houses on it), and raised pavements.

New buildings mixed with old: the Louvre and Tuileries, Notre-Dame, Les Halles and the Bastille were old; the École Militaire, next to the Champ-de-Mars, the Invalides, the Palais-Royal (a sort of arcade encompassing such oddities as the Café Américain), and the Panthéon, built over the old church of Sainte-Geneviève and completed only in 1790 (it became a necropolis for heroes, just as Saint-Denis was a necropolis for ancient kings) were new. Mansart roofs were a commonplace. Place Louis XV was at the west end of the Tuileries; two kilometres east on the Ile de la Cité, stood the Conciergerie and the Châtelet. In 1793-94 their inmates were brought by tumbrils through mocking, jeering crowds to Place Louis XV, by then called the Place de la Révolution, for execution. Their route was the Rue St Honoré, the very heart of revolutionary Paris.

Parisians, about to become French in the fully modern sense of the word, were justifiably proud of their city. Often their English neighbours failed to admire Paris for reasons that were perhaps centuries-old: resentment and jealousy, aimed at the French themselves. William Cole, a Cambridge clergyman, wrote in 1765 that if only each 'vain and Fantastical' Frenchman could see London, then 'if Truth will not make him acknowledge the *Petitesse*, the Littleness, the Nothingness of Paris in respect to the Beauty, Grandeur & Superiority of London, he must be ashamed of nothing; indeed a Very Frenchman.'

The Revolution

The storming of the Bastille was followed by an uprising in the countryside, which created a panic known as the Great Fear. Châteaux were burnt, tax-collectors murdered and clergy attacked. It soon passed, but meanwhile the National Assembly felt constrained to enact legislation abolishing feudal dues, serfdom and tithes, and nationalizing the church and clergy. Louis XVI approved this legislation in his new capacity as 'constitutional' monarch. Perhaps to save their necks, landed aristocrats and higher clerics in the Assembly voluntarily turned over their estates for redistribution to the peasants. 'They've all gone mad!' said one startled observer. At the same time, confiscated clerical lands were made the basis of a new currency, the *assignat*, which solved neither currency problems nor inflation, and was soon worthless. Most people continued to deal in *sous* and *livres*.

In October, inspired by radical orators (and *agents provocateurs* of the duke of Orléans, Louis XVI's cousin, now known as Philippe Égalité), a crowd of lower-class Parisian women trekked to Versailles with shouts of '*Vive la Nation*', and forced the royal family to accompany them back to Paris. Food and grain shortages, inflation and unemployment were the harsh realities of city life for these women, and they reckoned the king could better look after them – and himself be kept free of corrupt advisors – in the Tuileries.

The women were in no mood to argue. Jeanne Martin, a nurse, reported that she was forced to go with them on pain of being beaten if she refused. On the return to Paris they had sport with Queen Marie Antoinette, whom they threatened to butcher and eat, while some of the men with them fired guns over the queen's head. For the king they still could feel affection; Marie Antoinette was simply *l'Autrichienne*.

The cry '*Vive la Nation!*' indicated a new mentality, soon rooted throughout France. Early on there occurred the inevitable attempts to use the revolution to separate the provinces from Paris. These failed. Federations of villages and towns formed, brought together by the revolutionary spirit behind the slogan 'Liberté, égalite, fraternité'. Their representatives, called *fédérés*, went to Paris and brought with them a sense that all France was at last a nation united by common popular action to overthrow the old order.

REVOLUTIONARY GOVERNMENT

The National Assembly, now meeting in a hall next to the Tuileries Palace, struggled with a variety of problems in 1789–91. They were frequently intimidated by mobs who believed that now the *nation* had replaced the feudal order, their opinion would be wanted by the legislature and government. The Assembly solved no major problems, although they did hammer out a constitution, completed in September 1791. France was divided administratively into *départements*, the king no longer ruled by divine right nor could he absolutely veto legislation, the Assembly became permanently part of government, and the Rights of Man were formally spelt out. The way was also left open for future change.

That change would include emancipation of women – a century and a half later, at the conclusion of the Second World War. At the time, liberation for women was an unrealized ideal. The revolutionary intellectual, the Marquis of Condorcet urged it, pointing out that 'either no member of the human race has any natural rights or they all have the same; and anyone who votes against the rights of another, whatever their religion, their colour or their sex, has from that moment abjured his own.' Madame de Condorcet also urged female emancipation, as did such women as playwright Olympe de Gouges, who wrote the tract *Declaration of the Rights of Women and the Citizen*, Théroigne de Méricourt, often credited with being unofficial leader of those who sat in the gallery at the National Assembly, and Manon de Roland, a major figure in the Girondiste party and later a victim of the guillotine.

Méricourt called upon French women to 'rise to the level of our destinies and break our chains,' adding that it was high time 'women emerged from the shameful state of nullity and ignorance to which the arrogance and injustice of men have so long condemned them.' French women repudiated the *ancien regime*, gave sons to the revolution, and died on the scaffold in its name. However, neither words nor deeds spoken or performed by French women in the revolution had any lasting effect.

Political parties had formed even before the revolution began. Now they filled the Assembly and jockeyed for position. In 1791 the Girondins (liberals) were in power, led by Jacques Brissot. Other parties included the Jacobins (radicals), led by Camille Desmoulins and later by Georges Jacques Danton and Maximilien Robespierre; the Hébertists (socialists) led by Jacques Hébert; and the *enragés* (communists) led by a former priest, Jacques Roux. The marquis of Lafayette fluctuated between moderate monarchism and conservative republicanism, and created the National Guard from among the bourgeoisie of Paris to keep order and protect the revolution from reactionaries. Philippe Egalité (the duke of Orléans) played his own political game until he fell from favour. The duke went to the guillotine, it was reported, with an enigmatic smile on his face.

In the Assembly the basic political designations of subsequent times evolved: the President sat on a dais at the front; on his Left sat the radicals, on his Right the conservatives, and the moderates occupied seats in the Centre.

The Republic

In June 1791, Louis XVI tried to flee France with his family. They were caught at Varenne by the local *procurateur*, a grocer named Sauce, and returned to Paris. Until then Parisians shouted '*Vive le Roi!*' Now they shouted '*Vive la Nation!*' As they saw it, Louis had betrayed them. The proof, if more was needed, came in August when the duke of Brunswick issued the Declaration of Pillnitz, condemning the revolution and vowing revenge if harm befell Louis. French relations with the rest of Europe deteriorated rapidly. The Girondins argued for war as the best way to head off intervention – and to galvanize the nation into unanimous support for Paris and the revolution. After months of debate war was declared in April, 1792, and the inclination towards republicanism became a headlong rush.

THE SEPTEMBER MASSACRES

But first the nation had to root out the enemy within. In August a national convention was summoned to depose the monarch. Then on 2 September a massacre of political prisoners began, carried out by enthusiastic volunteers. They broke into the prisons and began systematically slaughtering the inmates: 1200 in all – priests, royalists, common criminals, and some for whom no actual crime was in evidence. Contemporary accounts describe incredible horrors and bestiality, including cannibalism. Princess de Lambelle was stripped, raped and her body mutilated; some were beheaded, some slashed to death with sabres, and others set on fire. On the other hand, some prisoners were simply released, and even escorted home by people smeared with the blood of others less fortunate. The English ambassador simply commented: 'What a people!' Authorities encouraged the bloodletting, or at least did nothing to discourage it, on the grounds that the mob was ridding France of internal enemies.

VALMY

Thus 'secured', the revolutionary army went off to confront their foreign enemies. They were ill-armed but highly motivated. Flushed by the heady idea of belonging to the Nation and of carrying forward a new order, they defeated the professionals of Prussia and Austria at Valmy. A dispirited Prussian officer commented: 'We have lost more than a battle.'

This was 20 September; the next day the Convention proclaimed the Republic and prepared to bring Louis XVI, now called Louis Capet, a symbolic repudiation of the entire monarchial history of France, to trial for conspiracy. In January 1793 he was convicted, condemned and executed. Marie Antoinette followed in October. The dauphin died of illness in 1795, after having been proclaimed in the courts of Europe as Louis XVII.

The *ancien régime* thus ended. Meanwhile, there were increasing manifestations of egalitarianism: *citoyen* (citizen) became the standard form of address; powdered wigs and fancy clothes disappeared; people gave their children 'revolutionary' names: 'Égalité' and 'Vertu', for example. 1792 was Year I of the First French Republic. But not everyone was happy. Manon Roland, wife of the Jacobin Jean Roland, a woman of intellect and ability and a driving force in the Assembly, feared that the horrors were far from over. She was correct. Her husband was forced into exile in 1793 where he committed suicide upon learning that she had been guillotined for speaking out against Jacobin excesses.

THE TERROR

At first things went well after Valmy, and the Girondins prospered. French armies annexed Nice and Savoy, captured Belgium and invaded the Rhineland. Everywhere they proclaimed the 'sovereignty of the people' and equated it with nationalism. 'Exporting revolution', a common twentieth-century phenomenon, was first practised in 1792 by the French.

Then the Girondins fell behind both in prosecuting the war and dealing with poverty, shortages and inflation. The public became agitated. In April 1793, the Jacobin leaders (called *Les Montagnards* because they sat on the top seats of the tiered Assembly Hall) forced through the formation of the Committee of Public Safety, an organization for centralizing power and keeping order. It was used first to overthrow the Girondins, whose leaders were hurried to the guillotine shortly after. On 17 September the Law of Suspects was established – anyone suspected of betraying the revolution *ipso facto* had done so – and the Terror began.

Danton ran the Committee, but the true architect of the Terror was Robespierre and his principal aides, the cold-blooded Louis de Saint-Just and the wily Joseph Fouché (as bloodthirsty as any *sans-culottes*). They formed a dictatorship based upon popular fear and hatred of 'enemies of the revolution', and used it to save France from enemies abroad.

A revolutionary army of conscripts was formed; supplies were requisitioned; and anyone who objected was executed for treason. Cries of '*La Patrie en danger!*' and '*Aux armes, citoyens!*' were all that was needed for the Committee to justify any action. The marching song of revolutionary cadres from Marseille (*La Marseillaise*) became the hymn of the Jacobin army. The Terror was Rousseau's law of the General Will gone mad.

During a year-and-a-half 20,000 people in Paris and double that in the country died by the guillotine: aristocrats, priests, ordinary people, former royal ministers – even Madame Du Barry, once mistress to Louis XV, was caught up. Thomas Jefferson, the United States ambassador and a staunch friend of France, thought it prudent to slip quietly away during this period. Equality of a sort had been achieved: no one was safe from the guillotine, neither aristocrat nor commoner, guilty or innocent. Meanwhile, Dame Reason was 'enthroned' symbolically at Notre-Dame Cathedral, and churches were pulled down throughout France, including the famous abbey at Cluny.

The Terror saved France from foreign enemies; at home it produced such tension that the populace wearied of it and began to doubt the revolution itself. There was a turn to the Right. The Jacobins, Hébertists, *enragés* and other extremists were brought down in 1795. Saint-Just, Robespierre – all but Fouché who went missing at the opportune moment – made the journey to Place de la Révolution. The prediction of the Assembly's President, Pierre Vergniaud, was realized: the revolution was 'devouring its children'.

THE DIRECTORY

Rule by another committee followed: the Directory. Composed of conservatives, it ruled unsteadily and insecurely through devious compromise, purges, by hitting alternately at Right and Left, and by relying on the army. It condoned squads of bourgeois bully-boys called *jeunesse dorée*, who roamed the streets with clubs looking for 'radicals'. But economic problems defied the Directory, as they had all of its predecessors, and populist protests, led sometimes by the National Guard, became epidemic. On one occasion a young Corsican brigadier in command of artillery used a 'whiff of grape shot' to break up an anti-government riot. His reward was command of the French army in Italy in 1796 – a mistake, warned Dupont de Nemours, an economist who served the Directory. It was.

The Corsican brigadier won stunning victories, made his own treaties with the Habsburg emperor, and conquered Egypt. Alarmed by his brilliance, independent-mindedness and popularity with his troops, the Directory summoned the officer home for disciplining. He came, but under the inspiration of his brother, Lucien, President of the Council of Five Hundred, the lower house of the Assembly, on 9 November 1799 he overthrew the Directory at gunpoint. The Council soon declared him First Consul of the French Republic. Napoleon Bonaparte had arrived.

Napoleon

The First Consul soon brought order out of the chaos. A plebiscite affirmed him in his powers by a large majority. He then declared that the revolution was ended. In the coming months Napoleon confirmed the peasants in their revolutionary gains, restored the church, established a code of laws (the Code Napoléon) which governed every aspect of life from the law courts to education, and set up a one-man dictatorship based upon the principle of authority: the father over the children, the husband over the wife, the employer over the employee, and himself over everyone.

Although Napoleon talked republicanism and nationalism, he behaved like an eighteenth-century enlightened absolutist bent on the rationalization of power. In 1804 he proclaimed himself emperor; he set aside his wife, the beautiful bourgeoise Josephine de Beauharnais, in order to marry a Habsburg princess; he personally constructed the French constitution to fit his view of the State; propaganda and censorship were constants of his rule; he allied capital with government through the Bank of France; tax collection was reformed, improved, and committed primarily to the maintenance of his armies; rioters were dealt with ruthlessly; prices were carefully regulated; he reinstated slavery in the French colonies after the revolution had abolished it; and he made an agreement with the pope (the Concordat of 1801) which gave the Church protected status, but left it entirely dependent upon the State. Even as First Consul he claimed the right to name his successors; his birthday was celebrated as a national holiday and coins bore his portrait.

Napoleon continued the principle of exporting revolution. Many Rhenish states were liberated from the oppressive rule of petty princelings, and German intellectuals such as Goethe and Beethoven (at

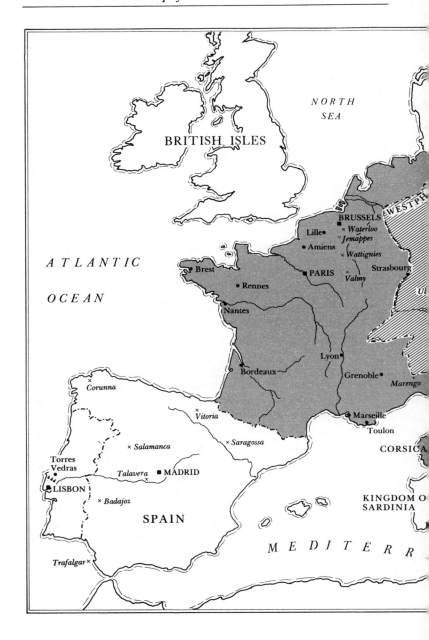

MOSCOW ■
×
Borodino

• Tilsit

PRUSSIA

GRAND DUCHY
OF WARSAW

Revolution and Empire

Areas ruled directly by Napoleon
Areas ruled by members of Napoleon's
family
× Battles

× *Leipzig*
na

AUSTRIAN EMPIRE
× *Austerlitz*

Wagram ×
■ VIENNA

BLACK

SEA

-DOM
-OF ITALY

E ■

-NGDOM OF
NAPLES

Naples

KINGDOM
OF SICILY

AN

S   E   A

first) regarded Napoleon as the true apostle of the Enlightenment. However, this, like his republicanism, was a sham. Nothing better revealed Bonaparte's disregard for the principles he exported – freedom, rights of man, and rule of law – than the incident of the duke d'Enghien. A French royalist apparently safe in the neutral German state of Baden, d'Enghien was abducted across the border into French-controlled territory, tried by summary court-martial, and shot as a conspirator against Napoleon. The reappearance of Fouché, who had survived office under the Terror and the Directory, as Napoleon's Minister of the Interior in charge of police, indicates further that Napoleon's rule was ultimately based upon ruthless, limitless and cynical power.

THE EMPIRE

Napoleon's plans included the reordering of Europe, and the overthrow of the balance of power in France's favour. When Louis XIV attempted this, the European powers took up arms to stop him. They did again now, but it took nearly fifteen years for them to succeed.

Napoleon repeatedly defeated the Habsburgs and forced concessions from them by the treaties of Campo-Formio in 1797 and Lunéville in 1801. But in 1798 at Aboukir Bay, at the Battle of the Nile, Admiral Horatio Nelson destroyed a French fleet, thus securing British power in the Mediterranean. In India Sir Arthur Wellesley disrupted French attempts to intrigue with Tippoo Sahib, Sultan of Mysore. The parameters of the Napoleonic wars were established by 1802: Napoleon could have his way on the continent – for the time being; but he could not overcome the British at sea. An invasion of Britain depended upon Admiral Villeneuve neutralizing admirals Nelson, Collingwood, Cornwallis and Pellew, which he could not do. Napoleon had to settle for isolating Britain diplomatically and commercially, but that, too, failed in the long run.

On the continent Napoleon went from strength to strength up to 1807: there were great victories at Marengo, Austerlitz, Jena and Auerstadt, among others; there were treaties with Denmark, Russia, the United States, Naples, Portugal, Turkey and – a treaty of mutual distrust – with Britain at Amiens in 1802. Napoleon overran the Rhineland in 1803, crowned himself emperor in 1804, became master of Italy in 1805, and in

1806 abolished the Holy Roman Empire (the Habsburgs now simply became Austrian emperors) and set up the Confederations of the Rhine. In 1807 he met Alexander I of Russia at Tilsit in Poland, where they made a secret peace. Napoleon was master of the continent then, his power at its apex. Britain was isolated, Russia neutralized, and the only world still to conquer was the British Empire.

BLOCKADE

The French emperor knew that until he mastered Britain there would be a gap in the solid front of his power. In an attempt to close the gap, he declared a blockade against all commerce with Britain: British goods were denied access to the continent, and no ship could land in both British and French harbours, or any European port under French control. Britain replied with its own blockade, whereby no neutral was permitted to trade with Napoleonic Europe. The emperor could only try to prevent Europeans from trading with England, for it had to be done through customs officials, whereas Britain had the fleet to enforce its blockade – and to run the French blockade. A lively commerce in smuggling soon developed, negating much of Napoleon's effort, while France's port economy fell into depression from lack of use. At the same time, shortages created by the British blockade raised anti-French resentment amongst dependent territories, despite Napoleon's propaganda which blamed it all on Britain.

DECLINE

Prince Maurice de Talleyrand, Napoleon's foreign minister and as skilled a survivor as Fouché, was in touch with the British in 1807, preparing for what he thought was the inevitable collapse of the Napoleonic empire. This was clearly treason, but when Napoleon learnt of it, far from having Talleyrand shot he merely verbally abused him, and ordered him to be sacked. Talleyrand had the last word. As he withdrew from the audience, the prince remarked loudly enough to be heard: 'How unfortunate that such a great man should be so ill-mannered.'

After this, things went badly wrong for Napoleon. Fouché also conspired with the British, and fled France altogether. The Spaniards were in revolt with British help; Napoleon called Spain the 'thorn in my side'. In 1808 Napoleon occupied Rome and arrested the pope, Pius VII, which cost him his good relations with the Catholic church. Jean-Baptiste Bernadotte, a former French marshal and now heir to the Swedish throne, intrigued with Austria to overthrow Napoleon, which intrigue was ended only by the emperor's victory at Wagram in 1809.

The next year, Tsar Alexander repudiated the Treaty of Tilsit, and in 1811 France faced an economic crisis brought on by costly attempts to maintain the blockade. In 1812, after a year of skirting around the issue of Russia, the emperor collected his 600,000 strong *grande armée* (far too large actually to manage efficiently under the limited supply and ordinance capabilities of the time) and invaded the Tsar's domain.

AND FALL

As Napoleon advanced, he found the Russians had denuded his path of the supplies so vital to his vast army. Victory at Borodino, 40 miles from Moscow, cost Napoleon tens of thousands of soldiers and many of his best marshals. The emperor occupied Moscow, which was deserted (save for a Russian aristocrat named Pierre Bezukhov, if we are to believe Tolstoy), and waited for Alexander to seek terms. No Tsar was forthcoming. Winter was, however, and the army was ill-prepared to face it. In October the *grande armée* retreated. Winter and Marshal Kutuzov's Cossack cavalry, fighting a form of guerilla warfare, caught up with them, and the retreat became a horror. There were conspiracies in Paris to unseat Napoleon who raced back to France to deal with them. Scarcely 90,000 of the original 600,000 survived to reach Poland.

Now Europe closed in for the kill. The Prussians joined their re-formed army to that of the Tsar; the Spanish drove the French out of Spain, and British armies occupied Gascony as far as Bordeaux. Napoleon was heavily defeated at Leipzig in 1813, and the Rhenish states rose against him. On 31 March, 1814, Tsar Alexander entered Paris at the head of an army, and Napoleon abdicated a week later.

In May, Louis XVIII, younger brother of Louis XVI, entered France after the victorious coalition had agreed to restore the Bourbon throne. Napoleon was granted a pension for life and tiny Elba off the coast of Italy for a kingdom. It seemed not a bad end to his career.

WATERLOO

But, being Bonaparte, he was not satisfied. In February, 1815, Napoleon returned to France. Louis XVIII fled, and the French cheered their emperor – but not too loudly, just as they had not cheered too loudly for Louis. 'We are not royalists so much as realists,' one former Napoleonic officer remarked. Napoleon was soon on the march. After a few victories, the allied armies, commanded by the Duke of Wellington, lured him into confrontation at Waterloo in Belgium, on 18 June 1815. It was Wellington's battle plan and the timely assault of the Prussians on the French flank which routed the Napoleonic army on that day. This time there were no mistakes. Napeoleon was taken by the English under guard to the tiny south Atlantic island of St Helena which was a British possession.

What was Napoleon Bonaparte? Monarchist, revolutionary, Byronic hero, mere adventurer, or all of the above? One thing is certain: he was an egoist who left a psychological mark upon France greater than any

Napoleon's bedroom at Malmaison

figure before or since. At St Helena, before his death in 1821, he wrote his *memoirs*. They were the last and greatest piece of Napoleonic propaganda, and created a legend that endured for more than a century.

THE CONGRESS OF VIENNA

Representatives of all Europe, great states and small, had assembled in Vienna in the autumn of 1814 to resolve the problems (fill the power vacuum, in other words) left by Napoleon's departure. The mood had been exuberant and Vienna a scene of unremitting celebration and revelry. Everyone who was anyone had been there. Europe had felt such relief that the treatment of France was to be lenient. Then 'the monster' escaped Elba. The statesmen panicked. Their *joie de vivre* vanished, and when Napoleon was again penned up, their mood was subdued and unforgiving.

Prince Metternich, foreign minister and later chancellor of Austria, and Lord Castlereagh, British foreign secretary, were the architects of the treaty of 1815 and the system of international relations by which Europe was restored, as nearly as possible, to pre-1789 configurations. France lost territory, paid indemnities, and was occupied by 150,000 allied troops for three years. A system of international congresses was devised to deal with insurrection and other problems that might arise, and the balance of power was reaffirmed. The first congress met at Aix-la-Chapelle in 1818, where France formally became a signatory to the treaty. This was so that Europe could keep better control of France. There was to be no more Gallic revolutionary and military fervour.

The Restoration

This was perfectly acceptable to Louis XVIII (1814–1824), who understood the fragility of his position, and was determined to compromise; not unlike Charles II when he returned to England in 1660. If the new constitution, the Charter, favoured property and wealth, it also continued parliamentary and administrative institutions left over from the revolution and Napoleon. The church, the Jesuits, various reactionaries hoping to restore the old order, and *émigrés* demanding compensation returned with Louis. He listened less to them than to the liberal duke of Decazes. Officials were encouraged not to turn back the clock. In one famous instance an *émigré* nobleman, a naval cadet in 1789, demanded to be made a Rear-Admiral since he might have achieved that rank had not the revolution driven him out. The authorities got around the problem with similar logic: they admitted his claim, but informed him – sorrowfully – that he had been killed at Trafalgar in 1805.

The French economy was in recession, industry was only beginning to modernize, and the common people were none too ecstatic at having the Bourbons back. However, under Louis's prudent rule, recovery began. A cartoon of 1815 showed an eagle (Napoleon) leaving the Tuileries' back door as five fat geese (the Bourbons) waddled in at the front. It was apt; it also missed the point. Neither Louis nor the nation wanted more adventure, at least for the time being. They wanted peace.

Charles X

The Bourbon honeymoon was short, however. Charles X (1824–1830) had none of his brother's intelligence; he had neither forgotten nor learnt anything. The new king was crowned at Reims where he performed the ritual of touching for scrofula, an indication of things to come. He dismissed liberal ministers and raised his reactionary followers, such as the duke of Polignac and the count of Villèle. Both Polignac and the king belonged to the Congregation of the Virgin, a reactionary lay society dedicated to restoring the old church and old order. Charles intrigued to reduce the powers of the Assembly and alter election laws, so as to render the Assembly almost wholly a province of the landed aristocracy.

Revolution: 1830

It was not to be. The bourgeoisie had prospered under Louis XVIII and were not to be set aside by his reactionary brother. In 1830 a bad harvest, economic crises, intellectuals up in arms, and anti-Bourbon propaganda produced another revolution.

In July the barricades went up in the street of Paris; on 2 August Charles abdicated, and a week later, the duke of Orléans, son of Philippe

Égalité, sponsored by the ageing but still popular marquis of Lafayette, mounted the throne as Louis Philippe (1830–1848), the 'July Monarch'.

INDUSTRIALISM

The industrial revolution, which had begun in England in the eighteenth century, started in France between 1830 and 1848. France expanded its iron and coal production, revolutionized the technology of the cotton industry, and increased the number of its spinning factories, power looms and mechanized paper mills. A national railway scheme was drawn up in 1842. Lille became an industrial city, Lyon was highly capitalized as the silk centre, and bankers and industrialists took the place of landed aristocrats as the important men of the nation. Industrialism informed the socialist writings of Henri Saint-Simon, who romanticized it, and Charles Fourier, who repudiated it in favour of a bucolic communism. Louis Blanc and Auguste Blanqui were advocates of industrial socialism in the Assembly before 1848.

Industrialism contributed to a widening gap between the classes. Tensions rose steadily between landowners and peasants, factory owners and workers; the working conditions for the latter were even more appalling than had been the case among eighteenth-century industrial labourers. There was now more production of crops and goods as improved technology expanded agriculture and industry equally, but rapid population growth increased demand for land, jobs and food.

Bad harvests were more devastating than ever before. Land and factory-owners feared the classes beneath them, and they in turn resented and hated the classes above. In between were the petty bourgeoisie of doctors, lawyers and teachers, often only a generation removed from being peasants or workers. Some of them defended the industrial social system because they profited from it, or hoped to; others wanted to change the system because they felt excluded from it. Discontent and dislocation, endemic to industrialization in any case, was evident on all sides.

ROMANTICISM

Discontent, if not dislocation, was part of the new outlook in art, literature, music and ideas called Romanticism. Both a product of, and a reaction against, the Age of Reason, Romanticism stressed the imagination and emotion, was both reactionary and progressive, and looked for individualistic and non-rationalist solutions to problems. Romanticism included Jules Michelet writing heroic history; Eugène Delacroix painting Turkish Janissaries massacring Greek peasants; Hector Berlioz horrifying Paris audiences with a guillotine sequence in *Symphonie Fantastique*; Chateaubriand finding the 'genius' of traditional Christianity; Stendhal parodying reactionary society; and the image of Napoleon Bonaparte's son dying of tuberculosis. Romanticism was many things with many variations. What it was not was tranquil.

The July Monarchy

Industrialism and Romanticism were both revolutionary, in their way, and revolution defined the parameters of the July Monarchy of Louis Philippe. It began with revolution, ended with revolution, and feared revolution every day of its existence. The regime's members were anti-revolutionary, because all were connected with revolution from earlier days: Louis Philippe fought at Valmy and Jemappes; the duke of Broglie was Madame de Staël's son-in-law (she was a great memoirist of the revolution, and was later persecuted as a critic of Bonaparte); Casimir Periér's father led the revolt of the Dauphiné Estates; Adolph Thiers' father was ruined by the revolution; François Guizot's father was a Girondin and guillotined; and some of Louis Philippe's generals had served under Napoleon Bonaparte. The July Monarchy was bourgeois and practical, a perfect example of nineteenth-century monarchy, and had no love for the *ancien régime*. The king, himself a banker, strolled the avenues of Paris, unattended, umbrella in hand, like any member of the bourgeoisie. Louis Philippe was industrially-minded, progressive, and opposed to sharing power with any but those whom Guizot termed 'men of the rich and enlightened classes'.

There was opposition from the start: from legitimists because Louis Philippe was not a Bourbon; from socialists because they disliked the system; and from Louis Napoleon (who worked hard to cultivate a Romantic image in his early years), one of the nephews of the late emperor, because he aspired to re-establish his uncle's throne. However, no legitimist rising took place, socialist outbreaks usually responded to the resolution of specific grievances, and the only attempted *coup* in 1836 by Louis Napoleon failed utterly. It raised only mild curiosity at the time – except within the government, where fear of revolution was only equalled by fear of Bonapartism. This was not a régime which felt secure. There were 15 governments before Guizot assembled an administration in 1840 that lasted until 1848. More than one attempt was made on Louis Philippe's life.

Like Louis XVIII, Louis Philippe tried to balance between conflicting forces within French society. The July Monarchy retained the basic 1815 Charter, which was revised to nearly double the electorate. At the same time, the Assembly was filled mainly with landowners and industrialists. Royal ministers appeared to be in charge, with the king as a sort of constitutional father-figure. However, in reality Louis Philippe was the power in the State and merely encouraged the appearance that he was not, simply in order to remain above party and politics. He wished to remain above, for example, the continuous controversy over whether the Church or the State should run elementary education, a question which has been either a rallying cry or a political graveyard for French politicans since 1815.

Louis Philippe was unable to maintain his balancing act over foreign policy. Conservatives wanted to stay out of European politics; their memory of anti-French coalitions before 1815 remained keen. Radicals and nationalists wanted an aggressive, interventionist foreign policy – naval rivalry with Britain in the Mediterranean, for instance – in order either to wipe out the 'humiliation' of 1815, or to 'export revolution' once again. Louis Philippe sided with the conservatives. He stayed clear of involvement in Belgium in 1831, and in Egypt in 1840; but the radicals were given a colonial war against Abd-el-Kader in North Africa as a sop, from which France acquired Algeria and the legendary French Foreign Legion. It was not enough. Radical and nationalist opinion became alienated from the government over foreign affairs.

1848: The Revolution of the Intellectuals

Between 1844 and 1847 bad harvests drove up food prices and caused shortages. In 1847 an economic crisis accrued from short-fall in credit, and a business slump followed. The state was overcommitted to expenditure for the size of its budgets, something which raised fears of tax increases or else government bankruptcy. Unemployment increased steadily. Guizot was unpopular both for his pro-Austrian foreign policy and his refusal to reform the electoral system, and charges of corruption were frequently voiced. Anti-régime propaganda was endemic, and usually scurrilous.

When, in February 1848, the government cracked down on public demonstrations, barricades immediately went up in the streets of Paris. Troops fired and people were killed. Insurrection quickly spread through the city. On 24 February Louis Philippe abdicated, and radicals seized the Assembly. They declared the Second Republic and elected the poet Alphonse de Lamartine to lead it.

The new government at once prepared a republican foreign policy – proposed aid to Italian rebels – and set about reforming financial and economic conditions. The first produced mainly impassioned speeches, and the latter National Workshops and a commission to look after the workers' interests; neither of which solved any problems. Meanwhile, the provinces wearied of dictatorship from Paris and revolted on their own. A civil war followed, expanding quickly into the terrible June Days when peasants, who understood little of the Republican rhetoric but a good deal about hunger, rose against landlords and anyone else who stood in their way.

1848 was a revolution of Romantic intellectuals, informed by liberal and constitutional idealism, who could not bring themselves to extend the revolution to the social and economic systems. Therefore they lost control of it, and after the June Days the intellectuals looked to strong men to save them: to the republican General Cavaignac first, then to a representative of that tradition in France which claimed to reconcile revolution, authority, Catholicism, liberalism, external glory and social amelioration. That representative was Louis Napoleon Bonaparte.

THE MAN ON HORSEBACK

In 1848 the electorate was increased from 250,000 to over nine million, but it returned an Assembly of aristocrats and bourgeoisie. Alexis de

Tocqueville described this Assembly as merely going through the motions of 1789, and rather pathetically at that.

Then, after the June Days, when conservative deputies demanded monarchy, Lamartine made an impassioned speech demanding a presidency based upon popular sovereignty. 'It is in the nature of democracy to find its personification in a Man,' he said. Doubters feared that such an office might bestow too tempting a degree of personal power. Lamartine carried the day; the doubters carried history. The first national election for a President of France was in December 1848. It returned Louis Napoleon Bonaparte by a 75 per cent margin.

Louis Napoleon spent the next three years gathering his political strength: speaking in republican tones, posing as the friend of the working class, being the hero of liberals by criticizing the pope and subsidizing the press, and currying Catholic approval by favouring religious primary and secondary education. Clearly a Man for All Seasons; clearly, too, a Man on Horseback.

In December 1851, the Assembly played into his hands by trying to remove the vote from some three million Frenchmen. Louis Napoleon executed a *coup d'état*: he arrested the leaders and shut the Assembly down; then, with much fanfare, he restored universal suffrage and submitted the *coup* to a plebiscite. Opposition was light, and that which developed was quickly repressed by military force. The plebiscite overwhelmingly approved the action. Louis Napoleon now held dictatorial power, and by a species of popular approval.

One act remained. For another year, Louis Napoleon consolidated his position. Then, on 2 December 1852, the anniversary of the *coup*, he put on the crown of Bonaparte and rode into Paris as the Man on Horseback as the Emperor Napleon III. It was curiously anomalous: monarchy enthroned by popular vote. How well would monarchy and democracy cooperate? It remained to be seen. In any event, the era of revolution was at an end.

CHAPTER EIGHT

Second Empire, Third Republic
1852–1914

The era of revolution ended in 1852, but the search for an acceptable political system went on. Significant segments of the population remained politically radical, but a social conservatism emerged during the Second Empire and dramatically affected the Third Republic which followed it. Rumour had it that while the French still wore their hearts on the Left, they now wore their wallets on the Right. It was no rumour.

The Second Empire

Napoleon III traded on his name. But he was nothing like his famous uncle, save that he too was an adventurer in foreign affairs. The new emperor was lazy, quiet, cautious, reluctant to make hard decisions, and liked war only in theory, only when it was absolutely 'safe'. He tried to be all things to all people: liberal, authoritarian, defender of property, friend of the workers, pro-Catholic and anti-clerical. The Empress Eugénie was a Spaniard with a touch of the bohemian; that is, she presided over what the stiff-necked Paris bourgeoisie regarded as a 'loose-mannered' court.

Napoleon III was successful to a remarkable degree, for all of his limitations. He modernized France politically and economically, and made it competitive with its neighbours. After the first dictatorial years of his reign, the emperor moved steadily leftward in domestic affairs. In 1859 he declared an amnesty for his political opponents; in 1860 the powers of the Senate and Assembly were extended, and the next year the press was allowed to publish verbatim accounts of Assembly debates. In 1863 government ministers began explaining policy in the Assembly, and in 1867 the Assembly was granted the right to question the government. A parliamentary opposition emerged as a result of these changes. Napoleon regarded this as a positive step, and in 1870 introduced parliamentary government with Émile Ollivier as the leader of a government majority. A plebiscite approved all of Napoleon's reforms. Once again, he had won a vote of confidence from the public. The Assembly, meanwhile, was less widely based and also less popular. This gave Napoleon a slight edge over the Assembly. He may have been lazy, but he was astute.

The Second Empire encouraged economic enterprise and expansion at every turn. Financiers and speculators had a field day; fortunes were made – and lost – on the Paris Bourse, and French industrialisation hit its full stride. Railroad mileage quadrupled; seaports expanded; mining developed rapidly; French engineers were everywhere, planning, designing and building: a Paris ship canal, an Alpine rail tunnel under Mont-Cenis, and, one of the greatest triumphs of all, Ferdinand de Lesseps' Suez Canal, which opened in 1869. A channel tunnel was

The Opera House, Paris

planned with grudging British approval, but never materialized. Paris was also modernized. Napoleon gave Baron Haussmann, prefect of Paris, *carte blanche* for 'urban renewal'. The plan was at once to beautify Paris and make it safe from revolutionary barricades. The old, narrow, crowded central city gave way to broad avenues, boulevards and quays, stately and tree-lined, such as the Champs-Elysées which stretched from the Louvre to Napoleon I's Arc de Triomphe. Parks, churches, hospitals, markets, railway stations (the Gare de l'Est and Gare du Nord) and the modern sewage system were Haussmann's work. The Ile de la Cité was swept clean, save for Sainte-Chapelle, Notre-Dame and the Conciergerie, and remodelled. Many elegant old buildings were razed, and many of the new were gaudy and frivolous. Second-Empire France was frankly materialistic and not always tasteful, and Haussmann's Paris boldly asserted the fact.

Napoleon III, always conscious of his populist base, looked after the interests of ordinary people as well as those of the middle and upper classes: 'Saint-Simon on horseback,' Sainte-Beuve once called him. He encouraged advances in public health and slum clearance, was responsible for an array of new financial institutions which welcomed small investors as well as large ones: the Société Générale, Crédit Lyonnais and Crédit Foncier – and Crédit Mobilier, before it collapsed amid scandal.

The emperor was a free trader, as the tariff-reducing 1860 Cobden-Chevalier commercial treaty between Great Britain and France attested. But he also espoused the collective rights of workers against exploiting manufacturers. Trade unions and strikes were legalized, and when Napoleon died in 1873, in exile in England, the only Frenchmen at his funeral were trades unionists.

French Colonialism

Colonial expansion was now a regular part of overseas policy. Even Republicans approved it. Napoleon pressed French interests in Indo-China (Cambodia, Laos and Vietnam), Syria, Africa and Mexico; the Suez Canal was both a commercial adventure and a communications link with outposts in India and the Far East. Colonialism had its drawbacks. The other colonial powers were impressed at French achievements, but also feared them. Meanwhile, colonialism gave Napoleon's opponents at home another stick with which to beat him: Republicans, essentially nationalistic at heart, wanted the emperor to go further; conservatives questioned whether he was wise to go as far as he did. Certainly his Mexican adventure did not display much wisdom.

MEXICO

A civil war ended in Mexico in 1860, and the next year the new government of Benito Juárez suspended payment on foreign debts incurred by the deposed President Miramon. Britain, Spain and France jointly occupied Veracruz to protect their investments, and Mexican *emigrés* in Paris – conservative and Catholic – persuaded Empress Eugénie that only a strong monarchy could save the church and restore order in Mexico. She pressed her husband to intervene. Over-confident after his own success at 'democratic empire', Napoleon decided the concept would work in Mexico as well. He put forward Prince Maximilian von Habsburg, a former viceroy of Lombardy, as emperor of Mexico. In 1862 Spain and Britain withdrew their troops. They knew that the United States' Monroe Doctrine would not tolerate European interference in the Western Hemisphere. Indeed the Americans were furious; but, caught up in a civil war of their own, they could do nothing to stop the French. In 1864, armed with a dubious Mexican plebiscite in his favour – but, more to the point, behind the bayonets of French troops under Marshals Bazaine and MacMahon – Maximilian entered Mexico City.

Napoleon was already having second thoughts about the venture, but Maximilian and his empress, Carlotta, had the bit in their teeth. Theirs, they reckoned, was a holy mission of restoration, and they persuaded Napoleon to continue French military support. He did so, but with declining enthusiasm.

Napoleon's doubts stemmed from the Americans' antipathy to the venture, and from the fact that in Mexico democratic imperialism was not democratic. Maximilian also had hoped for an enlightened régime, but he was supported mainly by reactionaries to whom enlightenment was anathema. They, not Maximilian, ultimately shaped policy. President Juárez's followers, meanwhile, were finding caches of weapons and ammunition along the banks of the Rio Grande between Texas and Mexico, seemingly misplaced by the United States Army. With these weapons the Juaristas resisted Maximilian with rising success. The emperor was then persuaded to suppress liberal ideas and shoot suspected Juarista sympathizers out of hand.

In 1865 the American Civil War ended. Napoleon saw the writing on the wall and withdrew French support from Mexico. He was encouraged in this by the United States government using language so firm as to be almost threatening. Violation of the Monroe Doctrine was a *causus belli* in American eyes, if it continued. In 1867 the last French troops withdrew from Veracruz. Maximilian declined to go with them, still believing he had the Mexican people on his side. This seems doubtful, but who will ever know for sure? In the event, Mexico City fell, he was captured, and on 19 May 1867 the victorious Juaristas executed him before a firing squad. The Mexican venture was over. It left Napoleon discredited and the treasury depleted. Equally important, France had been humiliated.

FOREIGN POLICY

The Second Empire fared well in foreign policy before the Mexico fiasco. In 1854 Napoleon involved France as an ally of Britain and Turkey in a war against Russia in the Crimea. The clash was classically European: a war to maintain the balance of power by limiting Russian access to the Mediterranean. It ended with the Peace of Paris in 1856, over which the French foreign minister presided, thus allowing Napoleon to appear as the grand arbiter of European destiny. French pride was satisfied, even if little else had been gained.

The Crimean War was on a small scale, more troops died of cholera than in combat, and military competence was at a premium. The most famous episode, the British cavalry charge at Balaclava, was an utter débâcle. The French commander, General Saint Arnaud, said of it: '*C'est magnifique, mais ce n'est pas la guerre.*' (It is magnificent, but it is not war.)

Léon Gambetta supposedly said much the same thing years later about London's newest marvel, the St Pancras railway station: '*C'est magnifique, mais ce n'est pas la gare.*' (It is magnificent, but it is not a railway station.)

ITALY AND AUSTRIA

Napoleon always fancied an Italian confederation allied with France against Austria. In 1858 he met secretly with Camillo Cavour, the prime minister of Piedmont-Sardinia, the most important north Italian state, and they signed the treaty of Plombières, an agreement to drive Austria out of Italy jointly. The alliance was sealed by the marriage of Clothilde, daughter of the Piedmont-Sardinian monarch, to Jérôme, Napoleon's nephew. Dutiful daughter that she was, Clothilde told Cavour: 'Send Prince Jérôme to me, and if he is not actually repulsive, I shall marry him.'

In 1859 the Austrians provided an excuse and war broke out. Marshal MacMahon was victorious at Magenta in June, and Napoleon entered Milan in triumph. Later he personally commanded at Solferino – and was so horrified at the carnage that he offered an armistice, practically on the spot. The peace of Villafranca and the Treaty of Zurich ended the war officially, giving Nice and Savoy to France while Austria gave up Lombardy and kept Venice. The Italians had wanted this war to lead to the unification of Italy and they therefore felt that Napoleon had betrayed them, and his stock plummeted. It fell still further in 1867 when French troops occupied Rome to protect the pope from Garibaldi. On the other hand, the Austrian emperor, Franz Joseph, thought well of Napoleon's generosity after Solferino, and back in Paris, even Republicans cheered him for the territorial gains. French troops were still in Rome when the Franco-Prussian war began in 1870. Otherwise, after Villafranca, Napoleon left the Italians to their own devices.

THE FRANCO-PRUSSIAN WAR

This war justified Napleon III's fear of war; it cost him everything.

Otto von Bismarck became Prussian prime minister in 1862; his policy thereafter was to enhance Prussian security in Germany and then German security in Europe. The first aim was fulfilled in 1871 when the German Empire was formed, with Berlin its capital and Prussia its heart and soul. By 1867 Bismarck had made Prussia supreme in Germany through successful wars against Denmark (1864) and Austria (1866).

The possibility of German unification was now clear. French nationalists, believing that France's 'natural' eastern frontier was the

Rhine, were not pleased. A sizeable portion of the west bank was in German and Prussian hands, and detaching it from a united German state would be next to impossible. On his side, Bismarck regarded France as the only stumbling block in the way of convincing the Rhenish German states to accept Prussian hegemony.

In 1868 a member of a cadet branch of the Prussian ruling family was nominated to take the recently vacated Spanish throne. 'Encirclement!' cried the French nationalists, and the candidate withdrew. It was not enough. Agitation mounted in the Assembly, and in May, 1870, Count Benedetti, the French ambassador to Prussia, approached King Wilhelm at Ems, on the matter of obtaining a guarantee regarding the Spanish candidacy. *'Jamais encore'* (never again) was the promise that France wanted. The interview was peaceable, and Bismarck received an account of it by telegram. He reworked the telegram to make it appear that the king had rebuffed the ambassador, and that the ambassador had insulted the king. The note was then leaked to the press in Paris and Berlin. Sabres were rattled on both sides. Napoleon III faced an irate Assembly, Bismarck an outraged Reichstag – exactly the mood he wanted from them. The nationalist press in Paris and Berlin was in a martial frenzy. Napoleon did not want war – his meeting with Bismarck at Biarritz the year before had been hopeful – but he was left with no choice. War began in July.

For France it was utter disaster. The Prussians outflanked, outgunned and outgeneralled the French. Marshal Bazaine was trapped at Metz, and Marshal MacMahon at Sedan, where his proud regiments were torn to pieces by Prussian artillery. Napoleon was ill and not able to keep up with the deteriorating situation. He tried to stop the slaughter by getting himself killed at the front, but only managed to be captured. This simply enhanced French humiliation. A Prussian photograph depicts Napoleon and Bismarck, in uniform, seated together in campaign chairs outside of Bismarck's tent. Napoleon looks abjectly miserable; Bismarck resembles nothing so much as the cat who has just finished off the canary.

When news of Napoleon's capture reached Paris, radicals seized control of the Assembly, declared a republic, and formed a provisional government. On 27 October Bazaine surrendered Metz, and the Prussians besieged Paris. Léon Gambetta escaped from the city in a hot-air balloon and made his way to the Loire Valley, where he tried unsuccessfully to raise an army in the name of the new republic. On 28 January 1871, Paris capitulated and the war was virtually over – just three days after the Prussians humiliated France still further by having the German Empire proclaimed at a ceremony in the *Galerie des Glaces* at Versailles.

An election in February 1871 returned a National Assembly full of moderates and conservatives; radicals, for the most part, were not elected. The mandate was clearly for peace. The Assembly selected Adolphe Thiers, a conservative, to head the provisional government, which set up its headquarters at Versailles. Thiers then negotiated the draconian treaty of Frankfurt which ended the war. France had to pay five billion francs in indemnities and lost Alsace and part of Lorraine. The Assembly approved it by 546 votes to 107, and the treaty was signed on 10 May.

The Paris Commune

The Assembly outraged Paris by making the château of Versailles, the symbol of the old order, its meeting place. Municipal elections in March 1871 returned a radical council, or commune. (George Clemenceau, a future prime minister, was elected for Montmartre.) This commune rebelled against Versailles. The Paris Commune was never communist, as many at the time – and later – made out; it was, in fact, extremely bourgeois. Nevertheless it was also revolutionary, and after two months an army under MacMahon besieged it. The Tuileries Palace was burnt down in consequence.

The Commune held out for six weeks, but could not withstand MacMahon's peasant soldiers for whom Paris was not sacred. When the city fell, the government took vengeance. All told, twenty thousand were tried and summarily shot, imprisoned or transported to French penal colonies. Thus was born the Third Republic.

The Third Republic

All of the forces which had been factors in French political and social life since 1815 were manifested in the Third Republic: monarchism, republicanism, reaction, radicalism, clericalism and Bonapartism. Nursed along by Thiers and then by the monarchist soldier, MacMahon, the Republic was officially established only in 1875, and then more or less by default. It came about simply because the Assembly accepted the Wallon amendment. Deputy Wallon said:

> My conclusion is that it is necessary to leave the provisional. If monarchy is possible, show that it will be accepted, propose it. If ... it is not possible, I do not say to you: decide for the Republic, but I say: recognize the government now established, which is the government of the Republic. I do not ask you to proclaim it as definitive – what is definitive? But all the same do not call it provisional.

This was hardly an oratorical *tour de force*, but it was effective. There was no constitution, only laws having constitutional ramifications: a seven-year renewable presidency; a Senate, one-third chosen for life, the rest for nine-year terms, a third to be elected every three years; and a Chamber of Deputies, elected by constituencies. None of it worked quite as expected, but it did survive, right down to 1940.

REPUBLICAN ISSUES

The royalist cause had scant hope of success, but both the Bourbon count of Chambord and the Orléanist count of Paris had followers. So too did the Bonapartists, and when Napoleon III's son died in 1879, fighting in the British army invading Zululand, the *sense* of Bonapartism continued in strongmen – or would-be strongmen – such as General Georges Boulanger. Meanwhile, clericalism and anti-clericalism dominated the politics of Right and Left, and the strength or weakness of the presidency was of concern to all.

GENERAL BOULANGER

A self-advertising soldier, General Boulanger was a useful minister of war who reformed the army. But his ambitions went well beyond that. Early in the game, radical politicians like Clemenceau supported him.

Soon Boulanger took for himself the Bonapartist mantle, and made himself a dangerous and popular force on the Right. In 1889 he was overwhelmingly elected to the Assembly for Paris. Huge mobs surrounded him on election night crying '*À l'Élysée!*', the Élysée palace in the Rue du Faubourg Saint-Honoré now being official residence for the president. A *coup* seemed inevitable.

But the general hesitated. Why is not clear. He did nothing, and when the government moved to arrest him – or appeared to – he fled to Belgium and his mistress. Boulanger faded from French history at that point, appearing only for an instant a few years later to prove that Romance still informed the French mentality: when his mistress died Boulanger lay down across her grave and shot himself.

SCANDAL

The word is almost synonymous with the Third Republic. Even as Boulanger was proving a broken reed, a scandal erupted over Ferdinand de Lesseps' failure to repeat, in Panama, his triumph in Suez. The controversy concerned corrupt officials, and even more corrupt financiers, such as Cornelius Herz. The Republic stumbled grimly through this, and trauma piled upon trauma. Panama drove Clemenceau briefly from public life; public unrest turned into violence, and President Sadi Carnot was assassinated. Meanwhile, church–state conflict erupted into the infamous Dreyfus scandal.

THE DREYFUS AFFAIR

'Clericalism – there is the enemy!' proclaimed Léon Gambetta, and after he passed from the scene Jules Ferry continued the theme. Republicans felt threatened by the church, and Catholics felt persecuted by the Republic. Education was increasingly laicized, '*école sans Dieu*,' in Albert de Broglie's phrase, and the Republic made no pretence at allowing for equality between lay and religious education. The result was a church-state dualism in education which persists to the present day.

In the 1880s, a progressive papacy encouraged *railliement*, a policy of reconciliation between Church and Republic. A 'democratized', and even on occasion radicalized, priesthood went into proletarian neighbourhoods and improved the church's image. *Railliement* had only limited success among traditional secular anti-Republicans, however. They gave up on monarchism, but created a New Right: anti-Semitic, pro-Catholic, and aimed at seizing control of the Republic.

Such was the state of affairs when in 1896 Captain Alfred Dreyfus, the only Jew on the army general staff, was arrested for selling military secrets to the Germans. The evidence against him was worse than spurious; it was non-existent. He was tried because he was a Jew in an army dominated by anti-Semitic aristocrats and Catholics, who regarded the army as their private preserve. For most of them Dreyfus proved his unsuitability for membership in this élite by refusing to commit suicide when confronted with arrest.

At first it was generally believed that Dreyfus was guilty; even by Clemenceau and Jean Jaurès, who also feared that he might escape punishment. Dreyfus should be hanged, said Clemenceau, usually an opponent of the death penalty. The anti-Semitic press, represented by Édouard Drumont's *La Libre Parole*, had earlier built a case against Jews in the army, and now led the public attack on Dreyfus. The captain was convicted without opposition on the strength of forged evidence and shipped to Devil's Island. The case was closed.

MAJOR PICQUART

But not quite. Major Picquart of military intelligence, as anti-Semitic as any other Catholic officer, was curious why Dreyfus, a rich and happily-married man, would sell secrets. Picquart found no reason; but he did find evidence pointing to a transplanted Hungarian officer, Major Esterhazy – profligate, always in debt, notoriously without scruple, but devotedly Catholic and aristocratic – as the guilty man. Picquart had come too close to the truth. Soon he was in Tunis inspecting fortifications. Colonel Henri, the intelligence officer who compromised Dreyfus in the first instance, wanted no one rocking the boat.

DREYFUSARDS AND ANTI-DREYFUSARDS

The Dreyfus family never stopped protesting, and by 1898 important people began to believe them. The novelist Émile Zola published his famous *J'Accuse*; Clemenceau changed his opinion, and came out in support of reopening the case. France was divided between those who thought Dreyfus innocent – or at least saw in this an opportunity to bring down their political enemies – and those who thought him guilty, or at least a convenient scapegoat. The issue was the survival of the Republic, and for a decade the controversy was very ugly.

The Republic survived. Dreyfus was exonerated and returned to his post with a promotion. Strong governments under René Waldeck-Rousseau and Émile Combes brought the most troublesome anti-Dreyfusard elements of church and army under control. But scars were left, not least among which was open anti-Semitism and a mood and style highly suggestive of fascism.

ACTION FRANÇAISE

After the Dreyfus Affair, the Right regrouped, mostly as conservative Republicans. But early in the twentieth century *Action Française* appeared. Extremist Catholics, aristocrats and even royalists converged into a league built upon the proto-fascist, anti-Semitic theories of Charles Maurras and Léon Daudet. Maurras's journal, called *L'Action Française*, was one propaganda channel for the league; another was a volunteer corps of *Camelots du Roi*, who wore uniforms and were not above using violence against individuals and groups of which the league disapproved. *Action Française* was small and not very influential; but it reflected a disease of the spirit which would greatly affect the ability of France to function democratically in the years to come.

THE LEFT

Meanwhile, the socialist and trade-union Left was beginning to flourish. Jean Jaurès and Jules Guesde led the Socialists, although they did not agree on their Marxism. Jaurès established *L'Humanité* as the leading socialist newspaper, and in 1899 *L'Internationale* replaced *La Carmagnole* as the party song. Labour was grouped largely in the Confédération Générale du Travail, which was anarchist rather than socialist. By 1909 it had nearly a million members. Among CGT leaders was Aristide Briand, author of the movement's General Strike ideology: shutting down everything through industrial action in order to force social and political change. It was more myth than reality: there were strikes, and they were often violent, but there was never a General Strike.

ECONOMY AND SOCIETY

The French population grew by only three-and-a-half million between 1870 and 1914, rapidly falling behind Britain and Germany. Half of the French people lived in rural areas; half of French labour was agricultural, and half of them worked on farms of less than two-and-a-half acres. This population was relatively prosperous after 1871. France trailed after only the United States and Russia in grain production, and only after Italy in wine. Phylloxera nearly destroyed the French wine trade in the 1860s but grafts from immune American vines revived it, and by 1885 it was again prospering. Farm houses now had wooden floors, and the blue blouse and wooden *sabot* of the peasant was disappearing. Pressure for change was therefore less now than in earlier decades.

Meanwhile, industry expanded rapidly even though raw materials often had to be imported. By 1914 steam-power use had multiplied ten-fold, coal production doubled, cast-iron multiplied by four and steel by twelve. Yet the industrial workforce was only half of the total labouring population, and a majority of these worked in shops with less than five employees. Large enterprises remained relatively less common than in Germany or Great Britain. The reality, if not the concept, of the industrial masses was not so evident in France as elsewhere. Politically radical, socially conservative just about sums up French society under the Third Republic.

COLONIES

The French were frugal, and vast amounts of savings were available to invest abroad in capital loans or for development of territories already acquired as colonies. Despite the unease about overseas ventures that had been inspired by Napoleon's Mexican *débâcle*, statesmen of the Third Republic expanded French colonialism well beyond Second Empire limits. Some statesmen, indeed, firmly believed in colonialism: for Jules Ferry it was a supply mechanism for the industrial revolution; Gambetta and other Republicans agreed, and also saw the possession of colonies as the measure of being a great power; and the French Catholic church was a leading exporter of Christianity, and therefore a supporter of colonial expansion. Three-quarters of Catholic foreign missionaries in these decades were French. In 1881 Tunis became a French protectorate;

Tonkin (North Vietnam) in 1885, and Laos and Cambodia five years later, fell to France, giving the Republic control of some of the richest areas in south-east Asia. Madagascar became a French possession in 1896, and other parts of Africa soon followed. By 1898 France controlled a colonial empire second only to that of Great Britain, and well ahead of Germany's.

CULTURE

If French colonialism achieved eminence under the Third Republic, French culture achieved pre-eminence. True, bureaucrats and the conservative bourgeoisie attempted to dictate taste as they had done under the Second Empire – it has been said that the Third Republic held advantage over the Second Empire in public building only in that there was less of it – and to some extent succeeded. The Third Republic was responsible for the basilica of Sacré-Coeur, Gustave Eiffel's Tower (for the Paris Exhibition of 1889), and the Statue of Liberty in New York Harbour, all of doubtful artistic merit. But this was a small part of the picture, and after 1870 France again emerged as the cultural inspiration of Europe.

In 1863 Édouard Manet was rejected by the *Salon des Beaux Arts* in Paris, the arbiter of respectability. The *Salon* ran to such refinements as imposing fig leaves on nude statues by Auguste Rodin. The same year, Manet held a rival exhibition with other rejected artists called the *Salon des Refusés*. His painting *Déjeuner sur L'Herbes* was included, shocking Parisians not because it featured a nude woman picnicking with male companions, but because she was depicted as a tart rather than as a Venus.

IMPRESSIONISM AND OTHER STYLES

A revolution was in the making, and the *Salon des Refusés* began it. The Impressionists abandoned strict definition of line and colour in order to achieve new effects with the play of light on objects. The idea soon spread beyond Impressionist purists, who insisted on limiting their work to landscapes and other exteriors, and an entire generation manipulated the Impressionist principle to create their own individual styles. Claude Monet's painting of a water-lily pond was a misty, dreamy experiment with light; Georges Seurat's pointillism – piling different coloured dots on the canvas until they achieved the desired form and value – was an impressionist extreme; so too was Pablo Picasso's Cubism, though in the opposite direction. Soon every subject was fair game. Revolution in style merged with revolution in subject matter and purpose: Gustave Courbet insisted that his paintings of peasant life embodied Proudhonian socialism; Paul Gauguin's Tahitian motifs incorporated a vague naturalism; and Henri Toulouse-Lautrec applied Impressionist technique to the bohemian life of the Montmartre. Never have so many great names marched through French art together: Camille Pissarro, Edgar Degas, Paul Cézanne, Henri Matisse, Pierre-Auguste Renoir, and Vincent Van Gogh, among others. Paris was their spiritual home, but not their only venue: much of the time Monet was in Normandy, Gauguin in Tahiti and Van Gogh in Provence, when he was not in an insane asylum.

After the *Salon des Refusés*, sculptors, painters, composers and writers moved away more and more from convention into experimentation with impressionism, realism and naturalism. Auguste Rodin and Jules Dalou were leaders in sculpture. With *Carmen* in 1875, Georges Bizet gave France an operatic style which departed from both the Italians and Richard Wagner. He was soon followed in other musical *genres* by Maurice Ravel, Claude Debussy, Camille Saint-Saëns, Erik Satie and Paul Dukas. Gabriel Fauré and Saint-Saëns helped establish a musical theatre at Béziers intended to be a French rival to Wagner's Bayreuth.

Realism and naturalism – the anatomy of life as lived – informed Gustave Flaubert's *Madame Bovary*, Émile Zola's *Nana* and *Thérèse Raquin*, Guy de Maupassant's three hundred short stories, and Charles Baudelaire's *Les Fleurs du Mal*, which linked realism with romanticism through eroticism, lesbianism and other forbidden themes. Six of the poems in *Les Fleurs* were condemned in a court case and stricken from the published volume. In 1911, Paris was shocked again – but by now was more resigned to it – by the erotic and disturbing implications of Igor Stravinsky's ballet *Le Sacre du Printemps*, stage set by Pablo Picasso and with choreography by Sergei Diaghilev.

Philosophy too was radically alive. Auguste Comte created Positivism, a sort of religion of science based on the laws of social progress, from which evolved sociology. It was fundamentally politically conservative, although methodologically innovative. So too were Hippolyte Taine (also a Positivist), who hated democracy and feared revolution, and Émile Durkheim, whose group, or mass, sociology sought to expose the irrationality of democratic action. By contrast, liberal rationalism was evident in Ernest Renan's 'biography' of Christ – but not among his colleagues at the Collège de France, who deprived Renan of his chair of Hebrew history over the book. Meanwhile, in the field of science, the Third Republic basked in the glow emanating from Henri Poincaré in mathematics, Marie Curie in radiology, and Louis Pasteur in bacteriology.

FOREIGN POLICY

After 1870 France recognized that it was not a match for Germany alone. There were years of sabre-rattling ahead, over the indemnity and the loss of territory, and the cry *'revanchisme!'* (revenge) was a part of political rhetoric at the hustings and in the Assembly. But realists saw the way the wind now blew. In the early years, Bismarck, Chancellor of the new German Empire, maintained alliances and relationships designed to keep France isolated: the Three Emperors' League (Germany, Russia and Austria), and later the Triple Alliance (Germany, Austria and Italy). He also maintained good relations with Great Britain, whose traditional policy was to keep a watchful eye on the balance of power in Europe and, if possible, to stay out of it. French policy would have to change. No more French mastery over Europe. Even survival might now depend on outside help.

ANGLO-FRENCH RAPPROCHEMENT

Great diplomatist that he was, Bismarck was not infallible. In 1884–85 he revised his basic policy and wooed France with the aim of isolating Great Britain. But France was not to be wooed. The effort resulted in France and Britain together looking distrustfully at Germany. In 1890 Bismarck was dismissed from office by the new emperor, Wilhelm II, who wanted an aggressive, expansionist world policy. In 1894 France made a mutual defence pact with Russia, aimed specifically against Germany, and French isolation was broken.

Théophile Delcassé, foreign minister from 1898 to 1905, was anti-

German at heart and wanted to go further than an understanding with the Tsar. His policy was to strengthen the Russian bond and reconcile France to Great Britain. A common enemy, in short, or potential common enemy, achieved a reversal of Anglo-French antagonism that was 900 years old. How long it would last, no one could say. But no matter: for now, Delcassé arrived at amicable solutions to Anglo-French imbroglios in Egypt, the Sudan and Morocco, and in 1904 constructed the Entente Cordiale with Britain.

The Entente in its particulars covered everything from disputes in Egypt and Morocco to Newfoundland fisheries claims, and when the first Moroccan confrontation with Germany occurred in 1905, the agreement was transformed into a mutual Mediterranean defence pact aimed directly at Germany. German Mediterranean policy had worried Delcassé, and the German naval expansion programme had irked Britain, for some time before then. After 1905 Europe was, in effect, divided into armed camps.

Europe Divided

Wilhelm II seemed intent upon stirring every available pot. He publicly proclaimed Germany's sympathy with the Boers in South Africa, and tested the Entente Cordiale by claiming a share in the Moroccan investments in 1905 and again in 1911. Britain and France had shared Morocco between themselves alone, and had no intention of doing otherwise. Wilhelm was rebuffed, but such confrontations as these heightened tensions throughout Europe. Faced with the emperor's posturing, and his aggressive colonial and naval policies, Great Britain joined France and Russia in the Triple Entente, signed in 1907. Europe's six major powers were now grouped in two mutually suspicious and, on occasion, hostile alliance systems.

Tension then piled upon tension: Germany financed a railway system linking Berlin to Baghdad, which was interpreted as a German threat to Britain's control over the Suez Canal; Austria annexed Bosnia on the Adriatic Sea; Russia backed an anti-Austrian *coup* in Serbia; German generals trained Turkish armies; efforts to initiate international disarmament talks fell flat; and Balkan states at war with Turkey in 1912–13 were armed and trained by the French. The Middle East, meanwhile, to which the Balkans were the European gateway, was of rising importance well beyond the need to control the Suez Canal.

The new ingredient was oil. Middle East oil production was still small in 1914, but clearly it would increase. European navies were beginning to transfer from coal to oil-powered engines, and the age of the automobile and oil-powered factories was beginning. Through all of this, Europe's leaders did the routine things and went through the usual diplomatic motions, and pretended that the world could go on as it was forever.

Paris was lovely in the spring of 1914; so too was Provence, the Dordogne, and the beaches of Brittany, where the French would soon spend their summer holidays. Some thought about the disturbing implications of Marcel Proust's *À la Recherche du Temps Perdu* (Remembrance of Times Lost), the first volume of which was published in 1913.

Then the summer came; it was the hottest that anyone could ever remember.

CHAPTER NINE

France in the Century of Total War
1914–1945

In a sense, the European nineteenth century ended with the outbreak of the First World War in 1914. For the next thirty years, Europe was in a state of waging, recovering from or preparing for general war. France was squarely in the middle of it all, and the experience transformed France quite as effectively as had the wars of the Revolution and of Napoleon.

The First World War

Archduke Franz Ferdinand, heir to the Austrian throne, visited Sarajevo, in Bosnia, on 28 June 1914. Gavrilo Princip, a Bosnian nationalist, was one of a half-dozen student terrorists sworn to assassinate him. It was a confused, messy business. The archduke did not appear when or where he was meant to on the route out of the city, and Princip thought he had missed his chance. Disconsolate, he sat at a table in a pavement café. An open car stopped in the square opposite. Incredibly, inside sat the archduke and archduchess. Without hesitation, Princip dashed into the street, leaped onto the running-board, and fired six shots at the pair before the startled bodyguards could move. Both Franz Ferdinand and Sophia died of their wounds. So too, in a manner of speaking, did Princip, who was executed for this murder. But his place in history was assured. His six shots were the first heard in what came to be known as the First World War.

No one expected this event to produce a general war; after all, Balkan crises were nothing unusual. But Austria , seeking to turn the assassination to advantage against Russia in the Balkans, declared war on Russia's client, Serbia, on 28 July. Russia reacted; Germany reacted to Russia;

alliances were invoked and armies mobilized; ultimata flew back and forth; and war began on 3 August, unexpectedly and disastrously. British foreign secretary, Sir Edward Grey, uttered perhaps the most subsequently quoted words from that moment: 'The lights are going out all over Europe. We shall not see them lit again in our lifetime.'

France at War

There was no great agitation for war as in 1870. All the same, nationalism was rampant. Jean Jaurès, the only pacifist voice in the Assembly, was assassinated on 31 July. President Raymond Poincaré called for national unity, and, for once, got it. Every shade of political opinion believed German aggression lay behind the war, and so backed the government. There was no French Fifth Column in 1914.

Unity did not, however, guarantee competence. As in the past, the General Staff set out in 1914 to fight the preceding war instead of the present one. Of course, so did everyone else. The Commander-in-Chief, Marshal Joseph Joffre, along with the General Staff, expected a short war on the order of 1870, to be decided by a single, sharp offensive.

In the early days of the war – and as in 1870 – it looked as if the Germans were winning. Following the Schlieffen Plan, Germany's order of battle in the West, General von Kluck drove across Belgium, into France and towards Paris. The government withdrew to Bordeaux, just in case, after reorganizing to include Socialists, Radicals and Conservatives in the cabinet. The national union was secure; the nation was not, however, and on 5 September Paris itself seemed likely to fall.

But General Gallieni, commander of the Paris garrison, counterattacked that day on the Marne, with reinforcements sent from Paris literally by taxi cabs. Von Kluck was stopped. Over the next four months, with the help of the British Expeditionary Force, the lines were stabilized with ten *départements* in enemy territory, and the armies in trenches which stretched from the Swiss frontier to the North Sea. In these first four months of war France suffered 850,000 casualties. Sadly, they were only a foretaste of losses to come.

The French command continued committed to the concept of the large offensive, to which soon was added attacks by troops who sallied forth from the trenches in small numbers. The main effect was large-

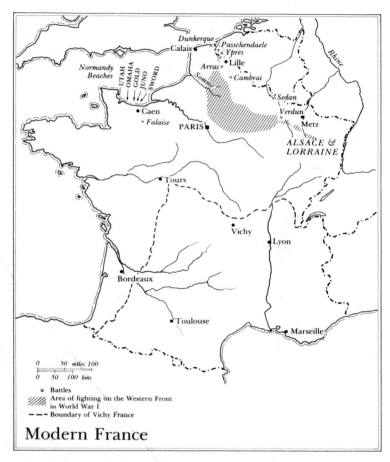

Modern France

scale slaughter, to little apparent purpose. It was the style on all sides, and casualties mounted steadily through 1915. Political and military nerves grew frayed, hence the symbolic tragedy of Verdun.

VERDUN

In February 1916, the Germans attacked Verdun, near Sedan. Aristide Briand, now premier, knew that if Verdun – strategically unimportant but a symbol of the national will to resist – fell, public morale and his government would fall with it. Verdun had to be held. Briand ordered a counter-offensive, led by General Philippe Pétain. Pétain saved the fortress and made his reputation; but between Verdun and the Somme offensive in July to relieve pressure on the fortress, there were half-a-million French casualties – and Marshal Joffre lost his reputation. Public disillusionment set in, and the government embarked on an extensive propaganda campaign to sustain public support for the war. Joffre was its victim, and was dismissed at the end of the year. His successor, General Nivelle also failed; Marshal Foch played the game better and lasted until 1918.

1917

This year was the turning point in the war and in twentieth-century European and French history. The United States entered the war, and would subsequently play a role in Europe; mutinies broke out in the allied armies, chiefly as protests against the endless slaughter; in France radical journals of Left and Right, *Le Bonnet Rouge* and *L'Action Française*, for example, stirred civilian unrest; first the Briand and then the Ribot and the Painlevé governments fell, the latter caught up in a scandal involving the famous German spy, Mata Hari; strikes, absent in France since the war began, now were widespread, given impetus by the Bolshevik Revolution in Russia in November; and Georges Clemenceau became premier. Like Britain's David Lloyd George, Clemenceau was an able and ruthless politician who would stick at nothing to bring order out of the sudden chaos. The war ground on.

THE VERSAILLES TREATY

The war ended at last on 11 November, 1918. The Kaiser was forced to abdicate and a Republic was declared in Germany. At the end, German armies were in full retreat before Allied armies led by British, French and American generals. When the Americans arrived in France early in 1918, General Pershing probably did not actually say: 'Lafayette, we are here!' – a reference to French contribution to American independence. However, American president Wilson did urge upon Europeans the ideals of open diplomacy, national self determination, and a League of

Nations through which nations would arbitrate their differences. Clemenceau remarked: 'God gave us ten commandments we couldn't keep. Now Wilson gives us fourteen!'

In the spring of 1919, the victorious powers met in Paris to work out the peace at a conference which much resembled – or so many historians have thought – the Congress of Vienna a century before. France had been the battleground for much of the war, and had moral force on its side. Behind Clemenceau's leadership, France got most of what it wanted. The treaty returned Alsace and Lorraine, reduced the German military to 100,000 with no air force or submarines, demilitarized the Rhineland (Clemenceau would have preferred a separatist Rhineland, but Lloyd George, looking to the future, would not permit it) and assessed heavy reparations against Germany.

The treaty was signed on 28 June 1919 in the *Galerie des Glaces* at Versailles – sweet revenge for 1871. The Germans had no input; for them the treaty was a 'diktat', and a growing source of resentment in the interwar years which made no small contribution to the rising tide of German fascism and the coming of the next war.

WHAT PRICE GLORY?

The war cost the earth. France had 1,322,00 dead and 3 million wounded soldiers; a quarter of the dead were under 24 years of age. Consequently, the birth-rate plummeted after the war. In 1938 France had only half the number of 19- to 21-year-olds it would have had without the war. In 1919 France was short of 3 million workers, and the gap had to be made up by foreigners, whose mere presence created resentment among French labourers. Ten *départements* had been laid waste by the Germans, including mines, blast furnaces, roads, railways, agriculture, sometimes whole towns. The population of Reims dropped from 117,000 to 17,000, Soissons from 18,000 to 500.

The war also played havoc with the nation's finances. The national debt in 1919 was 175 billion francs, five times greater than in 1913. Prices had risen 400 per cent since 1914, and the income tax introduced to pay for the war ate into everyone's income, especially among the bourgeoisie.

There were advances, too. Mass production was introduced on a large scale during the war, and many heavy industries expanded to make war materiél. They cut back in peacetime, but the principle of growth had been established and the industrial economy was ready for the take-off in productivity which began in the 1920s. Inflation pushed up farm prices further than costs, and the peasants were better off than before 1914. Trade unions at the war's end were accorded more respect than in the past, and the number of women teaching in schools increased.

WOMEN AND THE WAR

The status of French women hardly altered as a result of participating in the war. Women entered the war-work force in large numbers: they comprised 25 per cent of the munitions workers, for example, and at Renault were 4 per cent of the general work force in 1914, rising to 32 per cent by 1918. But working conditions were appalling. Women were resented by male workers, who saw to it that they had largely menial, and even dangerous, jobs. 70,000 industrial accidents reported in 1917 involved women. Sexual harassment was commonplace. After the war, the numbers of women in work increased, but shifted into 'light' industry and white-collar, mostly secretarial, jobs.

The sexual division of labour was not altered; and no 'feminist revolution' was in the offing. If French men could have had their way, French women would have stayed at home and had babies. French governments tended to agree: stiff penalties were invoked for distributing propaganda for birth control through the use of contraceptives, or against abortion. In 1922 an attempt to give the vote to women passed the Chamber, but was thrown out by the Senate. French women would have to wait for their political liberation until 1945.

POST-WAR

Meanwhile, the slaughter of those four years and the horrors of life in the trenches produced a disillusioned and pacifist generation. Even the most patriotic of returning soldiers were fervent partisans of peace at any price. Pessimism and malaise: these were the war's legacy.

POLITICS

In the 1920s, French politics operated on the principle of Buggins' Turn.

First the *Bloc National* had power; it was a Nationalist-Catholic alliance formed to protect the interests of big business and the Church. It was supported in the pages of *L'Action Française* and other extreme right-wing publications; Léon Daudet, an *Action Française* contributor, was elected to the Chamber for Paris in 1919. For the first time, the Third Republic had produced a Chamber in which the majority of members were practising Catholics. This was known as the 'Sky-Blue Chamber', Conservative and clericist.

The first item on the post-war agenda was reconstruction. But that would cost a great deal, and the *Bloc* had no intention of paying for it by raising taxes. Rather, the Germans could pay through reparations. This idea had wide sympathy on both the Left and the Right. In 1922 Raymond Poincaré, former president, became premier with a specific mandate to enforce reparations.

When Germany defaulted on the payments in January 1923, Poincaré activated a clause in the Versailles Treaty which allowed Marshal Foch to occupy the Ruhr Valley and enforce payment. The occupation force also encouraged Rhenish separatism: 19,000 German state officials were dismissed and replaced by pro-separatist Rhinelanders. The German government responded by flooding the Ruhr with inflated currency. The effect was to ruin the German monetary system and deprive France of the full allotted reparation bill. In 1924 Poincaré was forced to accept an American mediated reduction of reparations. His government fell soon after, and it was the turn of the *Cartel des Gauches* (Left Alliance) to govern, under Radical premier Édouard Herriot.

The *Cartel* was Radical-Socialist, with the Radicals in the majority. As a gesture to the Socialists, Jean Jaurès's ashes were installed in the Panthéon. Otherwise, Radicals and Socialists were miles apart. The Radicals advocated the free-market system, reducing government to a minimum; the Socialists expected the government to run the economy as well as the state. But the Socialists had no real power, and they were at odds with the Radicals over social policy, and with the French Communist Party and its 500,000-member trade union, the Confédération Générale du Travail Unitaire, over the Communists' insistence that political guidance must come from Moscow. The best the Socialists could do was help the Radicals fend off the *Bloc*. The Communists, like

Action Française (which temporarily lost credibility through a row with the papacy), were mainly a nuisance value in French political life.

THE ECONOMY

The Herriot government gave up only reluctantly on the idea that reparations could pay for reconstruction. But there was no choice. Serious inflation and a fall in the value of the franc came after 1924, and there were signs of incipient public rebellion as confidence waned. The government then forgot artificial solutions to economic problems and simply raised taxes and reduced expenditure. It worked. The economy was fundamentally sound and took off almost at once. Confidence in the government returned; the franc revived, and by 1928 the economy was as prosperous and progressive as it had been before the war.

FOREIGN POLICY

Foreign affairs remained the chief topic of interest throughout the 1920s. From the moment war ended, France looked for security. There seemed none to be had. The United States refused to ratify the Versailles Treaty, which left Europe bearing the responsibility for the League of Nations; in 1922 Britain sided with the Greeks against Turkey, whom France favoured. 'Perfidious Albion,' the French cried, grimly assenting to Clemenceau's lament in 1919: 'England is the lost illusion of my life! Not a day passes that I do not receive from one of our agents abroad reports indicating veritably hostile acts.'

Suitable alliances were sought: Belgium in 1920, Poland in 1921, and Czechoslovakia in 1924, the latter associating France with the 'Little Entente' of Czechoslovakia, Rumania and Yugoslavia. France did not wish to distance itself from Britain or from Soviet Russia, despite French antipathy to Bolshevism. Only Germany was a constant negative factor in foreign-policy considerations, and Britain's efforts to ease reparations payments, as at the Genoa Conference in 1921, met with a flat French refusal. France also fared better at the naval disarmament conference in Washington than did Britain; but in 1923 came the disastrous occupation of the Ruhr. French troops stayed on in the Ruhr until 1929 when there was a second mediated reparations reduction.

In 1924, Aristide Briand took over foreign policy. He was flexible, subtle yet idealistic, and took a different tack from his predecessors. He involved France in on-going disarmament talks, and drew upon the Francophilia of British foreign secretary, Austen Chamberlain, to arrange some accommodations with Germany that would recognize French apprehensions. The result was the Locarno meeting between Briand and the German foreign minister, Gustav Stresemann, in 1925, and a general agreement between them, the Treaty of Locarno. While problems were not solved, an atmosphere was created which promised a more constructive approach in the future. For this Briand was a hero in Paris.

The 'Locarno Spirit' operated in foreign policy for four years, during which French economic recovery continued, aided by expanding Franco-German trade. The idealistic high point came in 1928 when the multilateral International Treaty for the Renunciation of War as an Instrument of National Policy was constructed by Briand and the American secretary of state, Frank Kellogg.

The Crash of 1929

For every silver lining there is a cloud, to turn the adage around. In 1930 Briand derived a plan for Franco-German economic co-operation leading towards European integration, and then another for European Union. But Europe was not yet ready for a Common Market, and in any case, events were already in train which would undercut Briand's achievements.

The New York Stock Market crashed in October 1929. Subsequently President Herbert Hoover declared a moratorium on German reparations payments, while insisting that France continue to pay its war debts; in 1930 the Nazis gained 107 seats in the Reichstag, the German parliament, and in 1932 took control of it with 250 seats, in 1933 Adolf Hitler was named chancellor of Germany. In that year too, French unemployment reached 1,300,000, an indication that the general depression triggered by the Stock Market crash had reached France. Illusions of peace and prosperity were shattered. By 1935 production was down by 20 per cent; shares on the Bourse fell by 33 per cent, dividends by 50 per cent; agricultural income had dropped 33 per cent by 1934, and bankruptcy among small businesses had doubled. In 1938 French exports were down by 50 per cent, and the balance of payments was running a 3000 million franc deficit. The government had no idea how to deal with the crisis.

CRISIS POLITICS

Prime ministers came and went after 1924: Herriot, Painlevé, Briand, Poincaré, and in 1929 André Tardieu. Tardieu was a former henchman of Clemenceau, whom Bernhard von Bülow, German chancellor (1900–1909), once called 'the seventh greatest power in Europe'. Superior in every way, Tardieu was trusted by no one. He had sweeping political reforms in mind, including a Five-Year Plan for 'national retooling', but they came to nothing because of opposition from Radicals, Socialists and Conservatives. He left office in 1932.

A new *Cartel des Gauches* then emerged, and having learnt nothing from 1924, it named Édouard Herriot as prime minister. He again demonstrated his inability to grasp economic problems and soon left office. After him came Édouard Daladier and a succession of nonentities, until the formation in 1936 of the *Front Populaire* under the brilliant Jewish Socialist, Léon Blum. Crises continued, and still governments had no idea how to solve them. Extremists of the Right, on the other hand, thought that they did.

THE STAVISKY SCANDAL

Serge Stavisky, a prominent businessman, committed suicide in 1934 when it appeared that the police were closing in on him over some shady financial dealings. Revelation followed revelation, and it emerged that Stavisky was highly connected with the government. The situation was made to order for the extremists, and the journal *L'Action Française* lost no time in alleging in its pages that Stavisky had in fact been murdered to keep him from talking. On 6 February 1934, Right-wing demonstrators congregated outside the Chamber chanting anti-Republican slogans. The scene quickly deteriorated into a riot: 14 people were killed and another 236 were injured. Deputies were manhandled, and the rioting continued on into the night.

Republican politicians were sure all of this was part of a conspiracy to seize the government, that there was a fascist plot. They were not entirely wrong, but were far from correct. *Action Française* was not fascist, but had fascist traits: anti-parliamentarism, anti-Communism, nationalism, xenophobia, anti-Semitism and the cult of violence were part of the outlook of *Action Française, Jeunesse Patriotes, Solidarité Française*, and other extreme groups on the Right in the 1930s. They all had their blue-shirts, or other bully-boys to stir up trouble, do battle with the police and break shop windows in Jewish neighbourhoods. The *Croix de Feu*, run by Colonel de la Rocque, had nearly half-a-million members and was thought by the Left to be the most dangerous extremist group.

The intellectuals of the extreme Right urged what amounted to authoritarian models for government and society. They thought they knew best how to solve French problems; but the Right never came closer to taking control than the attack on the Assembly on 6 February 1934. This incident was not a failed *coup* so much as an indication of growing economic, social and political malaise, discontent with the Republic and successive governments, and exasperation over seemingly irresolvable economic difficulties.

THE FRONT POPULAIRE

The climate of the times was well illustrated by the brutal physical assault by an *Action Française* mob on Léon Blum, just five months before he formed his popular front government in 1936. Charles Maurras, editor of *L'Action Française*, was briefly imprisoned for inciting the attack, which merely heightened his popularity. Blum was not deterred by the assault; but his task was in any case formidable. A massive strike spread through French industry in April and May, in the belief that the election which had brought Blum to power was the start of the revolution. It was not. Blum's government attempted much; it achieved little.

The strike ended with some gains for the workers, and perhaps some increased disillusionment. Extremist Right-wing 'leagues' such as *Action Française* were dissolved (though *Croix de Feu* simply re-formed into a political party, *Parti Social Français*, which soon had 800,000 members). War industries were nationalized. Women were made government undersecretaries of state, even though they did not yet have the franchise. The rest of Blum's plans never went beyond theory. First, the Spanish Civil War began almost as Blum took office, and while he sympathized with the Spanish Republic against General Franco's nationalist rebels, it was not politically expedient to interfere. Second, capital began to flee the country, for investors had no faith in capitalism under a Socialist government. Soon the Blum régime paused, and then retraced its steps away from reform. At once it lost the support of the Left, including the unions. In June 1937 Blum resigned. After another year of nonentity governments, Édouard Daladier took office again as premier.

Under Daladier the Republic shifted permanently to the Right. The 40-hour work-week was extended to 44 hours in order to stimulate production, and the government made it clear that it would back employers against unions in this and other matters. An attempted General Strike in December 1938 fell flat. Daladier, Paul Reynaud and Georges Bonnet, the principals in the government, were Radicals. But French Radicalism had changed its oulook. Now it co-operated with the Catholic church; Jewish ministers were excluded from a reception for German foreign minister Ribbentrop; foreigners were subjected to strict security controls; the Radicals actively sought support from the provincial bourgeoisie, which once had leaned towards anti-Radical conservative groups and parties; and Radicalism now came to be identified with pacifism.

PRE-WAR

Once again foreign policy became the centre of interest in France. On domestic issues, the years from 1919 to the election of the popular front could be termed 'post-war'; in foreign affairs the years after 1933 were definitely 'pre-war'.

In October 1933, Germany left the Geneva Disarmament Conference and the League of Nations. Thereafter French policy was to search for a European system whereby Germany could be controlled – Collective Security was Stanley Baldwin's term for it – and, failing that, sought to appease Germany as an alternative to risking another general war. In 1934 foreign minister Joseph Paul-Boncour failed in his efforts to construct a Four-Power Pact of France, Italy, Britain and Germany, because France's eastern allies (Czechoslovakia, Poland, Hungary and Rumania) did not trust Italy. The same year, Louis Barthou as Paul-Boncour's successor, tried to create a Franco-Soviet arrangement that would isolate Germany. The Poles objected, and while Barthou was trying to reassure them, he was killed by an assassin's bullet intended for King Alexander of Yugoslavia. Barthou's successor, Pierre Laval, had no liking for Soviet Russia, and while in 1935 he signed a defence treaty with the Russians, he would not follow it up with staff talks and a military convention.

France participated with Britain and Italy in the Stresa Front agreement to guarantee Austria in 1935, and Laval agreed with British foreign secretary Samuel Hoare that Italy should keep its ill-gotten gains in Abyssinia, now modern Ethiopia. That pact was repudiated in Britain and France, but Laval continued wooing Mussolini and also tried to achieve a Franco-German rapprochement.

Until 1935 the Versailles Treaty had defined Germany's position among the European powers. But after a plebiscite in the Saar went overwhelmingly in favour of returning that industrially-rich region to Germany, Hitler threw off Versailles restraints. He announced his rearmament programme in 1935, remilitarized the Rhineland and announced the formation of the Rome-Berlin Axis in 1936. He then united Germany with Austria and incorporated the Sudeten region of Czechoslovakia, with its large German population, into the Reich in 1938 (with the acquiescence of both Britain and France). Throughout these developments, the French did little beyond drawing closer to Britain. General Maurice Gamelin, heard of the General Staff, insisted that nothing could be done to prevent the remilitarization of the Rhineland; Blum, Ivan Delbos and then Laval refused to consider any serious alliance with the Soviet Union; and they 'watched with interest' in March 1938, when German troops marched into Vienna.

MUNICH

The greatest blow to peace was the Munich Pact of September 1938. Hitler's aim was to create a large, powerful German state that could dominate Europe, without war if possible, with war if necessary. Through 1938 it appeared he could have it peacefully. The Czech

Sudetenland was home to three-and-a-half-million Germans, agitating to join the Reich. The Czech government used force to quell riots while Berlin protested and threatened. In response, Prague mobilized the Czech army, assuming it could count on the mutual defence pact of 1924 with France. Immediately, British prime minister, Neville Chamberlain, sought to mediate between Prague and Berlin, and France reneged on its treaty obligations in order to ensure Czech acquiescence. In accordance with German demands, Czechoslovakia was partitioned. Georges Bonnet thereafter claimed that Chamberlain had hamstrung French policy; in fact, the Munich Pact, by which Hitler, Mussolini, Chamberlain and Daladier formalized Czech partition, simply opened the door for France to renege on all of its eastern-European commitments. It was not an unpopular policy; 57 per cent of the French people approved the Munich agreement. Those who were perceptive, however, could read between the lines. Munich was the written evidence that France was no longer a great power.

War

After Munich there was little to do but wait. In December 1938, France signed a declaration recognizing Germany's right to expand in the East. In March 1939, Hitler annexed 'rump' Czechoslovakia and danced a jig on the steps of Hradčany Castle in Prague. Two weeks later the British unilaterally guaranteed the security of Poland. In the summer of 1939, both Britain and France made belated overtures to Soviet Russia, which were rebuffed dramatically in the Nazi-Soviet Non-Aggression Pact of 23 August. A week later, Germany invaded Poland, and on 3 September, after co-ordinating the timing, both western democracies declared war on Germany.

THE PHONEY WAR

Nothing much was to happen for the next eight months, save for the war in Poland and a few conflicts at sea. French and German armies looked at each other across fortified frontiers and waited. No bombs fell (except on Warsaw), no tanks roared across fields. It was the period of the 'Phoney War'. It ended as abruptly as a shot from a rifle. In April

1940, the German western offensive began. Belgium, Denmark and Holland fell. In June masses of French and British forces were forced back to the English Channel. 320,000 of these were evacuated successfully from Dunkerque to form the nucleus of an army which in three years time would invade North Africa and Italy.

But in the meantime, France was beaten by again fighting a war that had been fought a generation earlier. On paper the French army looked at least the equal of the German. But the paper did not take into account *blitzkrieg*, the armour-air combined assault strategy devised by General Guderian. As they had been in 1870, and nearly were in 1914, the French army was outdone in 1940 by thinking in terms of the last war. The General Staff had not paid attention to such war theorists as the Englishman, Captain Basil Liddell-Hart, who understood the uses of the tank, nor to their own Colonel Charles de Gaulle, who had read Liddell-Hart.

Italy declared war on the Allies on 10 June; the next day the government fled to Bordeaux – again – and the day after, General Weygand ordered a general retreat. Two million Parisians fled the city, joining another 6 million refugees clogging the roads and interfering with the movement of troops. On 14 June the Germans entered Paris, and on 16 June Paul Reynaud resigned as premier, replaced by Marshal Pétain who sued for peace. It was granted on 22 June, effective from 25 June. On 10 July, after having been hounded and harangued by Pierre Laval, the National Assembly voted 468 to 80, with 20 abstentions, to give Pétain full power to revise the constitution.

The Third Republic thus died. In its place was the *État Français*, headquartered at Vichy and subject to the victorious Germans. It would rule directly over about half of the country; the rest, including Paris and all coastal regions, was occupied by the Germans.

Vichy

The story of Vichy France is not a pretty one. It was ruled until 1942 by Marshal Pétain, vainglorious, haughty, using as part of his title the royal *nous*. In 1942 Pierre Laval, whom Pétain did not like, took actual control of the régime as premier. So far as the Germans would allow it, he ruled

France on his own. Vichy may not have been a puppet state in the technical sense, but its leaders were sufficiently collaborationist that the difference made small odds. French workers went off to feed the German war economy – three workers sent gained the release of one French prisoner-of-war; French police rounded up Jews for the death camps; and French agents ferreted out members of the *Résistance* and sometimes summarily executed them. Laval claimed that he 'policed' France in order to keep the Germans from doing it, and he and Pétain both claimed that their collaborationist régime 'saved' France from destruction by Germany. The cost of saving France proved to be very high.

The Vichy régime embodied most of what the extremist Right-wing had long advocated. Indeed, Pétain himself was sympathetic to *Action Française*, though he was not strictly a follower of Charles Maurras. Vichy was authoritarian, anti-parliamentary, anti-Semitic, racist, xeno-phobic, clericist – for a time education was put back into the hands of the Church – and moralistic, in a totalitarian manner. The economy strove for corporatism, as in fascist Italy, but fell short of success. Women were regarded officially as baby machines. Pétain, Laval, Pierre Flandin and Admiral Darlan, the principal officers of the régime at various times, all tried to fit France into Hitler's new European order. They succeeded; by 1944 Vichy existed only in name, and Germany controlled everything.

Sadly, there were many French Nazis ready to applaud: Robert Brasillach, Jean Luchaire and Jacques Doriot, among others; Joseph Darnand's *Milice Français*, a sort of French SS, brought ideological collaboration to its worst depths. Sadly too, Vichy was not an aberration. The roots went deep into the Third Republic. At the same time, having seen the produce of the roots at their ugliest, post-war France would never be content simply with a re-creation of the old order. Interesting times lay ahead.

THE FREE FRENCH

In 1940, Charles de Gaulle was a very minor French general, with a position in the War Office. His major contribution at that point was in refusing to surrender to Germany. He escaped from Bordeaux to England, where over the next three years he persuaded the British, the

Charles de Gaulle

Americans, and finally the French themselves to recognize him as the symbol of French resistance as head of the Free French Forces. It was not easy. Churchill found him trying (though also a 'man of destiny'), Roosevelt considered him impossible and not altogether trustworthy, and the French, or those prepared to defend Vichy – which in 1940 was a very great many indeed – thought he was a traitor. The Vichy regime sentenced him to death *in absentia*.

THE RÉSISTANCE

Within France itself, in everything from cold-shouldering Germans to blowing up railway bridges, thousands of French patriots in the occupied areas and Vichy fought back. In the north they fought against an invader; in the south, the *Résistance* struggle had the characteristics of a civil war. Every ideological persuasion from Catholic to Communist, and every social category from peasant to aristocrat, was involved. (Six members of the du Granrut family went to concentration camps for *Résistance* activity, for example.) It was most dangerous in the occupied north; it was most political in the south, where resisters hoped to combine anti-

Nazi and anti-collaborationist activity with planting the desire to change France once Hitler was defeated.

The groups included *Combat, Libération, Franc-Tireur, Témoignage Chrétien*, and the essentially guerilla *Maquis*, among others. Jean Moulin, working for de Gaulle, unified them and persuaded them to accept de Gaulle as their symbolic head, regardless of their political or ideological preferences. Moulin established MUR (*Mouvements Unités de la Résistance*) before he was betrayed in 1943 and tortured to death by the infamous Klaus Barbie, the 'butcher of Lyon'. Moulin was replaced by Georges Bidault, later de Gaulle's enemy over independence for Algeria.

Liberation

On 6 June 1944, the allies effected a landing in Normandy and began the operation of liberating France. All *Résistance* groups, Left and Right, agreed that a mass uprising should take place both to throw out the Germans and remove the odour of Vichyism. De Gaulle agreed; but when such a rising occurred, German reprisals were swift, brutal and thorough. The *Parti Communiste de France* was the most firmly committed to a mass rising. The Paris Free French were commanded by Communist Colonel Rol-Tanguy, and key posts within the 'secret army', as the *Résistance* had come to be called, were held by Communists. On 22 August Paris insurgents were at war with the Germans.

De Gaulle despaired at the idea of a Communist take over of France, and the allies shared his concern. Paris was not strategically important; politically it was a vital symbol, and General Eisenhower dispatched American and French troops, the latter commanded by General Jacques Leclerc, an officer in the French colonial army in Africa when the war broke out.

The German commander, General von Choltitz, surrendered to Leclerc on 25 August, and de Gaulle entered Paris that afternoon. He drove straight to his old office at the War Ministry, to symbolize that in his view Vichy was an illegal establishment and that officially the Third Republic still existed. On 26 August he led a giant demonstration and parade on the Champs-Élysées, despite the fact that there were still snipers in the city.

COLLABORATIONISTS

For France it was all over but the shouting – and the revenge. Perhaps 9000 summary executions of collaborators took place. In the Dordogne Valley there was a virtual reign of terror. 'Horizontal collaboration' – liaisons between French women and German soldiers – was dealt particularly severe punishment: the women were publicly humiliated, often paraded naked through the streets with shaved heads. Official purging of collaborators accounted for about 767, including, famously, Pétain and Laval. Pétain's death sentence was commuted to life imprisonment by Charles de Gaulle. The others were shot.

De Gaulle was no fool. Getting rid of collaborationists did not mean getting rid of every civil servant or official who had served the Vichy régime. Élites were swept away, to be replaced by a new kind of élite, the veterans of the *Résistance*; but left-over officials from the Vichy régime remained in the civil service. In 1948, for example, 97 per cent of *inspecteurs de finance* had been employed by Vichy, and in the 1960s Maurice Couve de Murville, a high civil servant of Vichy, was President de Gaulle's foreign secretary. Couve de Murville was among those who had practised 'wait and see', and skipped out the moment it was clear who was winning.

Post-War

De Gaulle established a provisional government, and later claimed that he had saved France from Communism. This was not true: there was no serious Communist expectation of seizing power in 1944, 1945 or even 1946. For one thing, the Anglo-Americans would never have permitted it. De Gaulle certainly did battle with the Communist Party, but more important, he held onto power until some order came out of the chaos. The country was in ruins in 1945, far more than in 1918: 55,000 factories and business houses, 135,000 agricultural buildings and 2,000,000 dwellings were destroyed; 4000 kilometres of railways and 7500 bridges were gone; inflation was rampant; antagonism between town and country operated at a high level of intensity; and industrial production was only 50 per cent that of 1938.

De Gaulle resorted to a time-honoured French tradition and held a plebiscite. On 21 October 1945, 96 per cent of French people voted '*non*' on the Third Republic. At the same time elections to a Constituent Assembly (women voting for the first time) produced a Chamber with few Radicals, slightly more Rightists, and large Socialist, Communist and Christian Democrat (*Mouvement Républicain Populaire*) parties, the latter led by Georges Bidault. De Gaulle remained aloof from party. In January 1946 he resigned his provisional leadership, disgusted because his views on a powerful presidency were not accepted. He would return.

In May, a new constitution was drawn up. It looked remarkably like the old one: a weak presidency, a premier forced to balance parliamentary parties which again were looking like mainly self-interest groups. It was approved by a mere million-vote majority; but approved it was, and the Fourth Republic was born. In 1947 it became as operational as it ever would be.

CHAPTER TEN

Contemporary France

1945 was a crossroads for France. The French could continue to stagnate, the national condition since 1918, or they could, in Charles de Gaulle's words, 'marry their century' and liberate themselves from the decadent aspects of their past, just as they had finally liberated themselves from the Germans. The choice, however, was not so simple as it might appear.

IDEAS

The problem of stagnation and the search for solutions to it began in 1918 and affected both mind and body. Liberation of the one entailed liberation of the other. In 1919 Paul Valéry wrote: 'We civilizations now know that we are mortal ... We see that the abyss of history is large enough for everyone. We feel that a civilization is as fragile as life.' So it was. French intellectuals now believed that traditional civilization had been swept away by war, and searched for new, often perverse and always despairing, alternative values. The Dadaists had celebrated mindless destructiveness in the 1920s; then the Surrealists exalted 'the dream; the subconscious; love, freed from all moral or social fetters; revolutionary fervour; flamboyant atheism'. Marcel Proust had pioneered stream-of-consciousness in the novel, while André Gide, failing to resolve the ambiguities of the universe, experimented with Henri Bergson's concept of the 'gratuitous act,' devoid of purpose or meaning. These and the ideas that came after them, found expression not only in literature, but in art, music, theatre and the cinema.

Despair deepened in the 1930s. For artists and writers Paris might be a 'moveable feast', as Ernest Hemingway phrased it, but the fare was sometimes nearly indigestible. Louis-Ferdinand Céline's nihilism revealed 'a satanic vision of the godless world, rolling helplessly through space and infested with crawling millions of suffering, diseased, sex-obsessed, maniacal human beings'.

Despair produced a desire for action, if it could be justified: André Malraux found *engagement* in neo-romantic exploits in Indo-China, the Spanish Civil War and the *Maquis*. Or, if action could not be justified: Jean-Paul Sartre considered the role of Existential Man, alone in an absurd and irrational universe, absolutely free to choose. Existentialism never caught on; the burden of absolute freedom was too heavy. Moreover, it was at odds with Sartre's own Communist beliefs. Meanwhile, Simone de Beauvoir's legendary book *Le Deuxième Sexe* encouraged the advance of feminism within a vaguely Existentialist context.

In the 1950s *engagement* gave way to *dégagement* (disengagement) and an aloof, intellectual élitism. In the 1960s Claude Lévi-Strauss's Structuralism – everything can be understood because societies are collections of simple structures, eternally coherent and much alike – caught on with sociologists, planners and the *Annales* school of historians. Structuralism faded in the 1970s into Post-Structuralism, a loosely-grouped collection of extremely complicated variations of Structuralism. Critics called Post-Structuralism a 'glorious cerebral game', and noted that simple ideas did not become sophisticated merely by dressing them up in unintelligible jargon.

The old, mainstream ideas of the French tradition, Rationalism and Humanism, were not displayed by these fruits of intellectual despair and extremism. Albert Camus cogently illuminated the fact by moving beyond Existentialism toward moral responsibility. If the world seems absurd, he argued, human beings are not thereby excused from trying to make sense of it, or improve it, or from fighting against fanatics, tyrants or saviours who offer themselves as substitutes for God. Frenzied intellectualism from Dada to Post-Structuralism offered no lasting alternative to Voltairian scepticism, Marxist materialism and Christian humanism. On the other hand, it paralleled in time the evolution of twentieth-century politics and society. It was no mere coincidence that Existentialism was in vogue in 1945, at the moment when France faced choosing its path into the future.

The Fourth Republic

In 1947 Communists and Socialists found that they could not co-operate after all, and a centrist 'third force' formed. It allied Socialists, Radicals and the *Mouvement Républicain Populaire* (MRP). In 1948 the Socialists fell back as the political centre of gravity shifted rightward. Charles de Gaulle's *Rassemblement du Peuple Français* and Pierre Poujade's populist shopkeeper and peasant bloc kept the pressure on. The Gaullists had ideas, at least, even if they were vague. Poujadism had 'as much intellectual content as a scream'.

Between 1947 and 1958 governments lasted an average of six months. At best they fended off crises and maintained slim majorities in the lower house, renamed the National Assembly; at worst they tried actually to govern, to meet crisis head on, and were thrown out of office. French government balanced precariously between negative interest groups: the Fourth Republic had died, said one cynic, and had been replaced by the Third.

RECOVERY

While witty enough, this judgement was neither fair nor true. Progress was made in every sphere but the political. Women finally had the vote and constitutional guarantees of equality of rights. Coal, gas, electricity and the four largest deposit banks were nationalized, a comprehensive welfare state emerged with social services far more comprehensive than anything before the war, and the Communist party was now one of the largest political forces in the country – though less effective than its numbers implied. A birth-rate revolution reversed the negative population growth rate, pushing upward the demand for more schools, social services and jobs. Even old Radicals now conceded defeat on the most eternal of education questions, and agreed to schemes which gave state assistance to church schools in order to meet the expanding needs of primary and secondary education.

Meanwhile, forward-looking newcomers to 'social management' had their eyes fixed firmly on economic planning and European integration as the way to the future. Jean Monnet's Planning Commission drew up a series of Four-Year Plans which, fuelled by United States' Marshall Plan aid, revived industry and technology. Production increased 50 per cent by 1953 over 1938. The Communist party led strikes against this 'American imperialism' in 1947 and 1948. Jules Moch, the Socialist interior minister, blunted them successfully, largely because the public was suspicious of Communist motives.

THE TREATY OF ROME

Robert Schuman was the architect of the European Coal and Steel Community, which linked France, Western Germany, Italy, Belgium, Holland and Luxembourg. The Six, as they were known after 1951, formed the basis of the Common Market, founded by the Treaty of Rome in 1957. René Pleven was less successful with his European Defence Community (EDC), which was to include Western Germany. (The idea of integrating Germany into western Europe as quickly as possible was in the forefront of all enlightened French political thinking in the first post-war decade, and for obvious reasons.) The EDC died of neglect in 1954. By then defence was in the hands of the North Atlantic Treaty Organization (NATO), which was dominated by the United States and Britain. The Americans believed that European defence was too important to be left to Europeans. Apparently the British felt the same, even with the socialist Labour government in power.

Only agriculture made no significant progress in this period. Inflation wiped out gains made at war's end. Uneconomical small farms and antiquated farming methods, which nevertheless produced an almost constant surplus, kept agriculture in a state of permanent depression. A conservative peasantry resisted modernization: the number of tractors increased from 16,000 in 1938 to 630,000 in 1959, but they apparently were used less for tilling fields than for blocking roads during frequent demonstrations against falling farm prices. Eventually, the national trend towards urbanization reduced the rural population significantly, and those who remained began to prosper. The advent of the Common Market provided an expanded agricultural market, which helped even more.

Decolonization

'Retreat from Empire' was a major theme of European post-war reorganization. The retreat was not without incident. In France it brought down the Fourth Republic.

The French had hoped to retain their empire after the war by democratizing it. Social and economic reforms were introduced; the French Union, an idea not unlike the British Commonwealth but within which the colonies acknowledged that their allegiance was first to France, pretended to integrate the colonies into policy-making. But the Paris government failed to understand the depth of nationalism among most native populations or the extent to which *les colons* (French colonials), particularly in Algeria, were prepared to resist any kind of change, which might take local political and economic power out of their hands.

INDO-CHINA

While Syria and Lebanon became independent during the Second World War, almost by default, the British spearheaded liberation from the Japanese in Indo-China (Cambodia, Laos and Vietnam) in 1945, and handed control back to the French. Indo-China was raised to the status of an Associated State of the French Union in 1949. The Vietnamese were not impressed.

Vietnam claimed independence even as the Japanese withdrew. After that its Vietminh nationalists, led by Paris-educated Ho Chi Minh, waged war against France. Ho was a Communist, as the French rightly understood; he also was a nationalist, which they did not grasp, and had the support of the bulk of the Vietnamese people. The war dragged on, justified as an anti-Communist struggle. The cost was enormous in manpower, money and disillusionment. In 1954 Dien Bien Phu, important strategically and symbolically, fell to the Vietminh after a long siege. Dien Bien Phu inspired a deeply romanticised film, *Jump Into Hell*, in 1955; who knows what impact it may have had on inspiring American intervention in Vietnam a decade later? Pierre Mendès-France, a Radical, was summoned to the premiership specifically to bring an end to the struggle. He arranged an internationally arrived-at settlement, signed in Geneva. That the French were relieved to have the nightmare over was evident when the Assembly voted 471 to 14 in favour of the settlement.

NORTH AFRICA

Mendès-France did not stop with Indo-China. His talks with the Tunisians led to their independence in March 1956. Morocco followed in a few days, which left Algeria. In June 1956 a law passed the Assembly paving the way for future independence for all of France's African colonies.

Algerian nationalists were not prepared to wait. A nationalist uprising and campaign of terrorism, begun at the end of the Second World War, now intensified. By 1955 170,000 French troops, many of them veterans of Indo-China, were in Algeria. In 1956 the Socialist Guy Mollet became premier, was shocked at the *colons'* hostility when he proposed to negotiate with the rebels, and reversed government policy. Reinforcements poured into Algeria, swelling the French army to 350,000 while the rebel FLN numbered perhaps only 15,000. All the same, the French were unable to crush them.

THE SUEZ CRISIS

In 1955, Gamal Abdel Nasser, president of Egypt, nationalized the Suez Canal. The British government feared the effect on Arab nationalism throughout the Middle East; the French believed – or claimed to – that Egypt was arming the FLN. An Anglo-French plot was hatched, with Israel's co-operation, to take the Canal back and perhaps overthrow Nasser into the bargain. French interest in this affair was Algeria.

The Suez adventure would have succeeded – the actual invasion did succeed –had not the United States threatened intervention, backed by the American Sixth Fleet, and also declined to support the wavering pound. The United States was fearful of the moral advantage, if nothing else, which the Soviet Union might gain among Arabs (who sat upon much of the world's known oil reserves) from this recrudescence of European imperialism. Anglo-French forces withdrew. Thereafter French policy was more determined than ever to 'keep Algeria French'.

ALGERIA

However, the resolve was not universal. In 1958 matters came to a head. The French public wearied of another costly colonial war, and entertained doubts as to how 'honourable' was the French army's role in it: brutal torture was being employed; a village was bombed against government orders, provoking a furore which bought down the Félix Gaillard government; and on 13 May, when it was rumoured that Premier Pierre Pflimlin intended to negotiate with the FLN, a *colons'* revolt broke out. In Paris, sympathizers took to their cars and began tooting horns to the beat of '*Al-gér-ie-Fran-çaise*'; it was unnerving. Some army units went over to the *colons*, and on 24 May, paratroopers behind General Salan, a rabid supporter of French Algeria, invaded Corsica. A military *coup* seemed to be in the making.

Two things prevented it: the army rank and file, and General Charles de Gaulle. Ordinary French soldiers in Algeria, unlike the paratroopers whose special *esprit* was shaped largely by the 'humiliation' of Indo-China, were not prepared to follow extremist officers into rebellion. De Gaulle, the great hope of the Right, refused to lead a *coup*. Committing himself to no party or faction, he made it widely known that he 'stood ready to serve' should the nation summon him. With no acceptable alternative, the nation – in this case the Assembly and President René Coty – did call him on 29 May. Only the Communists were solidly opposed.

A sense of relief and optimism spread across the nation. At his insistence, de Gaulle was given power to rule by decree as premier for six months rather in the manner of an ancient Roman Consul, or yet another Man on Horseback. He used the time to introduce reforms and a new constitution, drafted by himself and Michel Debré, the justice minister. This constitution was approved in a national referendum by 80 per cent. The Fourth Republic was consigned to oblivion.

The Fifth Republic

The ghost of Louis Napoleon was much in evidence during the autumn of 1958. The new constitution recognized the president as the representative of the national sovereignty. The Assembly continued to function as a parliament, but with its powers over the government curtailed and its sessions limited to six months in the year. Legislative power passed to the premier and cabinet, which was no longer entirely responsible to the Assembly, and the premier was now the choice largely of the president.

De Gaulle used national referenda much as had Louis Napoleon, and with similar success: favourable votes of 80 per cent in 1958, 75 per cent in 1961, and 91 per cent in April 1962. At first he was elected president by 80,000 electors chosen by local government units. In 1962 de Gaulle took the step no regime had been willing to take since 1870: he made the presidential election subject to direct universal suffrage. Louis Napoleon had been the last leader selected in such fashion, and scepticism showed in this referendum passing with only 62 per cent in favour.

Meanwhile, Assembly elections gave de Gaulle's *Union pour la Nouvelle Republique* (UNR) 200 seats, a rightist independent-peasant bloc 118, the MRP 56, the Socialists 44, the Radicals 13 and the Communists a mere ten. The UNR had a plurality rather than a majority, but with de Gaulle's overwhelming popularity there was little chance of conflict between the executive and the legislature, at least for the time being.

THE OAS

One outstanding piece of old business remained before the new Republic could get down to new business: Algeria. In 1959 de Gaulle annouced a policy of Home Rule. In January, 1960 a coalition of army officers, *colons*, and such former Gaullists as Georges Bidault and Jacques Soustelle, attempted a further revolt. They naïvely expected it to inspire a popular uprising against the president. Nothing happened and they tried again in April 1961, with General Salan as leader. This time de Gaulle went on radio to appeal for public support. Portable radios had been widely distributed among units of the French army so that ordinary soldiers could hear the speech. They listened, they were moved, and when their officers revolted, they had no stomach for a *coup*.

Thereafter disaffected officers, *colons* and former Gaullists, calling themselves the *Organisation de l'Armée Secrète* (OAS), made war against the regime. It was simple terrorism, and became one of the bloodiest underground conflicts of modern times: there were 12,000 victims in all, and 800,000 embittered *colon* refugees pouring into France, backing the OAS in sympathy if not with action. De Gaulle stood firm, and the OAS was crushed. The war, in its final phase, became the subject of a highly entertaining novel by Frederick Forsyth, *The Day of the Jackal*.

In March 1962 de Gaulle recognized Algerian independence. The two nations have got along reasonably well since. A film, *The Battle of Algiers*, made jointly by French and Algerian film-makers, celebrated the struggle for liberation realistically, honestly and with compassion, telling both sides of the story with remarkable objectivity.

De Gaulle

The president's policy from the start was restoration of French *grandeur*. This was perfectly consistent with his Catholic, royalist, aristocratic and military background. De Gaulle was first and foremost a *patriote* whose refusal to submit either to Vichy or Germany in 1940 made him the symbol of French pride and honour. His dedication to the interests of France informed his politics, and prevented him from trying to cling to power when the will of the nation was against him. De Gaulle came to be known affectionately as *le grand Charlie*. The sobriquet fitted him as well as *le Roi du Soleil* fitted Louis XIV, and for similar reasons. An American cartoon of the 1960s depicted portraits of Joan of Arc, Louis XIV and Napoleon Bonaparte in the Louvre; all wore de Gaulle's face. The metaphor was appropriate. It was around his style that patriotic, political and state activities revolved.

THE ECONOMY

When de Gaulle took office, the economy was in a perilous state: a massive financial crisis threatened the 'economic miracle' of the 1950s. Prices rose, exports fell, gold and capital fled the country, and the franc destabilized. De Gaulle introduced deflation and austerity: tax increases; reduction of state expenditure in veterans' pensions and food subsidies; a wage-price freeze; and devaluation of the franc. Meanwhile, import controls were relaxed in hope that foreign competition would revitalize domestic productivity.

This 'short-sighted archaic liberalism', as de Gaulle's critics termed his economic policies, appeared to work. Exports rose; capital returned; gold and foreign-exchange made gains; the franc stabilized, and the modernisation process was resumed. The gross national product increased 5 per cent annually from 1958 through 1967, and France turned into a major industrial power with the highest economic growth-rate in the Common Market. Appropriately symbolic, the Caravelle jet emerged to lead the European aviation industry. In the Gaullist decade, a majority of French people grew accustomed to the outward manifestations of an affluent society: television, automobiles (by 1973 63 per cent of French families owned a car), refrigerators, decent housing and holidays away from home.

But there was a price to pay. The gap widened between haves and have-nots, and the lowest stratum of society remained as impoverished and hopeless as ever. Modernization drove out marginal operations in business and industry: between 1960 and 1970 France built nearly 1000 supermarkets, while 100,000 small shopkeepers went bankrupt. Official tax, housing, social and credit policies benefited the prosperous strata, but at heavy cost to the rest. Meanwhile, French élitism enlarged rather than disappeared. Without a diploma from the École Polytechnique, the Institut d'Études Politiques, or the École Nationale d'Administration, a hopeful young technocrat could whistle for a place among the country's managers. Stress increased. The Left made steady gains in politics, and the Right protested with obstructionist acts, such as seizing local tax offices and destroying official records. For this they went to prison and Gaullist policies remained unchanged. In the long term, economic growth and stability was only marginally better under de Gaulle than it had been without him.

FOREIGN POLICY

Following the presidential-election referendum of 1962, the UNR won a landslide victory in Assembly elections. Gaullist power was now unshakeable, with a majority of seats in the Assembly and a strong president. As one observer put it, the referendum 'blew up the road back to the Fourth Republic'. De Gaulle could get on with the policy which mattered most to him: restoring French *grandeur* in foreign affairs.

Knowing that France could not compete alone with the post-war superpowers, de Gaulle set out to create a Third Force, a bloc of European and Third World nations, excluding Britain, with France as its leader. In constructing his Third Force, de Gaulle switched sides in the Middle East from supporting Israel to the Arab states (France was concerned over lack of oil resources); recognized the government of mainland China; made a treaty with the West German chancellor, Adenauer, aimed at transforming the old Franco–German enmity into friendship; and approached the Soviet Union amid much fanfare about a continental unity stretching 'from the Atlantic to the Urals'.

Meanwhile, he attacked both NATO and the Common Market, to which the Fourth Republic had committed France. These organizations would destroy French independence, he argued; and anyway, they were unworkable. Moreover, NATO was dominated by the United States and Britain. De Gaulle was not keen on either, lumping the Americans and British together as '*les Anglo-Saxons*' and accusing them of conspiring to rule Europe without reference to France. It probably rankled the austere general when the attractive young American president, John F. Kennedy, visited and drew large, enthusiastic crowds which he charmed beyond all reason by introducing himself as 'the man who came to Paris with Jacqueline Kennedy'.

De Gaulle wanted to take France out of both NATO and the Common Market. He succeeded only with the former. First he demanded a triumvirate leadership for NATO of Britain, France and the United States; when the Americans rejected this he began withdrawing French forces. In 1967 he invited NATO to remove itself altogether from French soil. From that point forward France no longer was part of NATO. The public, with five years of Gaullist chauvinism under its belt, heartily approved. Opinion was less keen, perhaps, for the development of the *Force de Frappe*, an independent French nuclear strike force. Its function was as much diplomatic as military: having 'the bomb' guaranteed French membership in the 'nuclear club', and that France would be consulted whenever there was an international crisis – which simply is one definition of a great power. The first atomic tests were carried out in the Sahara in 1960. Over the years the *Force* grew more costly, and its benefits are still uncertain. Most recently it has involved France in contretemps with both Australia and New Zealand over testing in the South Pacific.

De Gaulle could not undo the Common Market. It had wide support in France, where membership greatly benefited agriculture. Therefore he decided to make of it another pillar supporting French independence.

His policy was, first, to scoff the notion that the Common Market was aimed at European federation, and then to co-ordinate the foreign policies of the Six behind French leadership. For example, in 1963 and again in 1967 France vetoed British membership on the pretext that Britain simply was America's 'Trojan horse in Europe'. Actually, he feared that once in the Common Market, Britain would rival France for leadership. So it has come to pass since the British joined in 1969.

De Gaulle's *bête noire* in foreign policy remained *les Anglo-Saxons*, and he missed no opportunity to set France, and where possible other nations, against them. He challenged the world-wide influence of the dollar and sterling; he denounced America's role in Vietnam; and on a visit to Canada in 1967, he ended a speech in Quebec with the words: '*Vive le Québec libre!*' These actions did not endear de Gaulle to the English-speaking world.

1968

In May 1968, a student-worker uprising in Paris shook the foundations of the Gaullist state. Ironically, the president's New Year's Day message that year said: 'Amid so many countries which are being shaken by so many upheavals, our own country will continue to offer an example of effectiveness in the conduct of affairs.'

In 1968, 605,000 students attended higher educational institutions which were equipped to handle about 60,000 comfortably: inadequate classrooms, lack of access to teachers, an administration which treated students like second-class citizens, and at the end, no guarantee of a job. Moreover, there was then a world-wide student protest movement fuelled by the Vietnam War, but aimed against everything associated with traditional values. Paris students were no exception, and the Nanterre campus of the Sorbonne was a particular hotbed. Radical students like 'Danny the Red' Cohn-Bendit, a German national, were disenchanted with the orthodox Left, and embraced Trotskyism, Maoism, anarchism and other extremist, dissident ideologies. An explosion needed only an excuse to happen. The arrest of a student terrorist in connection with the bombing of American Express offices in France provided it.

A student strike (the 22 March movement) was called in sympathy for the arrested 'victim of imperialism', and clashes between students and police followed. In May, barricades went up (an old Paris tradition); students threw stones, Molotov cocktails and uncomplimentary epithets at police, who responded by beating them up and anyone else who happened to be handy. Abuse of power under the Gaullist régime thus became an additional protest issue. The trade unions called a General Strike in sympathy with the students, and on 13 May 750,000 students and workers marched through Paris against the régime. Eventually ten million workers joined the strike.

The workers' grievances were genuine: low wages, unemployment and obdurate employers. The students, mostly from the privileged classes, were seen as seeking to outrage civilized values and vent anti-establishment frustrations. The Communist party was dismayed that the workers joined them. Communist party chairman Georges Marchais called the students 'mindless anarchists', 'fascist provocateurs', or 'student adventurers'. Communist opposition to *les événements*, as the May rising was called, both divided and weakened its overall impact.

De Gaulle went on radio on 30 May and rallied support, which was manifested in mass demonstrations in his favour. In June the strikes ended, and Assembly elections gave the Gaullists a massive 291-seat majority. De Gaulle seemed to have won. The new Assembly sought conciliation: there were wage increases for industrial labour and drastic university reforms.

Actually, during the May crisis de Gaulle lost control. His government blundered along, and the Gaullist election sweep afterward was because there was no viable alternative to the president, not because he had handled the crisis well. Now his judgement failed him, for the first time in his political career. De Gaulle's first act after the elections was to replace a good premier, Georges Pompidou, with a colourless bureaucrat, Maurice Couve de Murville, who had been foreign minister. Then, having toyed with the idea of introducing government reforms (increased regional autonomy and reorganization of the Senate), he decided in 1969 to submit these reforms to a simple 'oui' or 'non' referendum.

The referendum failed by 53 to 47 per cent, and de Gaulle did a completely unexpected thing. He simply walked away: no resignation, no explanation, he simply retired to his home at Colombey-les-deux-Églises to resume writing his memoirs. The French nation, loyal to him for so many years, felt betrayed. But a year later he died, and in death they forgave him, his great contributions recalled. But Gaullism never fully recovered, either from the May crisis or from the General's peculiar exit.

After de Gaulle

George Pompidou, *bon vivant*, businessman and language scholar, followed de Gaulle as president and pledged to continue Gaullist policies. But Pompidou was not de Gaulle, and policy soon shifted: opposition to British membership in the Common Market was abandoned, and a classical *laissez-faire* policy was favoured in economics. The latter development encouraged revival on the Left, and a Socialist-Communist coalition was formed behind Socialist François Mitterand. It won impressive gains in Assembly elections in 1973.

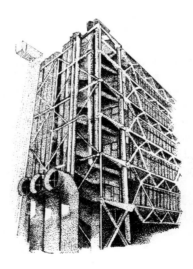

The Pompidou Centre

In 1974 Pompidou died suddenly of cancer. A new face and party pushed the Gaullists aside. Valéry Giscard d'Estaing, relatively youthful, energetic, aristocratic and very reminiscent of John F. Kennedy in style, led his conservative independent republican party to victory over Mitterand's coalition. Giscard promised an 'advanced liberal society' and introduced progressive tax reform, lowered the voting age to eighteen, relaxed controls on contraceptives and abortion, and emphasized concern for the ecology. But this bright outlook was quickly marred by a world-wide recession growing out of the oil crisis of 1973, when drastic increases in Middle East oil prices drove inflation through the ceiling. For the first time in twenty years, French industrial growth slowed, unemployment reached serious levels, and the government had to consider austerity. In 1977 the Left again challenged; and so did a sparkling young newcomer, Jacques Chirac, Giscard's own premier, for party leadership.

Giscard led a charmed life. He replaced Chirac with economist Raymond Barre, the Mitterand coalition suddenly collapsed, he held his own in the 1977 Assembly elections, and could look optimistically towards presidential elections in 1981. However, the Giscard luck was fleeting. The recession continued and Barre introduced austerity measures. He cut government programmes and froze wages and prices. Almost no relief was forthcoming, from unemployment, inflation or industrial slowdown as a result. Suddenly Giscard's charm had worn off, and he could not explain satisfactorily even a gift of diamonds from Emperor Bokassa, disreputable ruler of a former French African colony. Mitterand referred to the gift with annoying regularity during the election campaign, and with his coalition again intact, won the presidency in 1981 by 52 to 48 per cent.

France Today

On election night, thousands of young Parisians congregated spontaneously in the Place de la Bastille (the choice of site was not mere coincidence), to express their confidence that now things would change. In Assembly elections a few weeks later the Socialists swept to a landslide victory. Gaullist France was completely reversed; Mitterand was free to create a Socialist France, more revolutionary than social democracy, and more respectful of individual liberty than Communism.

In the first year, the régime introduced deficit spending in order to reinvigorate industry and cut unemployment (it was hoped that the other industrial nations would follow suit, thus ending the world-wide recession); nationalized large segments of the economy, and decentralized power from Paris to regional and local authorities; increased the minimum wage, family allocations and old-age pensions; expanded workers' rights and those of the expanding immigrant population; abolished the death penalty; and reduced over crowding in prisons with a programme of early release. But with all of this, the economy remained sluggish, inflation and unemployment increased, trade deficits rose, capital fled the country, and nationalized industries proved an economic albatross.

In the second year of the régime hope gave way to doubt, and Mitterand began temporizing his 'revolution'. This encouraged Right-wing opposition. In one instance, an Assembly bill to integrate Catholic schools into the national system had to be withdrawn when opposed by a massive popular demonstration. In another, the increased visibility of non-French residents, particularly blacks and Asians, attracted extremists of the Left and Right to Jean-Marie Le Pen's violently xenophobic and racist *Front National*, the ideological heir to *Action Française*. Le Pen was a former paratrooper and admirer of General Salan, the OAS leader in 1962. Assembly elections in 1986, influenced by rising unemployment, resentment against Middle East terrorists again using Paris streets for a battleground, and the scandal of French secret-service involvement in sinking the Greenpeace ship *Rainbow Warrior* in a New Zealand harbour, went heavily against the Socialists. Conservatives gained 286 seats to 212 for the Socialists, and 35 each for the Communists and the *Front National*. Mitterand had to select a Conservative, Jacques Chirac, as premier.

Socialist failure between 1981 and 1986 to turn France into a land of harmony, prosperity and social justice disillusioned many French people. At the same time, changes had been accomplished, even if they fell short of expectations. Above all, the myth that only Conservatives could be entrusted with governmental powers was dispelled. If Socialists had failed, they had done so no more dramatically or calamitously than had the Conservatives before them. In any event, the exclusion of the Left from political life was over, at least for the foreseeable future. In 1988, with the Right in shambles owing to Le Pen's rising influence, Mitterand won a second term with a 54 per cent majority, and appointed the moderate Michel Rocard premier, pending Assembly elections in June.

However, Rocard's was a minority government, and in May 1991, after three years of struggle in which he found himself increasingly stalemated by the opposition parties and unable to force legislation through the National Assembly, he resigned and President Mitterand took the unprecedented step of appointing a woman, Edith Cresson, to the post. The socialist Cresson was the obvious choice, he claimed. An engineer and economist, she was committed to European economic and political unification, set to begin in 1992 and be completed by the end of 1993. Thus Mitterand made clear that the cornerstone of French socialist policy was to see European Integration succeed, and with it the French economy strengthened. His policy for the future was Objective 1993, as the president termed it.

What had it all amounted to? Had the French 'married their century'? Unequivocally the answer is yes. Since 1945 France has been heavily urbanized; the population of Paris and its surrounding conurbation is 12 million, a fifth of the population of the country. The divorce rate has risen steadily, and a growing number of French people live alone, which suggests some major and fundamental alterations in values. Credit card and hire purchase are a way of life now (as is McDonald's and its French equivalents), and autoroutes are crowded on Friday afternoons with traffic heading for beach, mountains or countryside for 'le weekend', as it has come to be called. A higher percentage of French people than either Americans or British own a 'getaway' place outside their normal urban environment.

The gross national product of France is five times greater than in 1950; since 1960 the buying power of the average French person has doubled. High tech has replaced the dominance of traditional industry – the 'post-industrial revolution' – and there are now more white- than blue-collar workers. Correspondingly, only 12 per cent of the workforce belong to unions. Women are 43 per cent of the workforce, representing 72 per cent of women aged 25–49. Women sit in the Assembly: Pierre Mauroy's

1982 cabinet included five women, there were two women candidates for president in 1981, and Edith Cresson became France's first woman premier a decade later. Of course, a significant percentage of French men would still prefer that French women find fulfilment in fecundity.

Franco-German relations continue to be close, within the Common Market and on defence matters. Franco-British relations are more erratic, perhaps, but the joint Concorde SST project and the cross-channel tunnel popularly known as the 'Chunnel,' indicate more Anglo-French co-operation than since 1918, and perhaps yet more to come in future.

The Chunnel is a case in point. Scheduled to open in June 1993, it is more than simply the realization of a scheme first tried a century and a half earlier. The 32.2 mile tunnel 131 feet beneath the English Channel bed, which estimates say will carry 44 million passengers annually by the end of the present century, ends hundreds of years of English insularity from France and Europe. It is the perfect symbol for European economic integration in 1992. With a market of 350 million consumers, and a pan-European network of high-tech trains, including in France 5,000 kilometres of lines for the futuristic *le Train à Grande Vitesse*, among other developments, 1992 may mean a new European order and perhaps a new French order as well.

Or does it? Change and continuity blend in history. France today is different from the France of a hundred, or even fifty years ago. But there are similarities, if only symbolic. The Fifth Republic presidency has monarchial characteristics. Regional power bases compete with Paris. An *International Herald Tribune* headline in 1987 referred to mayors of regional cities who 'Reign like Omnipotent Dukes'. In similar vein, Bretons, Corsicans and Basques agitate for ethnic autonomy.

In the Pompidou Centre, France has a high-tech architectural monument which equals the symbol of industrializing France, the Eiffel Tower, in artistic bad taste. The traffic in Paris moves today at about the same rate of speed that it did in 1900, and only slightly faster than in 1610. Perhaps it should be no surprise that traffic congestion in central Paris, which today brings curses to the lips of frustrated motorists, in 1610 brought Henry IV within range of his assassin.

Sociologists argue that certain elements in French national behaviour are as old as France itself: the regionalism which contributes to a French tendency to denigrate foreigners and each other; and the undercurrent of individuality, perhaps also a product of ancient regionalism, which 'can't tolerate authority, yet at the same time ... considers it indispensable.' The sum of French history would seem to be this: *plus ça change, plus c'est la même chose*. 'The more things change, the more they remain the same.'

Chronology of Kings of the Franks and France

(Merovingian)

Merovich 447–458
Childeric I 458–482
Clovis I 482–511
Childebert I 511–558
Clothaire I 558–562
Caribert 562–566
Chilperic 566–584
Clothaire II 584–628
Dagobert I 628–637
Clovis II 637–655
Clothaire III 655–668
Childeric II 668–674
Thierry III 674–691
Clovis III 691–695
Childebert II 695–711
Dagobert III 711–716
Chilperic II 716–721
Thierry IV 721–737
(interregnum)
Childeric III 743–751 (died 754)

(Carolingian)

Pepin the Short 751–768
Charlemagne 768–814
Louis I, the Debonair 814–840
Charles I, the Bald 840–877
Louis II, the Stammerer 877–879
Louis III 879–882
Carloman 882–884
Charles II, the Fat 884–888
Odo, count of Paris 888–898
Charles III, the Simple 898–929
(interregnum)
Louis IV, the Foreigner 936–954
Lothaire 954–986
Louis V 986–987

(Capetian)

Hugh Capet 987–996
Robert II, the Pious 996–1031
Henry I 1031–1060
Philip I 1060–1108
Louis VI, the Fat 1108–1137
Louis VII 1137–1180
Philip II, Augustus 1180–1223
Louis VIII, the Lion 1223–1226
Louis IX (Saint-Louis) 1226–1270
Philip III, the Bold 1270–1285
Philip IV, the Fair 1285–1314
Louis X 1314–1316
Philip V, the Tall 1316–1322
Charles IV, the Fair 1322–1328

(Valois)

Philip VI *1328–1350*
John II, the Good *1350–1364*
Charles V, the Wise *1364–1380*
Charles VI, the Fool *1380–1422*
Charles VII, the Victorious *1422–1461*
Louis XI, the Spider *1461–1483*
Charles VIII *1483–1498*
Louis XII, Father of his People
   1498–1515
Francis I *1515–1547*
Henry II *1547–1559*
Francis II *1559–1560*
Charles IX *1560–1574*
Henry III *1574–1589*

(Bourbon)

Henry IV *1589–1610*
Louis XIII *1610–1643*
Louis XIV, the Sun King *1643–1715*
Louis XV *1715–1774*
Louis XVI *1774–1793*
(interregnum)
Louis XVIII *1814–1824*
Charles X *1824–1830*

(Orleans)

Louis-Philippe *1830–1848*

(Bonaparte Emperors)

Napoleon I *1804–1815*
Napoleon III *1852–1870*

Presidents and Heads of Government

THIRD REPUBLIC

Presidents:

ADOLPHE THIERS, 1871–1873
PATRICE DE MACMAHON, 1873–1879
JULES GRÉVY, 1879–1887
SADI CARNOT. 1887–1894
JEAN CASIMIR-PÉRIER, 1894–1895
FÉLIX FAURE, 1895–1899
ÉMILE LOUBET, 1899–1906
ARMAND FALLIÈRES, 1906–1913
RAYMOND POINCARÉ, 1913–1920
PAUL DESCHANEL, February–September 1920
ALEXANDRE MILLERAND, 1920–1924
GASTON DOUMERGUE, 1924–1931
PAUL DOUMER, 1931–1932
ALBERT LEBRUN, 1932–1940

Heads of Government:

LOUIS-JULES TROCHU, 1870–1871
EUGÈNE CHEVANDIER DE VALDRÔME, 1870–1871 (The Bordeaux Government)
ADOLPHE THIERS, February 1871–February 1875
LOUIS BUFFE, March 1875–February 1876
JULES DUFAURE, February–December 1876
JULES SIMON, December 1876–May 1877
ALBERT DE BROGLIE, May–November 1877

GAËTAN DE GRIMAUDET DE ROCHEBOUET, November–December 1877

JULES DUFAURE, December 1877–January 1879

WILLIAM H. WADDINGTON, February–December 1879

CHARLES DE FREYCINET, December 1879–September 1880

JULES FERRY, September 1880–November 1881

LÉON GAMBETTA, November 1881–January 1882

CHARLES DE FREYCINET, January–July 1882

CHARLES DUCLERC, August 1882–January 1883

ARMAND FALLIÈRES, January–February 1883

JULES FERRY, February 1883–March 1885

HENRI BRISSON, March–December 1885

CHARLES DE FREYCINET, January–December 1886

RENÉ GOBLET, December 1886–May 1887

MAURICE ROUVIER, May–November 1887

PIERRE TIVARD, December 1887–March 1888

CHARLES FLOQUET, February 1889–March 1890

CHARLES DE FREYCINET, March 1890–February 1892

ÉMILE LOUBET, February–November 1892

ALEXANDRE RIBOT, December 1892–April 1893

CHARLES DUPUY, April–November 1893

JEAN CASIMIR-PÉRIER, December 1893–May 1894

CHARLES DUPUY, May 1894–January 1895

ALEXANDRE RIBOT, January–October 1895

LÉON BOURGEOIS, November 1895–April 1896

JULES MÉLINE, April 1896–June 1898

HENRI BRISSON, June–October 1898

CHARLES DUPUY, October 1898–June 1899

RENÉ WALDECK-ROUSSEAU, June 1899–May 1902

ÉMILE COMBES, June 1902–January 1905

MAURICE ROUVIER, January 1905–March 1906

FERDINAND SARRIEN, March–October 1906

GEORGES CLEMENCEAU, October 1906–July 1909

ARISTIDE BRIAND, July 1909–February 1911

ERNEST MONIS, March–June 1911

JOSEPH CAILLAUX, June 1911–January 1912

RAYMOND POINCARÉ, January 1912–January 1913

ARISTIDE BRIAND, January–March 1913

LOUIS BARTHOU, March–December 1913

GASTON DOUMERGUE, December 1913–June 1914

RENÉ VIVIANI, June 1914–October 1915

ARISTIDE BRIAND, October 1915–March 1917

ALEXANDRE RIBOT, March–September 1917

PAUL PAINLEVÉ, September–November 1917
GEORGES CLEMENCEAU, November 1917–January 1920
ALEXANDRE MILLERAND, January–September 1920
GEORGES LEYGUES, September 1920–January 1921
ARISTIDE BRIAND, January 1921–January 1922
RAYMOND POINCARÉ, January 1922–June 1924
FRÉDÉRIC FRANÇOIS-MARSAL, June 1924
ÉDOUARD HERRIOT, June 1924–April 1925
PAUL PAINLEVÉ, April–November 1925
ARISTIDE BRIAND, November 1925–July 1926
RAYMOND POINCARÉ, July 1926–November 1929
ANDRÉ TARDIEU, November 1929–February 1930
CAMILLE CHAUTEMPS, February 1930
ANDRÉ TARDIEU, March–December 1930
THÉODORE STEEG, December 1930–January 1931
PIERRE LAVAL, January 1931–February 1932
ANDRÉ TARDIEU, February–May 1932
ÉDOUARD HERRIOT, June–December 1932
JOSEPH PAUL-BONCOUR, December 1932–January 1933
ÉDOUARD DALADIER, January–October 1933
ALBERT SARAUT, October–November 1933
CAMILLE CHAUTEMPS, November 1933–January 1934
ÉDOUARD DALADIER, January–February 1934
GASTON DOUMERGUE, February–November 1934
PIERRE-ÉTIENNE FLANDIN, November 1934–May 1935
FERDINAND BOUISSON, June 1935
PIERRE LAVAL, June 1935–January 1936
LÉON BLUM, June 1936–June 1937
CAMILLE CHAUTEMPS, June 1937–March 1938
LÉON BLUM, March–April 1938
ÉDOUARD DALADIER, April 1938–March 1940
PAUL REYNAUD, March–June 1940
PHILIPPE PÉTAIN, June–July 1940

VICHY

PHILIPPE PÉTAIN, 1940–1944
PIERRE LAVAL, 1942–1944

FOURTH REPUBLIC

Presidents:

VINCENT AURIOL (Soc.), 1947–1954
RENÉ COTY (Cons.), 1954–1958

Heads of Government:

CHARLES DE GAULLE (provisional), September 1944–January 1946
FÉLIX GOUIN (Soc.), January–June 1946
GEORGES BIDAULT (Chr.Dem.), June–November 1946
LÉON BLUM (Soc.), December 1946–January 1947
PAUL RAMADIER (Coalition), January–November 1947
ROBERT SCHUMAN (Coalition), November 1947–July 1948
ANDRÉ MARIE (Coalition), July–August 1948
ROBERT SCHUMAN (Coalition), August–September 1948
HENRI QUEILLE (Coalition), September 1948–October 1949
GEORGES BIDAULT (Coalition) October 1949–June 1950
HENRI QUEILLE (Coalition), June–July 1950
RENÉ PLEVEN (Coalition), July 1950–February 1951
HENRI QUEILLE (Coalition) March–July 1951
RENÉ PLEVEN (Coalition) August 1951–January 1952
EDGAR FAURE (Coalition) January–February 1952
ANTOINE PINAY (Cons.), March–December 1952
RENÉ MAYER (Coalition), January–May 1953
JOSEPH LANIEL (Coalition), June 1953–June 1954
PIERRE MENDÈS-FRANCE (Coalition), June 1954–February 1955
EDGAR FAURE (Coalition), February 1955–January 1956
GUY MOLLET (Socialist), January 1956–May 1957
MAURICE BOURGÈS-MANOURY (Radical), June–September 1957
FÉLIX GAILLARD (Radical), November 1957–April 1958
PIERRE PFLIMLIN (Chr.Dem.), May 1958

FIFTH REPUBLIC

Presidents:

CHARLES DE GAULLE (Gaullist), 1959–1969
GEORGES POMPIDOU (Gaullist), 1969–1974
VALÉRY GISCARD D'ESTAING (Cons.), 1974–1981

FRANÇOIS MITTERAND (Soc.), 1981–

Heads of Government:

CHARLES DE GAULLE (Gaullist), June 1958–January 1959
MICHEL DEBRÉ (Gaullist), 1959–1962
GEORGES POMPIDOU (Gaullist), 1962–1968
MAURICE COUVE DE MURVILLE (Gaullist), 1968–1969
JACQUES CHABAN-DELMAS (Gaullist), 1969–1974
JACQUES CHIRAC (Cons.), 1974–1976
RAYMOND BARRE (Cons.), 1976–1981
PIERRE MAUROY (Soc.), 1981–1984
LAURENT FABIUS (Soc.), 1984–1986
JACQUES CHIRAC (Cons.), 1986–1988
MICHEL ROCARD (Cent.), 1988–1991
EDITH CRESSON (Soc.), 1991–

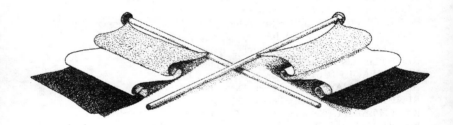

Chronology of Major Events

B.C.

A.D.

1122	Suger becomes abbot of Saint-Denis and advisor to King Louis VI
1130–60	Chrétien de Troyes and Marie de France write Arthurian stories
1152	Louis VII divorces Eleanor of Aquitaine, who then marries Henry II of England
1154	Henry II becomes King of England and establishes the Angevin Empire: Britain and Western and Southern France
1186	Philip II paves the streets of Paris
1200	Philip II codifies the study of medicine, civil and canon law; student riots at the University of Paris
1210	The Pope officially recognizes the University of Paris
1259	Henry III of England abandons Normandy, Maine, Anjou and Poitou, and recognizes French overlordship in Aquitaine
1280	Chartres Cathedral completed
1302	First meeting of the Estates General
ca.1310	*Parlement* of Paris established as judicial court apart from *Curia Regis*
1339	Beginning of the Hundred Years War
1346	French defeat at Crécy
1348	The Black Death
1356	French defeat at Poitiers
1358	Paris uprising and *jacquerie*
1411	Paul and Jean de Limbourg: *Les Très Riches Heures du duc de Berry*
1415	French defeat at Agincourt sounds death knell of chivalry
1420	Treaty of Troyes makes Henry V of England heir to the French throne
1429	Joan of Arc raises the siege of Orléans; Charles VII crowned at Reims
1431	Joan of Arc burnt at Rouen as a heretic
1435	Reconciliation of France and Burgundy at Arras
1438	Pragmatic Sanction of Bourges establishes the Gallican church
1453	French victory at Castillon virtually ends the Hundred Years War
1465	Rising of the League of the Public Weal against Louis XI
1484	The Third Estate recognized as part of the Estates General
1515	French victory at Marignano at the outset of the Italian wars
1516	Francis I persuades Leonardo da Vinci to settle at Amboise
1518	Budé's *L'Institution du Prince*
1523	Failed attempt of the duke of Bourbon to overthrow Francis I

1525	Battle of Pavia; Francis taken prisoner by Emperor Charles V
1529	Peace of Cambrai – 'Peace of the Ladies', Franco-Imperial alliance arranged by Louise of Savoy and Margaret of Savoy
1534	'Affair of the Placards', Protestant outburst in Paris
1536	Calvin's *Institution of the Christian Religion*
1544	Anglo-Imperial invasion of France
1554	Crespin's *Book of Martyrs*
1562–98	Wars of Religion between Huguenots and Catholics
1572	St Bartholomew's Day massacre and climax of Huguenot persecution
1576	Bodin's *De la République*
1588	Spanish Armada threatens England and Catholic League of Sixteen seizes control of Paris
1593	Henry IV converts to Catholicism at Saint-Denis
1598	Edict of Nantes grants religious toleration to Huguenots
1614	Last meeting of the Estates General until 1789
1618–48	The Thirty Years War
1628–29	Huguenots defeated at La Rochelle; Edict of Nantes reaffirmed
1630	Cardinal Richelieu, first minister of Louis XIII, subsidizes Sweden in the Thirty Years War
1635	*Académie Française* established
1635,40,45,70	Anti-tax riots
1637	Descartes's *Discourse on Method*
1638	Swedish-French alliance
1648	Peace of Westphalia establishes the principle of the European Balance of Power
1648–60	The Fronde and other rebellions against Louis XIV
1665	Colbert appointed first minister
1670	Molière's *Le Bourgeois Gentilhomme*
1675	Breton uprising against Louis XIV's Dutch War
1677	Racine's *Phèdre*
1682	The court moves officially to Versailles
1683	Death of Colbert
1685	Edict of Nantes revoked
1689	Grand Alliance of England and the Empire against France
1701–13	War of the Spanish Succession; the French are defeated at Chiari, Blenheim, Ramillies, Turin, Oudenaard, Lille and Malplaquet
1713	Peace of Utrecht ends the War of the Spanish Succession
1717	Watteau paints *L'Embarquement pour l'Ile de Cythère*
1740–48	War of the Austrian Succession
1748	Montesquieu's *L'ésprit des Lois*

1751	Diderot's *Encyclopédie*, first volume
1756–63	Seven Years War
1757–59	French lose India and Canada
1762	Rousseau's *Émile* and *Social Contract*
1763	British took over Québec and Louisiana passed from France to Spain
1778	France supports the Americans against England
1781	French navy help Americans win the Battle of Yorktown
1785	David paints *Oath of the Horatii*
1788	Paris *Parlement* forces summoning of the Estates General
1789	Declaration of the Rights of Man, Storming of the Bastille, and formation of the National Assembly
1792	Victory of revolutionary armies at Valmy: first victory of the Revolution against external enemies
1793	The Terror: Rule of the Committee of Public Safety
1796	Napoleon defeats the Austrians at Lodi and Arcola
1799	Napoleon's *coup d'état*
1802	Peace with Britain at Amiens
1804	Napoleon crowns himself French Emperor
1805	Lord Nelson crushes Franco-Spanish fleet at Trafalgar
1806	Confederation of the Rhine formed by Napoleon; Holy Roman Empire abolished
1807	Treaty with Russia at Tilsit
1812–13	French driven out of Russia and Germany
1814	Napoleon abdicates; Bourbon monarchy re-established
1815	Napoleon returns; Battle of Waterloo; Congress of Vienna partially restores the Old Order in Europe
1816	Saint-Simon's *Industry and Society*
1818	Occupation armies withdraw from France
1824	The newspaper *Le Globe* founded
1830	Reactionary policies of Charles X foment revolution; first performance of Berlioz's *Symphonie Fantastique*
1830–1881	Building the African and Indo-China empires
1839	Stendhal's *La Chartreuse de Parme*
1839	Daguerre introduces photography
1841	Child Labour law passed
1848	Revolution overthrows the July Monarchy
1851	*Coup d'état* of Louis Napoleon, Napoleon's nephew
1852	Louis Napoleon is crowned Napoleon III
1852–65	Baron Haussmann rebuilds Paris
1854–56	Crimean War
1859	Italian War of Unification; Peace of Villafranca
1860	Cobden-Chevalier free-trade treaty with Britain
1862	Hugo's *Les Misérables*

1863	Renan's *La Vie de Jésus*; Manet exhibits *Déjeuner sur l'Herbe* at Salon des Refusés
1864–67	Napoleon III's Mexican Empire experiment
1869	Suez canal opens; Flaubert's *L'Éducation Sentimentale*
1870–71	Franco-Prussian War, Napoleon III captured at Sedan
1871	Paris Commune
1874	Monet paints *Impression: Soleil Levant* – one critic mockingly dubs Monet and his friends the Impressionists
1875	Third Republic established
1876	Mallarmé's *L'Après-midi d'un Faune*; Renoir's *Moulin de la Galette*; France makes a gift of the Statue of Liberty to the United States
1880	Zola's *Nana*
1884	Trade unions legalized
1886	Seurat exhibits *Dimanche à la Grand Jatte* at the last Impressionist exhibition
1892	Panama Canal scandal
1892–4	Monet paints *Rouen Cathedral* series
1894–1906	Dreyfus Affair
1894	Franco-Russian alliance
1895	*Confédération Générale du Travail* formed; Lumière introduces cinematography; Cézanne given one-man show by the dealer Vollard
1898	*Action Française* founded; Marie Curie discovers radium; Zola's *J'Accuse*
1902	First performance of Debussy's *Pelléas et Mélisande*
1904	*Entente Cordiale* with Britain
1905	Legal separation of church and state
1907	Triple Entente with Britain and Russia; Bergson's *L'Évolution créatrice*
1908	Sorel's *Réflexions sur la violence; L'Action Française* becomes a daily newspaper
1909–10	Matisse paints *La Danse* and *La Musique*
1913	First performance of Stravinsky's *Le Sacre du Printemps*; Proust's first volume of *À la recherche du temps perdu*
1914	First World War begins; battle of the Marne saves Paris
1916	Struggle for Verdun, battle of the Somme; Sykes–Picot agreement divides the Turkish empire between Britain and France
1918	Armistice
1919	Versailles Treaty ending the war
1920–26	Alliances formed with Belgium, Poland, Czechoslovakia and Rumania
1922	Valéry's *Le Cimetière marin*

1923	French occupy the Ruhr
1925	Locarno agreements
1930	French troops leave the Rhineland
1932	The Crash of 1929 catches up with France; non-aggression treaty with Soviet Russia
1932–34	Failed disarmament conferences
1935	Franco-Russian mutual assistance pact
1936–37	Léon Blum's Popular Front
1938	Munich agreement dismembers Czechoslovakia, Daladier signs for France
1939	Anglo-French guarantee of Poland; Germany invades Poland
1940	Fall of France to Germany; Vichy state formed under Marshal Pétain
1943	Free French formed under General de Gaulle
1944	Allies land in Normandy; Sartre's *Huis Clos*; Paris liberated
1945	Third Republic ends; French women vote for the first time
1947	Camus's *La Peste*
1949	Organization of NATO
1951	European Coal and Steel Community treaty
1954	Fall of Dien Bien Phu, and France leaves Indochina; Algerian revolt
1956	Suez Canal invasion
1957	Treaty of Rome founds the Common Market
1958	*Colons* revolt in Algiers; Fifth Republic forms
1959	De Gaulle proclaimed first president of the Fifth Republic
1960	First French atom bomb tested
1962	Algeria becomes independent
1963	Anglo-German treaty of mutual cooperation
1966	Anglo-Russian rapprochement
1967	France leaves NATO
1968	Student-worker uprising in Paris
1969	De Gaulle withdraws from public life
1974	Valéry Giscard d'Estaing and conservatives push Gaullists aside
1981	Left coalition elects François Mitterand president
1984	Jean-Marie Le Pen forms the ultra-right National Front
1984–87	France extends military assistance to former African colonies; Mitterand favours US military presence in Europe; terrorist activities associated with Middle Eastern extremists; strikes and protests reminiscent of 1968
1988	François Mitterand re-elected president
1991	Edith Cresson appointed first woman premier of France

Major Universities and Founding Dates

Aix-en-Provence, 1409
Besançon, 1691
Bordeaux, 1441
Bourges, 1463
Caen, 1432
Clermont-Ferrand, 1854
Dijon, 1722
Lille, 1887
Lyon, 1896

Montpellier, 1289
Nantes, 1461 (transferred to Rennes in 1735)
Orléans, 1305
Paris, 1200
The Sorbonne, 1253
Collège de France, 1530
Strasbourg, 1566
Toulouse, 1299

Select List of Religious Buildings
(from the oldest dated remains)

Cathedrals:

AIX-EN-PROVENCE (Bouches-du-Rhône), Saint-Saviour, 11th century
ALBI (Tarn), Sainte-Cécile, 13th century
AMIENS (Somme), Notre-Dame, 13th century
ANGERS (Maine-et-Loire), Saint-Maurice, 12th century
ANGOULÊME (Charente), Saint-Pierre, 12th century
ARLES (Bouches-du-Rhône), Saint-Trophime, 11th century
AUTUN (Saône-et-Loire), Saint-Lazare, 12th century
AUXERRE (Yonne), Saint-Étienne, 5th century
AVIGNON (Vaucluse), Notre-Dame-des-Doms, 12th century
BAYEUX (Calvados), Notre-Dame, 12th century
BAYONNE (Pyrénées-Atlantiques), Notre-Dame, 13th century
BEAUVAIS (Oise), Saint-Pierre, 13th century
BESANÇON (Doubs), Saint-Jean, 12th century
BÉZIERS (Hérault), Saint-Nazaire, 13th century
BORDEAUX (Gironde), Saint-André, 12th century
BOURGES (Cher), Saint-Étienne, 13th century
CAHORS (Lot), Saint-Étienne, 11th century
CAVAILLON (Vaucluse), Notre-Dame-et-Saint-Véran, 12th century
CHÂLONS-SUR-MARNE (Marne), Saint-Étienne, 12th century
CHARTRES (Eure-et-Loir), Notre-Dame, 12th century
COUTANCES (Manche), Notre-Dame-de-Coutances, 13th century
DIJON (Côte-d'Or), Saint-Bénigne, 11th century
ÉVREUX (Eure), Notre-Dame, 12th century
LAON (Aisne), Notre-Dame, 12th century
LECTOURE (Gers), Saint-Gervais-et-Saint-Protais, 12th century
LE MANS (Sarthe), Saint-Julien, 13th century
LE PUY (Haute-Loire), Notre-Dame, 11th century
LIMOGES (Haute-Vienne), Saint-Étienne, 13th century
LISIEUX (Calvados), Saint-Pierre, 12th century

LUÇON (Vendée), Notre-Dame, 14th century
LYON (Rhône), Saint-Jean, 12th century
MARSEILLE (Bouches-du-Rhône), Notre-Dame-de-la-Major, 11th century
MEAUX (Seine-et-Marne), Saint-Étienne, 12th century
METZ (Moselle), Saint-Étienne, 13th century
MONTPELLIER (Hérault), Saint-Pierre, 16th century
NANTES (Loire-Atlantique), Saint-Pierre, 15th century
NARBONNE (Aude), Saint-Just, 13th century
NEVERS (Nièvre), Saint-Cyr-et-Sainte-Juliette, 12th century
NOYON (Oise), Notre-Dame, 12th century
ORLÉANS (Loiret), Sainte-Croix, 8th century
PARIS, Notre-Dame, 12th century
PÉRIGUEUX (Dordogne), Saint-Étienne-de-la-Cité, 11th century (replaced
   in the 17th century by Saint-Front)
POITIERS (Vienne), Saint-Pierre, 12th century
PONTOISE (Val-d'Oise), Saint-Maclou, 12th century
REIMS (Marne), Notre-Dame, 13th century
RODEZ (Aveyron), Notre-Dame, 13th century
ROUEN (Seine-Maritime), Notre-Dame, 12th century
SENLIS (Oise), Notre-Dame, 12th century
SENS (Yonne), Saint-Étienne, 12th century
SOISSONS (Aisne), Saint-Gervais-et-Saint-Protais, 12th century
STRASBOURG (Bas-Rhin), Notre-Dame, 11th century
TOULON (Var), Sainte-Marie-Majeure, 11th century
TOULOUSE (Haute-Garonne), Saint-Étienne, 11th century
TOURS (Indre-et-Loire), Saint-Gatien, 13th century
VANNES (Morbihan), Saint-Pierre, 13th century
VERDUN (Meuse), Notre-Dame, 11th century

Abbeys and Churches:

AMBOISE (Indre-et-Loire), abbey church of Saint-Denis, 12th century
CAEN (Calvados), Abbaye-aux-Dames, 11th century
CERNAY (Yvelines), abbey, 12th century
CHÂALIS (Oise), abbey, 12th century
CHARLIEU (Loire), abbey, 10th century
CHATEAUBRIANT (Loire-Atlantique), church of Saint-Jean-de-Béré, 11th
   century; Abbaye-de-la-Meilleraye-de-Bretagne, 12th century
CÎTEAUX (Côte-d'Or), abbey, 12th century
CLAIRVAUX (Aube), abbey, 12th century
CLUNY (Saône-et-Loire), abbey, 11th century
CONQUES (Aveyron), abbey, 11th century

FÉCAMP (Seine-Maritime), abbey, 7th century
FIGEAC (Lot), Abbaye-de-Saint-Sauveur, 11th century
FONTENAY (Côte-d'Or), abbey, 12th century
FONTEVRAULT (Maine-et-Loire), abbey church of Notre-Dame, 12th
  century
GORDES (Vaucluse), Abbaye-de-Sénanque, 12th century
GRANDE-CHARTREUSE (Isère), abbey, 11th century
GUINGAMP (Côtes-du-Nord), Abbaye-de-Sainte-Croix, 12th century
JUMIÈGES (Seine-Maritime), abbey, 11th century
LA CHARITÉ-SUR-LOIRE (Nièvre), abbey, 11th century
LANDÉVENNEC (Finistère), abbey, 10th century
LA SAUVE-MAJEUR (Gironde), abbey church, 12th century
LAVAL (Mayenne), Abbaye-de-Clermont, 12th century
LE BEC-HELLOUIN (Eure), Abbaye-de-Bec, 11th century
LE MANS (Sarthe), Abbaye-de-Notre-Dame-de-la-Couture, 11th century
MARMOUTIER (Indre-et-Loire), abbey, 4th century
MOISSAC (Tarn-et-Garonne), abbey, 11th century
MONCONTOUR (Côtes-du-Nord), Abbaye-de-Bouquen, 12th century
MONT-SAINT-MICHEL (Manche), abbey fortress, 8th century
NANT (Aveyron), Abbaye-de-Saint-Pierre, 12th century
NARBONNE (Aude), Abbaye-de-Fontfroide, 11th century
NEVERS (Nièvre), church of Saint-Étienne, 11th century
NOIRLAC (Cher), abbey, 12th century
NOYON (Oise), Abbaye-d'Ourscamp, 12th century
PARAY-LE-MONIAL (Saône-et-Loire), abbey, 10th century
PARIS: churches
  Sacré-Coeur, 19th century
  Saint-Étienne-du-Mont, 15th century
  Saint-Germain-des-Prés, 7th century
  Saint-Julien-le-Pauvre, 12th century
  Saint-Sulpice, 17th century
  Sainte-Chapelle, 13th century
PLOUGASTEL-DAOULES (Finistère), Abbaye-de-Daoules, 12th century
POITIERS (Vienne), Abbaye-de-Ligugé, 4th century
PONTIGNY (Yonne), abbey, 12th century
PONT-SAINT-PIERRE (Eure), church of Fontaine-Guérard, 12th century
PRADES (Pyrénées-Orientales), Abbaye-de-Saint-Michel-de-Cuxa, 11th
  century
REIMS (Marne), abbey, 12th century
ROMANS-SUR-ISÈRE (Drome), abbey, 9th century
ROUEN (Seine-Maritime), church of Saint-Ouen, 14th century
ROYAT (Puy-de-Dôme), church of Saint-Léger, 11th century
ROYAUMONT (Val-d'Oise), abbey, 13th century

SAINT-DENIS (Paris), abbey and cathedral, 3rd century
SAINT-GILLES (Gard), abbey, 8th century
SAINT-GUILHEM-LE-DÉSERT (Hérault), abbey, 9th century
SAINT-JEAN-DE-CÔLE (Dordogne), abbey church, 11th century
SAINT-MARTIN-DU-CANIGOU (Pyrénées-Orientales), abbey church,
    11th century
SAINT-PHILBERT-DE-GRAND-LIEU (Loire-Atlantique), abbey, 9th
    century
SAINT-PIERRE-SUR-DIVES (Calvados), abbey, 11th century
SAINT-SAVIN-SUR-GARTEMPE (Vienne), abbey, 9th century
SAINT-SEINE-L'ABBAYE (Côte-d'Or), abbey, 13th century
SAINT-WANDRILLE (Seine-Maritime), abbey, 7th century
SAINTE-MÈRE-ÉGLISE (Manche), village church, 12th century
SILVACANE (Vaucluse), abbey, 12th century
SOISSONS (Aisne), abbeys:
    Saint-Léger, 12th century
    Saint-Jean-des-Vignes, 11th century
    Saint-Médard, 6th century
SOUILLAC (Lot), abbey, 11th century
THORONET (Var), abbey, 12th century
TOURNUS (Saône-et-Loire), abbey church of Saint-Philibert, 10th century
VALMONT (Seine-Maritime), abbey, 12th century
VÉZELAY (Yonne), abbey, 9th century
VIENNE (Isère), church of Saint-André-le-Bas, 9th century

Selected reading on French history

Ardagh, John *France in the 1980s* (London, 1982)
Bates, David *Normandy before 1066* (London, 1982)
Briggs, Robin *Early Modern France* (Oxford, 1977)
Chamberlin, E.R. *Life in Medieval France* (London, 1967)
Cobden, Alfred *A History of Modern France*, 3 vols. (London, 1965)
Cronin, Vincent *Louis XIV* (London, 1964)
Druon, Maurice *The History of Paris from Caesar to Saint-Louis* (London, 1962)
Febvre, Lucien *Life in Renaissance France* (Cambridge, 1977)
Gies, Frances *Joan of Arc: The Legend and the Reality* (New York, 1981)
Greengrass, Mark *France in the Age of Henry IV* (London, 1984)
Hallam, Elizabeth *Capetian France* (London, 1980)
Hibbert, Christopher *The French Revolution* (London, 1980)
James, Edward *The Origins of France* (London, 1982)
Kendall, Paul Murray *Louis XI* (London, 1971)
Knecht, R.J. *Francis I* (Cambridge, 1982)
Lacouture, Jean *De Gaulle* (London, 1970)
Ladurie, Emmanuel Le Roy *Montaillou* (London, 1978)
Markham, Felix *Napoleon* (London, 1963)
McMillan, James *Dreyfus to De Gaulle* (London, 1985)
Scarré, Christopher, ed. *Ancient France* (Edinburgh, 1983)
Wright, Louis *France in Modern Times* (New York, 1987)

Historical Gazetteer

Numbers in bold refer to the main text

Aachen *(Aix-la-Chapelle)* The Rhineland city from which Charlemagne ruled his empire. Now part of Germany. **25–26, 122**

Aix-en-Provence One of the principal cities of Provence and site of a medieval university. Paul Cézanne and Émile Zola were born here, and Count Mirabeau, an architect of the French Revolution, was elected from here to the Third Estate in 1789. **8–9, 17, 64, 91**

Albi A Languedoc bishopric, Albi was the centre of the Albigensian heresy (anti-Roman, anti-clerical) in the thirteenth century. It also is the birthplace of Impressionist painter Henri Toulouse-Lautrec, in whose honour the Musée Toulouse-Lautrec was established within the walls of the Palais de la Berbie. **45**

Amboise (Château) Mainly the work of Charles VIII and Francis I, this Loire château hosted Leonardo da Vinci in 1516, among other masters of the Renaissance. **70**

Arles A city in Provence of Greek, Roman and French antecedents, Arles has been, variously, the capital city of the early Burgundian-Provençal king-dom and part of the Holy Roman Empire. It was joined to France only in 1481. Roman-style bull fights are still staged in the second-century Roman arena, and Vincent Van Gogh did much of his painting in Arles. **3, 8–10, 17**

Arras The capital of the Artois region and the scene of some of the most bitter fighting in the First World War. Arras also is famous for its tapestries and as a centre of economic and industrial activity since the Middle Ages. **147–151**

Autun This Burgundian city was a great educational centre in Roman times. Prince Talleyrand, Napoleon's foreign minister and a renegade churchman, was bishop of Autun just before the Revolution. Napoleon himself, and Lazare Carnot, a Revolutionary general, were pupils in the lycée. Marshal and president of the Third Republic, Patrice de MacMahon, was born at nearby Château de Sully. **9**

Avignon The city on the Rhône where for seventy years (1307–77) the papacy was held 'captive' by the French crown. A locally-produced wine was specially favoured by the papal palace, and has been named *Chateauneuf-du-Pape* ever since. Avignon was annexed to France in 1789. The Palais des Papes is a magnificent example of Gothic architecture. The English philosopher, John Stuart Mill, died in Avignon in 1873 and is buried in the Cimetière Saint-Veran. **10, 51, 64, 67**

Battles

AGINCOURT *(Artois)*, 1415: The English under Henry V destroyed the pride of the French aristocracy. **59–60**

BOURGES *(River Yèvre)*, 52 BC: Julius Caesar conquered this last Gallic stronghold. **9**

BOUVINES *(Flanders)*, 1214: Philip Augustus defeated John I of England, forcing him to give up most of England's French holdings. **43**

CASTILLON *(Gascony)*, 1453: A French victory here brought the Hundred Years War effectively to an end. **62**

CHÂLONS *(Champagne)*, 451: The Roman general, Aetius, stopped the advance of Attila the Hun towards Paris. Merovech, first king of the Salian Franks, was allied with Aetius. **10**

CHAMP-DE-MARS *(Paris)*, 52 BC: Julius Caesar defeated the Parisii and secured Roman power in the Paris Basin. **12**

CLERMONT *(Auvergne)*, 52 BC: Roman legions defeated rebel Gauls under Vercingetorix. **9**

CRÉCY *(Artois)*, 1346: The first major English victory in the Hundred Years War. **55–56**

DREUX AND ROUEN *(Loire and Normandy)*, 1562: Simultaneous sieges of Protestant strongholds by Catholic forces, opening the wars of religion in France. **79–80**

DUNKERQUE *(Artois)*, 1940: The Germans failed to prevent the evacuation of more than 300,000 British and French soldiers. **161**

FALAISE *(Normandy)*, 1944: The allied victory in the 'Falaise Pocket' was decisive in opening the way to the liberation of Paris. Appropriately, one of the greatest French warriors of all time, William the Conqueror, was born here in 1027. **164**

FORMIGNY *(Normandy)*, 1450: Dunois defeated English reinforcements. The most important French victory in the Hundred Years War, paving the way for Castillon three years later. **62**

JEMAPPES *(Flanders)*, 1792: French revolutionary armies defeated the Dutch and became the masters of Belgium. A future king, Louis-Philippe, fought in the Revolutionary army. **125**

LILLE *(Artois)*, 1708: The Anglo-Imperial armies of the duke of Marlborough defeated Louis XIV here. **99**

MALPLAQUET *(Artois)*, 1709: The French fought Marlborough to a draw; it was nearly the last gasp for France in the War of the Spanish Succession all the same. **99**

MARNE *(Champagne)*, 1914: Marshal Joffre rushed troops from Paris by bicycle, in taxis and on foot, to stop the German advance. They did, Paris was saved, and the First World War then settled into the long stalemate in the West which ended only in August 1918. **148**

MONT AUXOIS (*Cote d'Or*), 52 BC: Julius Caesar won another victory over the rebellious Gauls, bringing ever closer the final triumph of the Roman Empire. **9**

NORMANDY INVASION (*Normandy*), 1944: In June, allied landings on beaches between Cherbourg and Harfleur opened the final phase of the Second World War in the West. **164**

POITIERS (*Poitou*), 1356: Edward the Black Prince led the English to their second major victory in the Hundred Years War. **57**

RONCESVALLES (*Pyrénées*), 778: The Basques defeated the Franks, and - the epic poem, *Chanson de Roland*, was inspired by the death here of the Frankish leader. **65**

SAINTE-MÈRE-ÉGLISE (*Normandy*), 1944: On June 6, Units of the American 101st Airborne overshot their drop zone and landed in the very centre of this tiny village. The Germans shot them as they came down. Most of the company were killed. **164**

SEDAN (*Ardennes*), 1870: This battle opened the Franco-Prussian War. Emperor Napoleon III was taken prisoner. **135**

SOISSONS (*Champagne*), 486 Clovis overthrew Syagrius, the last Roman ruler in Northern Gaul. **19**

SOMME (*Picardy*), 1916: This bloody battle was fought to relieve pressure on the fortress at Verdun. **150**

TOURS (*Loire*), 732: Charles Martel, grandfather of Charlemagne, defeated an advance party of Moors (Moslems). The Moors penetrated no further into France. **22**

VALMY (*The Argonne*), 1792: Revolutionary armies defeated the duke of Brunswick, ending for the moment the threat of a counter-revolutionary invasion of France. **112–113**

VOUILLÉ (*Poitou*), 507: Clovis defeated the Aquitanians, establishing once and for all the supremacy of the Franks in Western and Southern Gaul. **19**

WATERLOO (*Belgium*), 1815: The duke of Wellington led an allied army to victory over Napoleon, ending his efforts at reestablishing his empire. Napoleon then was exiled to St Helena, a British-held island in the South Atlantic. **121**

WATTIGNIES (*Flanders*), 1793: A reorganized Revolutionary army defeated the Austrians. **112–113**

YORKTOWN (*America*), 1781: Admiral Count Grasse and General Count Rochambeau commanded French forces which backed George Washington against the British, and effectively ended Britain's hope of defeating the rebellious American colonists. **105**

Bayeux A Norman town where hangs the famous Bayeux Tapestry, which tells the story of the Norman conquest of England. It was commissioned in the eleventh century by bishop Odo of Bayeux, William Conqueror's half-brother. **37**

Besançon This city near Dijon in Burgundy, once a free city of the Holy Roman Empire, is the birthplace of Victor Hugo, Charles Fourier, Joseph-Pierre Proudhon, and Auguste and Louis Lumière, inventors of cinematography. The citadel fortifications were designed by Louis XIV's military engineer, Vauban. Besançon is the centre of the French watch and clock-making industry. **95**

Blois (Château) Francis I's favourite Loire château, and where Henry III summoned two meetings of the Estates General and plotted the assassination of the duke of Guise and his brother, the cardinal of Bourbon. **52, 71–72**

Bordeaux An ancient Roman town, now capital of the Aquitain region and an important port, Bordeaux produces some of the finest red wines in the world. Always closely associated with England, which possessed the region during much of the Hundred Years War. On three occasions, 1870, 1914 and 1940, French governments withdrew to Bordeaux in time of war when Paris was threatened. The philosopher Michel de Montaigne was mayor in the sixteenth century. **4, 7, 9, 14, 21, 45, 55, 88, 97, 120, 148, 161–162**

Bourges A Roman town, an archbishopric in the 3rd century, a ducal capital, and finally, briefly, capital of France under Charles VII when the English held Paris. Joan of Arc came here in 1429 to persuade Charles VII to drive the English out. Jacques Coeur, Charles's banker and one of the richest men of the age, was born here, as was Louis XI. Jean Calvin attended university at Bourges. **9, 60**

Cahors This city in the Lot Valley was briefly in Moorish hands in the eighth century, was governed by Thomas à Becket in 1159–60, and was nearly destroyed during the Hundred Years War. Pope John XXII and Léon Gambetta, a prime minister in the

Third Republic, were born here. **63**

Calais A town in the Artois region through which many English tourists enter France, Calais was an English possession for centuries. In 1347 Edward III captured it after six of its citizens gave themselves up for execution so that the town might be spared a siege. Auguste Rodin immortalized their sacrifice in sculpture. Calais was the last English possession to be recovered by the French, in 1558. **54, 56, 58**

Carcassonne For centuries a crossroads of trade between Aquitaine and the Mediterranean, this city in Roussillon was constantly under attack and, consequently, heavily fortified. Visigoths, Moors and Simon de Montfort during the crusade against the Albigensian heresy in the thirteenth century, attacked the city. The old town is probably the finest example of medieval fortification extant. **50**

Carnac This Breton coastal village is the centre of one of the most famous areas in France for neolithic remains. **5**

Chambord (Château) Francis I built it, Louis XIV visited often, and Molière created *Monsieur de Pourceaugnac* and *Le Bourgeois gentilhomme* here; in appearance the most medieval of Loire châteaux. **68, 71, 82**

Champ-sur-Marne (Château) Built in the eighteenth century by a wealthy army contractor who collapsed and died on the front steps when he was about to be arrested, probably for defrauding the government. The most famous resident was Madame de Pompadour. **103**

Chantilly (Château) Built near Paris by Louis XI, it later housed Anne de Montmorency, constable of France and friend of Francis I. **68–70, 72**

Chartres Fifty miles south-west of Paris, Chartres is famous only for its cathedral, which is the most important Gothic church in France. It is the subject of the most extensive explanation of the symbolic importance of cathedral decoration ever written, Henry Adams' *Chartres*. **66**

Châteaudun (Château) This northern Loire château was rebuilt in the fifteenth century, when it housed its most noteworthy owner, Dunois, bastard of Orléans and companion in arms of Joan of Arc. **61**

Chaumont-sur-Loire (Château) Queen mother Catherine de Medici forced Henry II's mistress, Diane de Poitiers, to trade it for Chenonceau. Diane presumably modelled for her classic sculptures elsewhere, for, not liking Chaumont, she rarely went there. **75**

Chenonceaux (Château) Henry II gave this Loire château to Diane de Poitiers, who lost it to Catherine de Medici. In the eighteenth century Jean-Jacques Rousseau stayed here as 'the cosseted guest of Mme Dupin, wife of a rich tax farmer'. It was built by Thomas Bohier, a tax farmer of the early sixteenth century. **75, 79, 81**

Chinon A small town in the Berry region, Chinon is where Henry II of England died in 1189, and Richard I may have done in 1199. Many Templars were imprisoned here during the suppression in 1308, Joan of Arc met with Charles VII here, and the region around Chinon inspired Rabelais' *Gargantua* and *Pantagruel*. **61**

Clermont-Ferrand The capital of the Auvergne region since Roman times,

a bishopric since the fifth century and an industrial town since the nineteenth. Pope Urban II both preached the first Crusade and excommunicated Philip I here in 1095. Blaise Pascal, Bishop Gregory of Tours, the chronicler, and Pierre Teilhard du Chardin, the Jesuit thinker, were from Clermont. **9, 17, 39**

Cluny This Burgundian town contains the ruins of what was once the greatest abbey in France, founded by Bruno of Baume in 909. Its greatest abbot, Hugh, orchestrated the famous reconciliation between Pope Gregory VII and Henry IV of Germany at Canossa in 1078. Peter Abélard died at Cluny. **38, 114**

Colmar One of the most fought-over towns in France, having belonged to both France and Germany on several occasions. In 1945 the retreating Germans put up stiff resistance here, leaving the town badly damaged. Sculptor Frederic Auguste Bartholdi was born in Colmar. **164**

Compiègne In this village north of Paris, Joan of Arc was captured by the Burgundians in 1430; in a railway car here in 1918 the Germans signed the armistice; as a symbolic gesture of retaliation, Hitler made Marshal Pétain sign the armistice of 1940 in the same railway car. Louis XV built a château here as an escape from Versailles; it is often described as a fine example of neo-classical decadence in design. **61, 150–151, 161**

Corsica An island off the south coast of France acquired from Italy in the eighteenth century, just in time to make Napoleon Bonaparte, who was born in the town of Ajaccio, a French

Dauphiné This Alpine province was autonomous until 1349, when it became an *apanage* of the crown prince, who was thereafter known as the dauphin. The first stirrings of the French Revolution were felt in Dauphiné. The winter Olympic games were held at Grenoble in 1960. **48, 57–68, 125**

Dijon The capital and principal city of Burgundy, and seat of its dukes for centuries. It also is the centre of one of France's richest wine-producing areas, and is known for its mustard. Famous Dijonnais include: Bishop Bossuet, the apologist for absolutism; Jean-Philippe Rameau, the composer; Gustav Eiffel; and Bernard of Clairvaux was born nearby. **59**

Domrémy-la-Pucelle The birthplace of Joan of Arc, near Nancy on the River Meuse. **60**

Étampes One of the oldest towns in the Ile de France, it was annexed by Hugh Capet, who maintained a palace there. Diane de Poitiers also lived there part of the time, and Ravaillac, Henry IV's assassin, was born there. **37, 46**

Foix The stronghold of the Albigensian heresy in the foothills of the Pyrénées. The village of Montaillou is in this region. **52**

Fontainebleau (Château) Northeast of Paris and the most famous château in France, Fontainebleau was started in the Middle Ages and expanded in the sixteenth century by Francis I. At Fontainebleau Philip IV was born and died, Louis XIII was born, Louis XIV signed the Revocation of the Edict of Nantes, Pope Pius VII, who excommunicated Napoleon, was imprisoned, and Napoleon signed his abdication. **71**

Fontevrault Isabella of La Marche, widow of King John of England, was incarcerated in the abbey here after she organized resistance to the French king in Poitou. Many Plantagenet kings of England were buried there. **37**

Gaillard (Château) Now a ruin on the Seine, this château was built in only two years by Richard I of England about 1190. It is one of the finest examples of High Medieval castle building. **43**

Gisors This Seine château was the favourite retreat of Henry II of England in his Norman duchy. It provided the setting for his Christmas meeting in 1182 with Philip Augustus. Eleanor of Aquitaine, Henry's wife, probably was there, and their four sons may have been. In any case, it was assumed that they were for purposes of making Gisors the backdrop of the film *The Lion in Winter*, which dramatised the tense relationship of Henry with his family and the king of France. **43**

Grenoble Famous for ski-ing, this city in Dauphiné also is the birthplace of Stendhal, Condillac, Casimir Periér, whose father led the revolt of the Third Estate in Dauphiné in 1788, and the seigneur de Bayard, the peerless knight of romantic song from the reign of Francis I. **68**

Grotte-de-Cougnac Cave paintings from the neolithic age. **4, 5, 32**

Grotte-de-Lascaux The most famous neolithic-age cave paintings, but not open to the public. **4**

Le Creusot One of the earliest

French industrial towns. The famous Le Creusot metal works helped spark French industrialisation in the early nineteenth century. **124–125**

Lille This commercial and industrial centre from the sixteenth century was the capital of ancient Flanders, until France took it in 1667. Lille also is a military crossroads. Louis XIV laid siege here in 1667, after which Vauban built the *citadelle*, one of the finest examples of military architecture anywhere. The Germans occupied Lille in 1914–1918. Charles de Gaulle was born here. **99**

Loches (Château) Louis XI and Louis XII used this Loire château as a prison. It contains the tomb of Agnes Sorel, Charles VII's mistress, and the famous portrait of her with one exposed breast. **62**

Lourdes In 1858 a vision of the Virgin Mary reputedly appeared to Bernadette Soubirous several times, and a spring appeared in the Grotte de Massabielle where she saw the vision. The Catholic Church ruled that she had seen what she claimed, and Lourdes became the largest centre of pilgrimage in the Christian world. Bernadette became a nun at Saint-Gildard, where she died in 1873.

Lyon The capital of Roman Gaul, then the kingdoms of Burgundy and Provence. It now is the third largest city in France, and the centre of one of France's richest agricultural regions. Thomas Aquinas died here, and Édouard Herriot, the Third Republic prime minister, was mayor in 1905. One of the first national financial institutions began here, Crédit Lyonnais. Famous Lyonnais include two

Roman emperors, Claudius and Caracalla, the poets Sidonius Apollinaris and Louise Labé, the economist Jean-Baptiste Say, the physicist André-Marie Ampère, and the aviation pioneer, Antoine de Saint-Exupéry. **3, 9, 11, 17, 20, 83, 124**

Maintenon (Château) Set in an extensive park on the Eure, Maintenon was given to Madame de Maintenon, Louis XIV's second wife, by her royal husband, when she was governess to his children. She derived her last name from the château. **93**

Malmaison (Château) Famous as the place where Napoleon, Empress Josephine de Beauharnais and their intimates held lively parties. She kept this retreat on the Seine as part of the divorce settlement, and died there in 1814. Napoleon III bought it, then sold it again. **115, 121**

Marseille The oldest city in France, dating to Phocaean times, it passed successively through Greek and Roman hands, and then was independent until it became French in the late fifteenth century. In the Revolution, city radicals sang Rouget de Lisle's *Chant de Guerre pour L'Armée du Rhin*, which, rechristened the *Marseillaise*, is the national anthem of France. The Château d'If in Marseille harbour, a sixteenth-century fortress, was the prison setting in Alexandre Dumas' *Count of Monte Cristo*. Desirée Clary, queen of Sweden as wife of Bernadotte, Adolphe Thiers, Émile Ollivier, statesmen, Honoré Daumier the cartoonist, and dramatist Edmond Rostand were born there. *Bouillabaisse* (fish soup) is the most famous dish served here. **6, 7, 17, 69, 113**

Montlhéry   The most troublesome royal fief in the Ile de France in early Capetian times. Its châtelains inspired Philip I's comment that the Montlhéry tower had 'made me old before my time'. **35**

Mont-Saint-Michel   The fortified abbey on a tiny island off the Norman coast was begun in 706. Over the centuries the Benedictines took it over, and it became so strong that Viking raiders could never sack it. At high tide it is completely surrounded by water; at low tide a sandy isthmus connects it to the mainland. Mont-Saint-Michel was suppressed during the Revolution and turned into a prison afterward. **32**

Nantes   This Breton city always has been a commercial centre, strategically located for trade. Henry IV issued the edict granting toleration to Huguenots there. Gilles de Rais, the infamous Bluebeard, was hanged and burned here in 1440. Jules Verne, René Waldeck-Rousseau and Aristide Briand came from Nantes. **82, 98**

Nîmes   A Roman town first, this Languedoc community still stages bull fights in the Roman manner in a Roman arena. It suffered at the hands of Simon de Montfort during the Albigensian Crusade. Its most famous landmark is the Pont du Gard, a Roman aqueduct which still functions. **8, 83**

Noyon   Charlemagne was crowned king of Neustria here in 768, and Jean Calvin was born here. Hugh Capet was elected King of France at Noyon in 986. Eligius, Dagobert I's relentless tax collector, was bishop of Noyon in the seventh century. **21, 31, 77**

Orléans   The road from Orléans to Paris was among the first major Roman highways in Gaul, an indication of the importance of this Loire city from the beginning. Early Capetian kings spent as much time in Orléans as in Paris. The city was besieged by Attila, Clovis and the English. Joan of Arc relieved the English siege in 1429, which was the turning point in the Hundred Years War. Orléans suffered from war also in 1594, 1870, and 1940–44. Jean Moulin, the legendary *résistance* leader was killed there by the Gestapo in 1943. Notable Orléannais include poet Charles Péguy. Marcel Proust did his military service in Orléans. **13–14, 19, 23, 31, 46, 61, 79–80**

Paris

ARC DE TRIOMPHE: Built to glorify Napoleon Bonaparte, it was completed only in 1836. It houses the tomb of the Unknown Soldier from the First World War. **131**

PALAIS-BOURBON: The meeting-place on the Left Bank of the Seine of the National Assembly, since 1795. Eugène Delacroix did five ceiling paintings in the building in the 1830s. **114–115**

BIBLIOTHÈQUE NATIONAL: One of the world's great libraries, founded in the nineteenth century but based upon the royal library assembled by Guillaume Budé in the reign of Francis I. **72**

BOULEVARD DU MONTPARNASSE: In the 1920s and 1930s, this Left-Bank street was the centre of Parisian literary and intellectual life. Ernest Hemingway wrote much of

The Sun Also Rises in the Café Closerie des Lilas. **167–168**

AVENUE DES CHAMPS-ÉLYSÉES: Built at the end of the seventeenth century, it connects the Arc de Triomphe with the Place de la Concorde. German troops staged a triumphal parade along this avenue following the armistice in 1940; four years later Charles de Gaulle led a march of jubilant Parisians along the Champs-Elysées in celebration of liberation from the Germans. **131, 164**

COLLÈGE DE FRANCE: Part of the University of Paris which grew out of the Regius lectureships established in 1530 by Francis I. **72, 144**

THÉÂTRE FRANÇAIS (COMÉDIE-FRANÇAISE): Opened in 1790, and the principal venue since for classical French theatre. Molière, Racine, Corneille and Voltaire are regularly performed there. **92, 99**

CONCIERGERIE: Here in 1792, on the Ile de la Cité, opposite the Châtelet, prisoners were dragged out and slaughtered in the September massacre. In 1793 their successors were taken to the Place de la Révolution (Concorde) to be guillotined, notably Queen Marie Antoinette. **108, 131**

ÉCOLE MILITAIRE: Completed in 1774 to house the new Military Academy, it was built near the site of Caesar's victory over the Parisii in 52 BC. In 1880 it became the École Supérieure de Guerre, a school for staff officers. **108**

GOBELINS FACTORY: Founded by Henry IV to house the Royal Tapestry workshops. **83**

HÔTEL DES INVALIDES: Built by Louis XIV as a hospital for wounded soldiers in 1671, designed by Libéral Bruant. In 1836 it became the house for Napoleon's tomb; also, Napoleon II, Vauban, Marshals Turenne, Foch and Lyauty, and Jérôme and Joseph Bonaparte, Napoleon's brothers. The Invalides actually is a complex, containing with the Hôtel a church, Saint-Louis-des-Invalides, also by Bruant, and the Dôme des Invalides by Jules Hardouin-Mansart. **108**

HÔTEL DE VILLE: City Hall; here Blanqui, Blanc, Lamartine and others made the impassioned speeches, and were censored for them, which sparked the Revolution of 1848. The present building dates from 1882; that which served in 1848 dated from the fifteenth century. It is on Place de l'Hôtel de Ville, opposite the Ile de la Cité, which, as Place de Grève, was used for public executions from 1310 to 1832. **126, 127**

ILE DE LA CITÉ: The place where Paris began, where Caesar camped in 53 BC, where Odo defended the city against the Vikings in 885–86, and where the first Capets lived (occasionally) in a palace on the site of the Palais de Justice. Notre-Dame Cathedral is the most famous building on the island, followed by the Gothic Sainte-Chapelle. **12, 31, 48, 108, 131**

ILE SAINT-LOUIS: The island in the Seine just behind the Ile de la Cité. Théophile Gautier and Charles Baudelaire were only two of the many literati who lived on the island, or frequented cafés there. **143**

LOUVRE: Started by Philip Augustus in the thirteenth century, added to by Charles V and Francis I, it was abandoned as a palace by Louis XIV who preferred the openness of Versailles. In 1793 it became an art museum, which it remains, housing one of the greatest art collections in the world. The Louvre, with all of its additions and extensions, dominates the Right Bank for nearly half-a-mile. **71, 95, 97, 108, 131, 175**

MONTMARTRE: The hill where Saint-Denis was martyred in 250, and where the Sacré-Coeur was built in 1876 fulfilling a vow taken by a group of dedicated Catholics in atonement for French defeat in the Franco-Prussian war. Montmartre was and is an artists' haven: Renoir, Utrillo, Valadon, Gauguin, Picasso and many others went there to paint. **11, 136, 143**

MOULIN ROUGE: The famous café in the Boulevard de Clichy, where Toulouse-Latrec sketched the characters who appeared in his paintings of the Paris *demi-monde*. **143**

NANTERRE: The Sorbonne campus where the student uprising of 1968 began. **178**

NOTRE-DAME: The great cathedral on the Ile de la Cité was begun in 1163 by Bishop Maurice de Sully, and finished in the fourteenth century. In 1793–94 it served as the 'Temple of Reason', and was restored afterward as a church. Napoleon was crowned in Notre-Dame in 1804; the cathedral was the backdrop for Victor Hugo's *The Hunchback of Notre Dame*. **12, 41, 45, 108, 114, 131**

OPÉRA: Commissioned by Napoleon III and built by Charles Garnier, it is typical of the garish style popular in the Second Empire. Opulent to a fault inside and out, it has been described as a place in which to be 'seen' fully as much as a place in which to see or hear. **130**

PALAIS DE L'ÉLYSÉE: The Paris residence of the Presidents of France in Rue du Faubourg Saint-Honoré. **138**

PALAIS-ROYAL: From this shopping arcade in 1789 crowds of Parisians gathered to start the march towards the Bastille which touched off the Revolution. **105, 108**

PANTHÉON: A necropolis for great heroes of France, built in the mid-eighteenth century on the site of the old church of Sainte-Geneviève. It houses the tombs of Rousseau, Voltaire, Hugo, Zola and Jean Jaurès, among others. **108, 153**

PLACE DE LA BASTILLE: Site of the fortress stormed on 14 July 1789, which began the Revolution, and the new Paris Opera house. **181**

PLACE DE LA CONCORDE: Once the Place de la Révolution, this square at the foot of the Champs-Elysées held the guillotine to which most of the principal actors in the Revolution sooner or later bent their knee: Louis XVI, Danton and Robespierre, to name but three. In Dickens' *A Tale of Two Cities*, Madame La Farge sat knitting while she watched the executions. **108, 114**

PLACE PIGALLE: During the last decades of the nineteenth century, the Café Le Rat Mort in Place Pigalle in Boulevard de Clichy was a recognized meeting place for lesbians. The writer Colette and her lover 'Missy', the marquise de Belbeuf, frequented the café. The area figured as a location in Zola's *Nana*. **142–143**

PLACE VENDÔME: Proust dined

here almost nightly to observe the decadence about which he wrote in *À la recherche du temps perdu*. Chopin died in a house in this square. **146**

PONT NEUF: Completed early in the seventeenth century, this was the first Seine bridge in Paris not to be lined with houses. Connecting the Ile de la Cité with both Left and Right Banks, Pont Neuf quickly became the heart of Paris. French literary heros – and anti-heros – often paused on the Pont Neuf to stare at the Seine's dark waters and contemplate suicide, as in the case of Sartre's Mathieu Delarue in *L'Âge de Raison*. **108**

QUARTIER LATIN: One of the oldest parts of the city, it has been a student and scholarly area since the second century. Abélard founded his school there in the cloisters of Sainte-Geneviève, a century before the University of Paris, also in the Quartier Latin. **13**

SAINTE-CHAPELLE: The exquisite Gothic church on the Ile de la Cité built in the thirteenth century by Louis IX. **48, 131**

SAINT-DENIS: The abbey church, a cathedral since 1966, was built by Suger beginning in 1136. It was the model for Gothic church architecture. Built on the site of churches dedicated to Saint-Denis since the third century, Suger's church continued the tradition of royal necropolis. Saint-Denis contains the remains of most French monarchs from Dagobert I to Louis XVII. **11, 13, 24, 38, 41, 52, 108**

THE SORBONNE: The theology faculty established in 1253 by Robert de Sorbon, Louis IX's confessor. In 1544 its faculty rather unwisely cen-

sored writings on religion by Francis I's sister, Marguerite of Angoulême. They quickly recanted. The Sorbonne is now part of the University of Paris. **64, 73, 77, 178**

TOUR EIFFEL: This symbol of industrial culture, standing at the northwest end of the Champ-de-Mars, was built in 1889 by Gustav Eiffel for the Paris Exhibition. **142, 184**

UNIVERSITÉ DE PARIS: Founded by Philip Augustus about 1200, formally recognized by the pope in 1210, and a centre of intellectual ferment ever since, this is one of the great universities in the world. In the thirteenth century it led the Christian world as a centre of theological and philosophical innovation and speculation. In 1968 its students seemed likely to start a revolution. There are campuses spread throughout the Left Bank area. **47, 64, 73, 77**

Pau The capital of Béarn, Queen Jeanne d'Albret of Navarre lived there in the sixteenth century, and her son, Henry IV, was born there. So too was Jean Bernadotte, who grew up to be first a Napoleonic marshal and then king of Sweden. **80, 83**

Plessis-les-Tours (Château) Louis XI's favourite residence on the Loire, where he died in 1483. **70**

Plombière-les-Bains This Vosges spa was a favourite watering place of Napoleon III, where he met Camillo Cavour, the Piedmontese prime minister in 1858 to plot the War of Italian Unification – which did not achieve that result, of course. **134**

Le Puy This small city in the Auvergne, surrounded by extinct volcanic cones, seems dedicated to religion as no French community has ever been: Bishop Adhémar of Le Puy joined Bernard of Clairvaux to preach the crusades; Louis IX brought the statue of the famous Black Virgin in 1254; and Le Puy lay across the route of pilgrims on their way to worship at the shrine of Santiago de Compostela in Spain. A rather pretentious statue of the Virgin and Child stands on a ridge outside of the town. **39–40**

Rambouillet (Château) Near Paris, this château is the summer residence for presidents of France. It has had a chequered career: Francis I died there, and in 1783 Louis XVI bought Rambouillet with the intention of making an experimental dairy farm. **75**

Reims The coronation city of French monarchs. Clovis was

Reims Cathedral

crowned there in 496; Joan of Arc brought Charles VII there in 1429; and in 1824, Charles X resurrected the old régime, at least symbolically, by being crowned at Reims and by touching to cure scrofula, a power attributed to French monarchs since Robert II (996). Reims also is the 'champagne capital' of France. **9, 14, 38, 41, 61, 92, 123, 151**

Rennes The capital of Brittany, the last of the great territorial principalities to be reconciled to rule from Paris. As there is now a Breton separatist movement (mostly limited to demands that the Breton language be recognized), it may be said that reconciliation is not altogether complete. General Boulanger was from Rennes. **51, 184**

La Rochelle One of the great French maritime cities and the first to trade with America, La Rochelle was also the central stronghold and last refuge of the Huguenots. It held out against the Catholics from 1573 to 1628, when a siege engineered by Cardinal Richelieu brought submission. Jean-Paul Sartre attended lycée in La Rochelle. **2, 78**

Rouen The capital of Normandy and William the Conqueror's seat until 1066. Joan of Arc was tried, condemned and burnt there in 1431; Corneille and Fontenelle were born there; and Flaubert was born, lived much of his life, and died in Rouen. The surrounding countryside was the setting for his *Madame Bovary*. **12, 21, 32–33, 61, 80**

Senlis A few miles outside Paris, Senlis was where Hugh Capet was crowned, and remained a royal residence from then until Henry IV. In 1352 a *jacquerie* massacred noble hostages, and in 1418 the Burgundians, and in 1914 the Germans, also massacred hostages in this town. **31, 63**

Sens   Near Paris, Sens was one of the earliest French archbishoprics, to which even Paris was subject until 1627. By the ninth century its prelates were titled Primate of the Gauls and Germania, and dominated the Ile de France. Here Archbishop Saint-Loups condemned Abélard's writings and had them burnt, in 1140. Its inhabitants enthusiastically supported the Catholic League during the religious wars of the sixteenth century. **38, 47, 66**

Strasbourg   One of Europe's oldest cities, Alsatian Strasbourg was an episcopal city-state until the seventeenth century, when it was joined to France. For a time its religious climate was very congenial for French Protestants. Rouget de Lisle composed what became the *Marseillaise* here, and Strasbourg has been the Council of Europe headquarters since 1949. Famous Strasbourgeois include Gottfried de Strasbourg, author of *Tristan und Isolde*, Raimond de Charbonnière, the geologist, and sculptor Jean Aup. Gutenberg worked on his printing press in Strasbourg. **76, 113**

Toulon   France's most important Mediterranean naval base, and a site of naval activities since the Romans used it for the same purpose. French royalists handed it to the British in 1791, and Napoleon took it back in 1793. The French fleet here was scuttled by its sailors in 1942 when the Germans occupied Vichy France. **87**

Toulouse   Capital of the old Languedoc region, this city on the River Garonne was first Roman, then Alaric the Visigoth made it his capital, in 419. Its independence later was crushed when the counts of Toulouse were caught up in the Albigensian Heresy. Toulouse was the centre of 'troubadour literature', of which Eleanor of Aquitaine was so fond. Jean Bodin and probably Michel de Montaigne attended the university here in the sixteenth century. Presently, Toulouse is headquarters of the French aviation industry, the home of *Caravelle*, *Concorde* and *Airbus*. **1, 8, 9, 17, 29, 34, 42, 45, 50–51, 78, 80, 91**

Tours   This Loire city is famous for the purity of its French and the quality of its food. Gregory of Tours, the first French chronicler, was bishop here in the sixth century, and Alcuin of York made it one of the great centres of learning in the early Middle Ages. Charles Martel defeated a party of Moors nearby in 732. Famous inhabitants include François Clouet, portraitist of Francis I, Louise de la Vallière, mistress of Louis XIV, and Honoré Balzac, the writer. **14**

Valençay   (Château)   Located in the Berry region, the château was built by the d'Étampes family in the sixteenth century, one of whom was mistress to Francis I. Prince Talleyrand bought the château in 1805 and remodelled it according to his own highly refined and imaginative tastes. **71–75, 119**

Valenciennes   Once called the 'Athens of the North', despite being in the centre of a heavily industrialised region, Valenciennes suffered heavy damage in the First World War. Its most famous product was Antoine Watteau, France's greatest rococo painter. **101**

Vaucouleurs Joan of Arc set out from this Meuse village on her mission of national liberation. Madame Du Barry, prostitute, mistress of Louis XV and victim of the guillotine, was born here. **60–62, 103–104**

Vercors This region of western Dauphiné was the centre of *maquis* resistance to the Germans and to the Vichy régime during the Second World War. The National Cemetery of Vercors located in Vassileux-en-Vercors commemorates the achievements of the *maquis*. **164, 168**

Vichy Located in the Auvergne region, this spa is famous for its water which was prized from Roman times to the present. Unfortunately, Vichy is also infamous as the seat of the collaborationist government of Marshal Pétain and Pierre Laval between 1940 and 1944. The town has lived down that episode and remains the most popular spa in France. **161, 163, 165, 175**

Villefranche (Villafranca) In 1859 Napoleon III and Franz Joseph, Emperor of Austria, negotiated an end to the War of Italian Unification, after the Franco-Piedmontese alliance won victories at Magenta and Solferino. This small city on the Côte d'Azur provided the venue. **134**

Index